Are You Lonesome Tonight?

Are You

Lonesome Tonight?

THE UNTOLD STORY

OF ELVIS PRESLEY'S

ONE TRUE LOVE

AND THE CHILD

HE NEVER KNEW

Lucy de Barbin and Dary Matera

VILLARD BOOKS

NEW YORK   1987

Title page photograph courtesy of Michael Ochs Archives/Venice, CA.

Grateful acknowledgment is made to Bourne Co. and Cromwell Music, Inc., for permission to reprint lyrics from "Are You Lonesome Tonight?" Words and music by Lou Handman and Roy Turk. Copyright 1926 by Irving Berlin, Inc., renewed by Bourne Co. and Cromwell Music, Inc. International copyright secured. All rights reserved. Used by permission.

Library of Congress Cataloging-in-Publication Data
De Barbin, Lucy, 1936–
Are you lonesome tonight?
Bibliography: p.
1. Presley, Elvis, 1935–1977. 2. De Barbin, Lucy, 1936–
3. Rock musicians—United States—
Biography. I. Matera, Dary, 1955–   . II. Title.
ML420.P96D4   1987   784.5'4'00924 [B]   86-40327
ISBN 0-394-55842-1

Manufactured in the United States of America
9 8 7 6 5 4 3 2
First edition

Book Design: Jessica Shatan

TO E. L. LANCELOT,
MY EVERLASTING LOVE

It was an intriguing tip, certainly worth investigating. An un-known daughter of Elvis Presley would be a marketable story. If there was any substance to it, a stylish presentation could lure a major magazine. If it was the more typical one-night-stand love child, a shot of rocket fuel in the prose would make the tabloid editors frenzied.

I pursued. She spooked. My contacts in Los Angeles informed me that the thought of an interview mortified her. I greeted her fear with mixed emotions. Not getting the story was disappoint-ing. The fact that she didn't want it told made it more plausible. I went on to other assignments, keeping this one in the back of my mind. Six months later I received a call at my home in Miami. It was Desirée. She was tentative, extremely cautious. She spoke in a soft, refined voice. She said that she might be interested in talking, but not then. She would contact me again. Now I was fascinated. She called a few more times over the next six months. She asked all the questions. What kind of story did I have in mind? In what publication would it appear? I tried to answer the best I could, but I had no idea what the story was. Whenever I probed for details, she retreated.

She called again and told me she would be laying over in Miami the following week, returning from a trip to South America. Could I meet her at customs? She described herself as tall and slender, with long black hair. She added that she would be wearing unusual sunglasses with alternate white and black frames.

"You can't miss me," she said. "I look like my father."

The plane was an hour late. I must have studied over a thou-sand faces streaming out the Miami customs gate; 99 percent of the travelers had black hair. Nothing clicked. I figured I missed her.

Then she appeared. There was no doubt. Her description was accurate—tall, nearly six feet in her heels, lean, with long black hair—but she left out an important adjective: beautiful. Her col-oring blended with the Latins swarming around her, but her fea-tures stood out. Her cheekbones were high and prominent. Her nationality was indeterminable. Not Latin, not quite European, a sprinkling of American Indian. She looked like something Calvin Klein might create.

As she moved closer, her beauty became chilling. I stood staring at her with my mouth agape. She looked so much like Elvis it was eerie. So eerie, she set off a subconscious recognition that raised goose bumps on my body.

I then noticed that she was wearing the odd sunglasses that were to be my clue.

Desirée was politely reserved when I introduced myself. She was guarded about everything, even her trip to South America. That was surprising. Despite our phone conversations and her prior reservations about the interview, I still expected a wide-eyed, giddy Hollywood starlet desperate for a break. She would theatrically express her story and cap it with the proclamation that she would carry the baton for Elvis from this point on.

She wasn't anything like that.

By that point in my journalistic career, I had interviewed more than two thousand people. With well-attuned reporter's antennae, I picked up her emotions. Tense. Afraid. Unsure. Wary. One wrong question and she would flee. Despite her bold appearance, she was a shy and somewhat naïve twenty-five-year-old woman unprepared to withstand the media attention that revealing her identity would generate.

I wasn't sure what I would do with the story, but at that point I ached to know it.

We small-talked about other things, then had a glass of wine. I got her to laugh. After an hour she loosened up.

"Okay, ask your questions."

As I fired away, my anticipation quickly became bewilderment. I had a suitcase full of questions, but she didn't have any answers. The first ten questions, mostly concerning her mother's relationship with Elvis, were met with a shrug or an "I don't know." She didn't know how or where her mother met him, nor how long they knew each other. In essence, she didn't appear to have an inkling how she came to be his daughter. She just knew she was. A less experienced interviewer might have accused her of being a fraud. In the course of my career, I frequently had the pleasure of going one-on-one with some of the best liars in the world. The standard liars on the regular newspaper beat, the politicians and pitchmen, are rank amateurs compared to the con men and women who hustle the extraterrestrial and parapsychology circles. These characters are classics. Strap them up to lie detectors and they pass with flying colors. Giving them the U.S. Army stress analysis test confirms that they just whizzed in from Pluto.

Yet, you can tell. You know they're lying. The smooth, practiced answers. The mannerisms. The sense that they're giving a performance. And they always slip up. A perceptive interviewer quickly learns to sift through the swindlers and crazies in order to locate the demure housewife or embarrassed forest ranger who did experience something strange, something real.

Desirée exhibited none of the affectations of dishonesty. What confirmed her credibility for me was her glaring lack of knowledge about Elvis. A fraud would have studied every detail of his life and weaved it into her story. A good fraud would have been able to field the toughest questions by calling upon her vast store of information.

Desirée didn't even know when Elvis entered the army. That was decisive. Her birthday was so close to that date that a couple of months either way would have exposed her. But she had no reason to check it out. She was telling the truth—what little of it she knew.

When it became apparent that the interview was going nowhere, Desirée merely laughed and said, "You're just going to have to talk to my mother. She has all the answers."

I certainly did want to meet her mother.

Another three months passed before it was arranged. What I didn't know was I had been the focus of a yearlong tug-of-war between Desirée and her mother. The mother, Lucy, wanted no part of any story. Desirée was unrelenting. She had to be. It was the key to her own quest.

Lucy finally agreed to meet me in Dallas at the Marriott Quorum. I was introduced to a petite, attractive woman with black hair, sparkling green eyes, and a bright but uneasy smile. We spent the first day sightseeing and getting to know each other. Late in the afternoon of the second day, Lucy began to talk. And she began to cry. I was totally mesmerized that afternoon, as I would be for the next twenty months. Lucy's story is both tragic and inspirational, one that transcends the simple elements of love, a secret child, and the fame of Elvis Presley. She fell in love with a boy, not an image. She loved a man, not a superstar. Their relationship never peaked, and in turn, never cooled. It was a dream love frozen forever at sixteen, an exhilarating first date that lasted twenty-four years.

It took almost two years for Lucy to recount her life. The details had been sealed inside so long that she had to shear them out piece by piece. Each session would leave her physically and emotionally devastated. I had interviewed people whose children were killed, wives who lost husbands, rape victims, individuals who had experienced every kind of grief imaginable, but I had never witnessed anyone wrenching out their soul as Lucy did.

Like Desirée, Lucy was convincing. She had a tremendous amount of intimate knowledge about Elvis, but all of it came firsthand. Anything outside her relationship with him was unknown, even things casual fans knew. She too didn't know the exact date he entered the army. She didn't know her blood type, Elvis's, or her daughter's, factors that are vital. Sometimes a passage in one of the many error-prone books detailing Elvis's life conflicted with her account. I'd insist that a meeting or event couldn't have happened as she said. She would gently inform me that she didn't know what the books said, all she knew was that it occurred the way she described. I'd dig further, question Elvis's associates, and uncover the facts or discover the mistake and realize she had been right all along.

She was never wrong about anything.

Lucy not only told the undeniable truth about having known, loved, and been loved by Elvis, she was unfailingly accurate about every aspect of their relationship from 1953 to August 16, 1977, the day he died.

She was also unbending. She emphatically refused to allow even the slightest deviation. Lucy wanted it recorded as it was, not scrubbed and glossed over to protect him or her. She asked him all the questions you would have asked him. The drugs. The self-destruction. The women. Why he clung to the Colonel. Why he surrounded himself with a gang of adolescents in sideburns. Why he married, then ignored Priscilla. His answers weren't profound. Elvis favored denial and avoidance over introspection. But through Lucy, a woman he trusted, who loved him prior to his fame and with whom he shared his most intimate feelings, we are given a renewed insight into the man. Lucy paints a portrait of an Elvis that even his closest associates may not recognize.

Which brings me to her memory. It was perfect. Not perfect in that she recalled everything, but perfect in that she remembered everything you and I remember about events in our past, and she forgot the things you and I forget. She recounted exact conversations but wasn't sure of the year they occurred. She could remember the color of the carpet and drapes in a hotel room but not the name of the hotel. I was unmerciful at times, pushing her for precise descriptions. Working together, we were able to pinpoint virtually every detail. It was an exhausting process.

Lucy's uncanny ability to remember long passages of conversation, while welcomed, did induce skepticism. I consulted Ginette Dreyfuss-Diederich, M.D., a professor of clinical psychiatry at the University of Miami School of Medicine and director of the Psychiatric Emergency Services, Jackson Memorial Hospital. Dr. Dreyfuss-Diederich's answer is enlightening.

"If a woman is given only a limited amount of time to spend with the man she loves, she endures the separation by constantly recalling and reliving every moment down to the finest detail. In Lucy's case, it goes even beyond that. Her moments with Elvis were the few pleasant experiences she had in a long, distressing life. She desperately had to hang on to them for sheer survival. The clarity and extent of her memory not only doesn't surprise me, I would expect it."

This is not to say that Lucy willingly confessed everything. She never lied, but she tried to hide a number of things from me, facts that were too painful to admit. I'd uncover them, become perplexed, and confront her. She would be evasive, confusing me more. My unwavering, insensitive journalist's demand for an airtight story usually blinded me to the reason. I would hate myself afterward for grilling her on such a sensitive, long-buried topic.

There was one final nagging question. Despite the anguish, tears, and long hours of work involved, Lucy and Desirée never asked for a dime. The story was originally conceived as a magazine article. I would get the money; Lucy would receive my thanks. It wasn't until I realized the power and depth of Lucy's recollections that I suggested writing a book. At first she rejected the idea. The slightest hint that she is exploiting her relationship with Elvis sends Lucy deeper into her protective shell. She and Desirée view the notion of making a claim against Elvis's estate as abhorrent. Their lack of greed was refreshing but left Lucy totally without motivation for revealing her secret. There had to be something more than my persistence, however dogged, that made Lucy agree to tell me her story.

The answer dropped on me like a bomb during the final interview. Desirée had no answers that day when we first met because she didn't know. Her knowledge ends with the lonely fact that, somehow, she is Elvis Presley's daughter. Lucy consented to uncover her life because she has been unable, by any other means, to tell her daughter the long, complicated tale.

Through me, Lucy has finally found the way to describe to Desirée the joy she had with Elvis and to explain the tragic circumstances that kept them apart. Making her story a public revelation is, in a sense, appropriate. Elvis gave everything to his fans, possibly even his life. It was Lucy's desire, not Elvis's, that their love be concealed. It was Lucy's decision to keep their daughter hidden, even from him.

Elvis would have shared them both with the world.

ACKNOWLEDGMENTS

I know of no place, either in advanced college courses or at newspapers and magazines, where journalists are taught or even made aware of the possible psychological damage caused by digging into someone's troubled life to withdraw an emotional story. To the contrary, we're taught to overcome our natural instincts not to interfere with someone's private moment of tragedy and plunge forward to get the anguished quotes that will help sell tomorrow's paper. Faced with this insight into my own insensitivities, I knew I needed help to delve into Lucy's dark past without leaving her mentally spent. No book would have been worth such a price. I was fortunate to interest an outstanding psychiatrist in Lucy's story. Her assistance in helping me understand Lucy was invaluable. In the process, she also helped me to understand the motivations behind the often quizzical actions of the main characters. I offer my special thanks to Ginette Dreyfuss-Diederich, M.D., assistant professor of clinical psychiatry, University of Miami School of Medicine, medical director of Psychiatric Emergency Services, Jackson Memorial Hospital, Miami, Florida. Dr. Dreyfuss-Diederich's French heritage and Catholic upbringing were added benefits in that they reflected Lucy's.

In addition, invaluable editorial assistance was provided by Fran Assalone Matera, Ph.D., School of Communication, University of Miami. Through her involvement in the book, Dr. Matera was able to share in the deep friendship that developed between Lucy, Desirée, and me.

On the other end, Lucy and Desirée had their own special adviser who encouraged them to go forward with the book and provided comfort and assurance when they were fearful of the consequences. We all are deeply indebted to Rafael Rodriguez, M.D., senior surgeon, Brotman Medical Center, Culver City, California, St. John's Hospital, and Santa Monica Medical Center, Santa Monica.

Although this book is basically one woman's story, it did entail a significant amount of additional research. Most of those I interviewed were not apprised of the full extent of this story. They

were sought for their knowledge of past events in the life of either
Lucy or Elvis that were appropriate to this project. They deserve
my sincere thanks for their willingness to share their time and
memories with me despite my being unable to fully disclose the
purpose of my inquiries.

In Monroe, Louisiana, special thanks to Mary Wilton Wade
and Jane Hayden; thanks also to Ginger Coats Tinsley, William
Hargiss, Phil Fishman, Gladyse Gallaspy, Mrs. J. D. Durrett,
Billye Adams, Gus Johnson, Bobbie Reis, Jenny Gonzalez, Mary
Taylor, Richard Wilcox, John Birdsong, Jr., Anna McCausland,
Monsignor George Martinez, Caroline Masur, Warren Antley,
Mary Jo Webb, Glenda Redden, Chris Ringham, and Eileen
Mark.

From KNOE Television, James Noe, Jr., Ansel Smith, George
Grubbs, Gene Milligan, Theresa Miletello, Alan Jones, Jack
Fisher, Leon Noland, Kenneth Purcell, Beth Breece, and espe-
cially to the Reverend James Cain.

In Shreveport, Louisiana, Billie Jean Horton, Horace Logan,
Maryetta Jones, Nel Twomey, Sammy Jones, Bill Cowen, and
Martha Fernandez.

In Alexandria, Louisiana, Sue Tudor Miller, Susan Blair, Effie
Schreiber, Mary de Barbin, Inez Jordan, Wileen Jordan, Irving
and Lily Goldstein, Neva Cestiva, Victor Bayone, Brenda Kaiser,
Bill Lynch, Thomas Easterling, M.D., George Bowden, Jr., and
Lee Huebner.

In Memphis, Edward Brown, Ph.D., of Memphis State Univer-
sity, Vester Presley, Eugene Smith, Patsy Gambill, Joe Alden,
Kathy Shelby, Beth Peace, Charles Wilson of the Memphis Zoo,
George Klein, Alan Fortas, and Jimmy Velvet.

In Los Angeles, special thanks to Currie Grant, Nan Morris
Robinson, and John O'Grady; thanks also to Joe Esposito, Marcia
Blaze, Paul Caruso, Mynna Dreyer, Dave Dreyer, Gerald Peters,
and Joan Deary.

In Dallas, Dave and Marty Harnden.

Also to Elizabeth Mansfield, Debbie Tkac, Sharon Faelten,
William Gottlieb, Carol Keough, Guy Kettlehack, Frankie Laine,
Les Share, Carol Powers, Arnold Taylor, Rodrigo Gatica, Wray
Lindersmith, Nelson Hendler, M.D., Pilar Wayne, Tommy
Thompkins, Nona Fried, Ray and Barbara Brown, Tom Congdon,
Susan Eilertsen, Carl Eisdorfer, Ph.D., M.D., of the University of
Miami, Billie Turnley, Jean Earl Tatum, Barry Lyon, Marilyn
Bradford DeVille, Nora Martin, Alanna Nash, Mike McGrath,
Angela Christi, Mike and Kathleen Assalone, and Mary Norris.

Very special thanks to Lucy's children: Deborah, Melody, Denise, Jacques, Jacqueline, and of course, Desirée Presley.

Infinite thanks to my agent, Connie Clausen, for her wise advice and support, and to my editor, Diane Reverand, for her skill and sensitivity.

And most of all, to Lucy, for allowing me to hear her story in its most intimate telling.

—D.M.

INTRODUCTION

I WISH I COULD HAVE FORESEEN THE horrible end to Elvis's life. Maybe I could have helped him hang on a little longer. Then again, maybe I was part of the reason he did the things that led to his death.

I don't know.

Looking back, that's what hurts the most. Not knowing.

I hope God will forgive me if I made the wrong decisions. I would have liked nothing better than to have been Elvis's wife. He asked me many times. It would have been easy to think only of myself and run to him. I wanted to, but I couldn't. There were too many people who would have been hurt. I never gave up hope of being with him. I loved him so much. The one thing he and I treasured was our ability to keep our love alive through all the troubled years.

I blame so many for what happened to Elvis. Those around him were supposed to protect and take care of him. Instead, they hurt him and allowed him to hurt himself. He was so trusting. He was sensitive. Those who betrayed him injured him more deeply than anyone knew. Each friend who turned his back cut out a piece of Elvis's soul.

I played my part. I hid a secret from him that nearly destroyed us both.

Or maybe it did.

I don't know.

I tried to run away. I hid. I tried to protect him. I did everything I could. Except one thing. I never tried to stop Elvis from loving me. I just couldn't. I needed him so much.

He was a man beyond the image everyone saw. The only man

I could love without being afraid. Before him, I was so afraid. He came and took the pain away. He was strong, indomitable, and sure of himself and his beliefs. He was tender, kind, gentle, and loving. He was my lover, my inspiration, and my deliverer.

He had faults. I won't try to deny that. But they were so few and small compared to his goodness. We've lost sight of that now. We've allowed some bitter people to distort our view of him. What he did for me, what he was to me, reveals the man he really was.

There remains a wonderful joy to hold on to. My daughter Desirée has grown so beautiful in body and spirit. She reminds me so much of him. She wants the identity I denied her for so long. I worry about her. She's so much like her father. She listens to everyone. She's much too trusting. Underneath her glamour lies a weakness, the same weakness that destroyed him. It's the sweetness that makes her give of herself and allow others to take. It's hard to explain, but I can see it. Those who were close to Elvis will also see it.

I'm so afraid someone will hurt her. She's been hurt enough. I hurt her. I only hope she knows that I was acting out of love. I pray she'll understand why I never told Elvis about her, or why I never told her about him. I thought I was protecting them. I thought I did the right thing.

I'm not sure anymore.

I recently dreamed that I was with Elvis again when he was struggling to launch his career. I was back with the real Elvis, the young man I knew at the beginning of the road, the boy with the quick smile and the beat-up guitar. He had a zest about him, a determination that would not be denied. Even when I'm awake, so many things remind me of him. I will never look at a star at night without thinking of Elvis. Falling leaves, green hills, autumn —it all reminds me of him. I hear his haunting voice on a distant radio station. I see his image laminated on wood at the county fair. Late at night, I turn the channel of my television set and see him singing and dancing through one of his movies, happy and carefree. It's almost as if he's still with us.

Except the phone is silent. There are no more midnight calls with him sky-high over his latest success, ranting about whatever upset him, or wallowing in despair over some minor defeat that he took much too hard.

His image remains, but Elvis is gone.

I realize I will be judged for my actions. I know people will look to see what part I played in his decline. Please try to understand. I did what I thought was best, not for me, but for him. I always put Elvis first. I need everyone to understand that, especially his fans, all of you who didn't know Elvis but loved him as if you did. I was among the fans at Graceland when he died. I too was on the outside. I saw the pain in your faces and tears streaming down your cheeks. You really cared. You cried with me. It gave me comfort.

Recalling my past hasn't been easy. Some of it is ugly. I held it inside so long. I banished it from my memory so I could heal. I pretend that the nightmarish images have slipped away. They fade, but they never go away. The memories of Elvis help. But now even they bring pain. My love is as intense as it was in 1953, when Elvis and I met. I thought that too would fade, but it hasn't. My grief remains as deep as it was in 1977, when suddenly he was gone.

The tears come less frequently now, but they've never stopped.

Even though I'm aware that I'll be judged, I have to tell the truth, all of it. An altered account would deceive not only the public, but my daughter as well. I can't do that. The only reason I've agreed to open up is to give my daughter a sense of her father and what we had, and to explain to her why I did the things I did. My daughter must know exactly how it was: the good times and bad, the passion and anger.

His few faults.

My many.

Desirée, my darling, I owe you this story and give it to you out of love. I kept it from you far too long. I've made you frustrated and angry. I understand. In a strange way, I respect you for that. Build strength around your anger. You're going to need it.

Are You Lonesome Tonight?

Chapter 1

I REMEMBER THE FIRE. IT WAS ONE OF my first memories. I was three years old. A crowd of relatives had gathered in the front yard and stood quietly under the tall oak trees. I saw some men splash a liquid around the base of our two-story, wood-frame house. A thin man threw a torch upon it and quickly jumped back. I heard a *whooosssh* sound and felt the heat against my cheeks as the fire devoured my home. No one tried to put it out. I held on to my mother's leg and stared into the bright orange flames, wondering what it all meant.

Everything had happened so suddenly. The memory is a blur of sounds, people, and colors. My father had just come home from a long trip. We had the usual feast to celebrate his return. Afterward, the children were shooed upstairs so the grown-ups could drink and carry on. I was still awake when the party ended, too excited by the noise to sleep. I crept downstairs and saw my father sitting in his rocking chair. He spotted me, smiled, and stretched out his arms. I ran to him and jumped in his lap.

My older sisters later described my father, Alfred Joseph de Barbin, as a tall, handsome man with blue eyes and thick, grayish-blond hair. He was always well dressed, usually in a three-piece suit accented by a dangling gold chain that led to the pocket watch he carried in his vest. He often tied a colorful cravat around his neck and was fond of knee-high boots, which he kept shiny and polished. He was born and raised in Paris, and some members of his family were said to be prominent in the French government. In the early 1900s a large group of my ancestors, from both sides, came to America and settled in Boston. My father met my mother when he was in his late forties and she was only sixteen. They were opposites. She was petite, just under five feet tall, with pale blue eyes set off by black hair that hung past her waist when she combed it out each night. During the day she wore it knotted at the nape of her neck in a chignon that was held in place by two large tortoiseshell hairpins.

Both families scorned their marriage. His people didn't think mother had the proper breeding. Her family was from Nice and believed that anyone from Paris was a scoundrel. Besides, he was much too old. Despite these misgivings, the marriage was solid. Mother had thirteen children, though only seven survived infancy. I was the last daughter and next-to-last child.

My family was part of a splinter group that migrated from Boston to Chalmette, Louisiana, a small French enclave a few miles from New Orleans. My great-grandfather, Louis James Bellevue de Barbin, had set off an earlier wave of immigration when the French government sent him to Louisiana as a munitions and customs official during the colonization in the 1700s and early 1800s, prior to the Louisiana Purchase. Many of his descendants chose to settle in Chalmette and New Orleans rather than return to France, so we were among friends and relatives. My father served as county sheriff for a while, and later had an interest in a cattle ranch in Houston that forced him to travel frequently.

He was seventy-five when I sat in his lap that night, but I had no conception of age. He was energetic and quick to laugh or sing. He was proud of his French heritage and made all his children learn French before they learned English. French was the only language I knew at the time and it was the only language my mother ever spoke. That night, as he held me on his lap, he said, "Ma petite Bee, you're going to be a beautiful woman one day and sing like a nightingale." He started to hum "After the Ball Is Over" and said "Ma chérie, sing with me." He sang it a few times, and I tried to parrot the English lyrics. All of a sudden, he started coughing violently. He ordered me to get him some water. I ran to the kitchen but couldn't reach the faucet. I ran back to tell him, but someone grabbed my shoulders and held me back. I peeked around their legs and saw my mother sitting on the couch with my father's head in her lap. She was hugging him and crying.

My father was dead. I found out later that he had tuberculosis.

As was the custom among the French immigrants, the relatives burned down our house the next day, thinking it would stop the spread of the disease. I had lost not only my father but my home as well. The family was placed under the dominating hand of my stern maternal grandmother, Aliscia Lachenye Luneau. She was a heartless old woman permanently unhappy about being uprooted from her beloved Nice. She hated America and Americans. She shrouded herself in mourning clothes, long black dresses and black bonnets, and peered down at us through wire-rimmed glasses. She walked with a cane, which she brandished about while condemning everyone to hell. My grandmother had never stopped hating my father, and that hatred spilled over to his children. We immediately became disposable.

We had so much when my father was alive. The house was large and well furnished. We never wanted for anything. After he died, everything vanished in the fire. Anything else he had was confiscated by my grandmother, and my family became impoverished overnight. My grandmother forced my mother to work as a common maid and sent my five-year-old sister Mary and me back to Boston. My younger brother and two sisters remained in Chalmette. I never knew why we were separated, but even at that young age I sensed that my grandmother disliked me most of all.

"Your parents both have blue eyes, but you have green eyes," she told me once. "That's a sign that you are evil."

In Boston we moved in with a widow named Nini Chaudoir, a kind woman in her sixties. No one ever explained who she was, though I recall someone saying she was the wife of one of my father's brothers. We called her Tante Nini. She lived by herself in a magnificent three-story house that was so tall I could see the lights of the city from my bedroom window. Despite the pleasant surroundings, I was unhappy about being away from my family.

When I was five I went on an outing with some older girls from the neighborhood. We were riding on a horse-drawn wagon in the country, making stops to gather flowers. I took off my shoes and sat on the wagon, dangling my feet over the side. The girls made me promise to sit there and not move while they ran off to play. I quickly became bored and decided to jump into the muddy water a few feet away. When I landed, I felt a sharp pain in my foot. I stepped out and discovered that my foot was bleeding. The girls ran over and pleaded with me to stop crying. They told me not to tell anyone what happened.

As the months passed the pain in my foot increased. The girls were still afraid of getting into trouble and repeated their request that I not tell anyone. I obeyed and withstood the pain.

Shortly afterward, Tante Nini told me I was too serious and sad for a child, and sent me back home to my mother. I was pleased, but the pain in my foot tempered my happiness. Back in Chalmette I attended a convent school and began limping. I was soon unable to wear a shoe on that foot because it was swollen and sore. The other kids at school thought I was crippled and avoided me.

With no friends, I turned my attention to schoolwork. I studied hard and won some merit awards. I learned English but found that it was my foot, not my language, that scared the other children away. I continued to endure the pain because of my vow to my friends in Boston. I didn't want to get them in trouble.

My uncle, Geoffrey Bellevue de Barbin, arrived unexpectedly from France one day. He was a jolly man who looked a lot like my father except his hair was darker and he sported thick, bushy sideburns. He was a doctor and asked me in French about my foot. I decided to confide in him. I told him about jumping off the wagon into the muddy water. He examined the scar and told me there was something inside that must be removed. He convinced my mother to send me back to Boston so he could operate.

When he opened my foot he found a green thorn. It had entered near my toe and in the year since the accident had traveled almost to the center of my foot. He said it was a miracle that I didn't lose my foot from an infection. I was elated because not only was the pain gone, but more important, I could wear a shoe! I could become just like other kids and wouldn't be shunned anymore. Free from the pain and stigma, my personality began to blossom. I soon had many friends.

My mother continued working as a maid, cleaning churches and large houses, scrubbing floors, washing windows, working herself to the bone. She would come home exhausted and depressed. She never smiled anymore. I knew her opportunities were limited because she couldn't speak English. My father's last words, about me growing up to be a beautiful singer, stuck in my mind. I wanted to be successful so I could help my mother. I practiced singing every day, learning everything from opera to popular tunes. I learned to control my voice and alter the tones. When I was eleven the nuns at the convent asked me to sing at a large, beautiful church, St. Anthony of Padua. I sang high soprano solos in Latin at Mass.

One day the housemother told me that my grandmother had come to see them. They said I would be moving away soon. I couldn't believe it. Here I was finally settling in somewhere and had to leave again.

When I got home, there was a party going on. The house was full of strangers, mostly men. A well-dressed woman introduced herself and told me to call her Aunt Victoria. After dinner I was asked to sing. That was routine at our parties and I loved performing. I had recently learned the song "Mother Machree" and dedicated it to my mother. I could see the tears in her eyes as I sang.

She told me later that the strangers were friends of my grandmother and had come to visit because of me. They were interested in helping me study music. They would furnish us with a nice home and things wouldn't be as hard anymore. My mother could give up her terrible job. I was thrilled! I was only eleven and already my singing had helped.

A few days later, my mother went off to live in a wonderful new home in Monroe, Louisiana. I was put in the care of Aunt Victoria. She was about forty and tall, with short, curly black hair. She was obviously wealthy because she had a closet full of fur coats and adorned herself with diamond rings, earrings, and necklaces. She began dressing me in her image. I loved the new clothes and acted out fantasies in the mirror, playing the part of a sophisticated lady out on the town. My hair was long and black like my mother's, and I experimented with different styles.

Aunt Victoria caught me primping one day and said, "Lucy, you're a very pretty girl and your breasts are very large. You look older than you really are. Some young man might be interested in you. Don't tell anyone how young you really are."

I didn't like that. I was self-conscious about my breasts. I wanted to look like my friends. Their bosoms were flatter, and they could wear smock dresses. I was always trying to hide my figure under baggy clothes.

Two weeks later Aunt Victoria said that my grandmother was

coming to discuss my future. She arrived promptly and ordered me to cooperate with the family's wishes. She said a green-eyed girl like me would go wayward if she didn't get married. I couldn't believe what she was saying. Married? I was just eleven. I had never even had a boyfriend.

"I don't know anyone to get married to," I said. "I don't want to get married. I have to study."

She told me I didn't have to worry about finding a husband. It was all arranged. There was a nice man who thought I was pretty and had agreed to marry me. I would be taken to him in Jackson, Mississippi.

"No. I will not do this," I said. "My mother will never agree to this."

My grandmother told me that if I didn't do as I was told, my mother would be thrown out of the new home and forced to work as a maid again. "Do you want to see your mother work herself to death?" she admonished.

I was then instructed to tell my mother that getting married was my idea and I would be happy. A week passed. I thought it had all been a horrible dream. Then Aunt Victoria and my grandmother came and told me to pack my things. They put me in a big black car and drove me to Mississippi. I was introduced to a man I remembered having seen at my house when I sang. He was tall, about six feet, thin, and had a ruddy complexion and dark reddish hair streaked with gray. He was at least forty-five or older and smelled of alcohol.

He was to be my husband. I had never been kissed and now I was to be the wife of a forty-five-year-old man.

I was taken to a wide, gray house with tall ceilings and dusty rugs. The man's sister came to stay with me and prepare me for the wedding. She looked like the house, drab and gray. She kept asking, "What's wrong with you?" because I was pale and frightened. I was so afraid that I kept throwing up in the bathroom.

A second woman, equally unpleasant, came in and handed me a dismal skirt, blouse, and jacket to wear as my wedding gown. I was told that the man didn't want anything special so as not to attract attention. I knew it was because of my age. The women left me alone to dress.

I stared in the mirror, trying to understand why all this was happening. I kept telling myself that God has a reason for everything. I thought of running away, but where could I go? I was in a strange city, and even if I did escape they would force my mother to go back to work. I tried to stay strong. I brushed away the tears so no one would see them.

I was taken outside and put in a car between the man and his sister. No one said anything. I remember it was raining and dreary. I was brought before a man dressed in black, a justice of the peace. He mumbled some words without smiling and then ordered me to say "I do." I did as I was told. With a strange man beside me, and two strangers standing behind me, I was married.

We were driven back to the house. The women left. I was alone with the Man. That night, I tried to stall as long as I could to keep him away. I knew something awful was going to happen, but I didn't know what. No one had told me anything. He kept approaching me and putting his hands on me. I pushed him away. I ran upstairs and hid in a closet. I got on my knees and begged God to let me wake up from this horrible nightmare.

Instead I heard a loud banging on the door. The voice was angry and cold.

"I know you're in there. I'm tired of waiting. You come on out right now."

I crawled deeper into the back of the closet. He started banging harder and shouting louder. He began throwing his body against the door. I was terrified and began screaming. The door burst open. He reached in, dragged me out, and threw me on the bed. He ripped off my clothes until I was completely naked. I was so ashamed. I tried to cover up, but he spread apart my arms, then took my body.

I'll never forget the pain.

To this day, Lucy doesn't realize, or has refused to accept, the fact that she was sold like a slave to the highest bidder. The party at her house was actually a discreet auction with Lucy as the prized property. "Aunt" Victoria was probably the wife of the local marriage broker, or possibly a marriage broker herself.

Lucy's singing performance was geared toward titillating the buyers and opening their wallets.

The winner of this auction was Richard "Dixie" W.D. Ware,* an underachiever whose stake came from a family aviation business and some minor real estate transactions. The house in Monroe that Ware offered Lucy's family may have been only part of the price he paid for a beautiful eleven-year-old "thoroughbred."

To some, this account may read as though it took place in another century. Actually, such marriages were not uncommon in 1947. The French have a tradition of arranged marriages and refer to them as *mariages de convenance.* A 1961 study by Wesley D. Camp, Ph.D., determined that the French had the highest frequency of marriages in the "younger ages" of all European countries.

In America, the 1980 census reported that among all married women, 3,284,682 were married at age fifteen or below. Broken down yearly, the National Center for Health Statistics reports that in 1982, the most recent year it surveyed, there were 9,214 girls in America who married at age fifteen or below, including 67 at age twelve, 198 at age thirteen, and 1,498 at fourteen. (No state allows legal marriages below age twelve, so there are no statistics for younger ages.) These figures don't account for people who lie about their age on their marriage license, nor do they include eight states that failed to report age breakdowns in their figures.

It is also significant that Lucy was brought to Mississippi to be married. In 1947, the minimum legal age a girl could marry with parental consent in Louisiana was sixteen. In Mississippi, the minimum age was twelve.

At the publication of this book in 1987, Mississippi had raised the age to fifteen, one year higher than Alabama and New York. If one is inclined to believe that we've progressed beyond such archaic practices, consider the turnaround of the state of New Hampshire. In 1925, the minimum marriage age for girls in this forward-thinking state was eighteen, the highest minimum in the United States and the age social reformers were pushing for as a national law. By 1987, the minimum age a girl could marry with parental consent in New Hampshire had plunged to thirteen.

---

*Richard Ware, known as "Dixie" W.D. Ware, and Lucy de Barbin should not be confused with Richard Ware and his late wife, Dixie Ware, of Monroe, Louisiana. Ms. Dixie Ware was a television personality on station KNOE in Monroe, where Lucy later worked. They are not related.

Chapter 2

I REMEMBER LITTLE OF WHAT HAP-
pened over the next five years. I've spent my whole life trying to
forget. Every time the Man forced himself upon me it was a
nightmare beyond description. I never got used to it. I couldn't
even resign myself to it. Each time I begged God that it would
be the last. It made my skin crawl whenever the Man came close.
The only thing that saved me was his frequent absences. He
traveled extensively on business and was away for months at a
time. Someone told me that he had a wife and family in another
city and spent most of his time with them. I didn't care. I wished
he would never come back.

Shortly after the marriage I was ordered to pack my things once
again and was sent to live near my mother in Monroe, Louisiana.
I was set up in yet another house, a Mediterranean-style home
with a large screened porch, and was left in the charge of a stern,
Brünnhilde-type woman, Mrs. Fowler, whom the Man had hired
to care for me. Spying on me is a better description of her duties.
She was a tall, stout, unsmiling woman with thick arms and legs,
rough hands, and short black hair. Her mood was soured by the
fact that the job as my overseer took her away from her husband
and family in Mississippi. She viewed me as the despised child that
kept her from her own beloved children.

I was allowed to continue my schooling at St. Matthew's, a
local Catholic school. Mrs. Fowler drove me back and forth every
day in a big black car the Man provided. I felt out of place at
school. I spoke with a heavy French accent, while my classmates
were more typical southerners. Monroe was settled by families
that had been in America for many generations, and their ethnic

origins had blurred. It was so different from the insulated French neighborhoods in Chalmette and Boston. I could barely understand my classmates' slow, thick speech patterns, and they looked at me like I was someone from outer space. It didn't really matter because I couldn't have any friends anyway. The Man had ordered me not to tell anyone about my situation. I wanted to fit in and live a normal life, but it was impossible.

I had to miss a lot of school because of my health. The Man continued to abuse my body. After one particularly harrowing encounter, I began bleeding heavily. Mrs. Fowler took me to see a doctor, a kind man named Glenn Gallaspy. He examined me, then told me I was pregnant and had miscarried. He kept asking me how old I was. Mrs. Fowler had ordered me to say seventeen.

"You're nowhere near seventeen. Tell me how old you really are," Dr. Gallaspy demanded. I was so afraid I kept insisting I was seventeen instead of eleven. He didn't believe me.

"Listen, I know you're very young. I don't know what's going on here, or even if I can do anything about it, but if you need help, or if you have any more problems, come to me."

It wasn't long before I was pregnant again. The Man went away for an extended period and by the time he returned I was showing and he wasn't as determined. I fought him off long enough to have the child. My first daughter, Deborah, was born six days after my twelfth birthday. My second daughter, Melody Charisse, was born two and a half years later in 1951. Life consisted of little more than cleaning the house, taking care of my children, and, when not hiding my pregnancies, going to school.

In the late summer of 1953 the local television station, KNOE, was auditioning for singers and dancers to be part of a music program. My circumstances had all but killed my dream of becoming a singer, but a few sparks of interest remained. I remembered what my mother told me before the marriage. The people who gave her the house wanted to help me pursue a musical career. It was a cruel lie invented by my grandmother, but I could use it as an excuse. I was more concerned with making money than singing. Money was the key to my escape.

At the same time my older sister Mary arrived in Monroe for a visit. She lived in Memphis, Tennessee. Mary was nineteen, beautiful, and had long blond hair like some of the women from my father's side of the family. She was the only sister I was really close to. When I told her about the auditions, she built up my confidence and encouraged me to go.

I went to the brand-new studio and waited with a small group of people for my turn. I sang "Spring Will Be a Little Late This Year" and was given the standard "don't call us, we'll call you" line. I was crushed. As I was leaving, a man named Pete McCausland asked me to audition for *The Mr. Music Show*, a hit-parade-type program KNOE was starting. He needed a dancer. I was a singer, not a dancer. I wasn't comfortable with the idea of dancing, but I wanted a job. I needed some kind of life outside my home, and the atmosphere of the television studio was exciting. I told Mr. McCausland that I wasn't sure I could do it, but he just smiled and told me to give it a try.

"We'll play the music. Make up a dance to it, practice a while, and we'll come in later," he said. He dimmed the lights, then left me all alone in the empty studio.

The darkness made me feel better. I could hide. The music came out of nowhere and startled me. It was a pretty song, the theme from the Italian movie *Anna*. The stage looked so inviting and magical I found myself walking out and pretending to be a famous dancer performing before a large audience. It was fun. Moving my body in sync with the music was exhilarating. I floated around the stage like a swan and really began getting into a spontaneous free-form dance. I wanted the music to go on and on, to dance away all my problems. When the song ended the lights snapped back on. A booming voice filled the large room.

"Very good! Excellent!"

I looked all around but couldn't see where the words were coming from.

"Up here. Above you," the voice said.

Mr. McCausland and two other men were applauding from what I later learned was the sound room. They had been watching my whole silly dance. I was so embarrassed I could have died! Mr. McCausland came down and said, "Okay, girl, you're hired. You start next week."

Mrs. Fowler, my keeper, was now the only thing keeping me from taking the first step in changing my life. I resorted to the oldest form of persuasion in the world—bribery. I didn't know how much the Man was paying her, but I figured if I shared some of my salary, she might keep quiet. I offered her ten dollars a week, almost half of the twenty-five dollars a week I was paid. To my surprise, she accepted.

The show and the dancing soon became one of the few bright spots in my life. My day was now full—school, studying, taking care of the children, and dancing on the program two nights a week. I spent what time was left refining my English and trying to lose my French accent. It all worked to occupy my mind and create a life removed from the Man. Like any normal sixteen-year-old, I began dreaming of falling in love.

I leaned more heavily upon my faith in God. I could endure anything with His help. Didn't Jesus have to endure suffering? God would find a way to deliver me from my pain. My faith renewed my strength. I was living such a split existence, as usual, always coming and going, never getting close to anyone. I didn't want the people at the television station to know about me, so I didn't socialize with anyone there. It was absurd to think that the Man wouldn't find out, and I dreaded the day he returned, which could be at any time. When he did, he was so withdrawn into his own world that I got by with it. He stayed only two or three days anyway, and he arrived on the weekends when the live show wasn't on.

My deception was so effective that he began to think there wasn't enough to occupy my mind. If I wasn't busy, he figured I would do something bad. He cut the electric cord on the washing machine and ordered me to wash all the clothes and diapers by hand in the sink, extending my work by hours. I hated him even more for this. The scrubbing and harsh detergents roughened and cut my hands, often causing large sores. When I looked at them I'd run into my room and cry. I wanted my hands to be beautiful and graceful so I could use them in my dances; they were the key to my expression. My battered hands came to symbolize all the abuse he inflicted upon me. The sores were like flashing lights warning me that both my physical and mental well-being were beginning to dissolve under the strain. I had to find some way to escape.

My first attempt was a miserable failure. Relying on my faith in God, I went to Monsignor Marsh, a parish priest at St. Matthew's. He met me in his formal attire, a long black robe with rows of covered buttons, red piping, and a black sash around his waist. He had white hair and a flushed complexion. He was the absolute picture of godly authority, and I begged for help. Instead of offering it, the monsignor coldly turned me away.

"You don't go to the store, buy a pair of shoes and wear them, then decide you don't want them anymore," he admonished.

"But Monsignor, I didn't want to be married. I was forced to. I wasn't married in the church."

"That was your first mistake," he said. "You shouldn't have been married outside the church. But that doesn't mean you can walk away from it. You are married, so go home and be a good girl and stay married."

I was devastated. If the church was against me, I could never get away. That had been my only hope. I missed the bus home, so I walked in the pouring rain for a long time and ended up at a Protestant church. I stood in the alcove and cried my eyes out. I would never depend upon or trust anyone again.

That knocked me down for a while. It was back to washing clothes in the sink and dreading the moment the Man would walk through the door. My only inspiration during those bleak morning hours was listening to Paul Harvey on the little wooden radio on the kitchen table. He spoke of heroes, achievers, and underdogs who fought their way out of dark circumstances. His broadcasts gave me the courage that I too could overcome my problems.

The television work was only part-time. After taking out the taxes and the bribe to Mrs. Fowler, there was only about ten dollars left each week. I decided to try to get a job at Silverstein's, a large department store that sold the finest clothes in town. I put on my best outfit, a sleeveless black linen sheath covered by a white, double-breasted jacket and accented by a white bag and white high-heel shoes, the first heels I ever owned. White gloves covered the sores on my hands. I was trying to look older and sophisticated so I could fit in at the fancy store. I bought the clothes with my first few paychecks from the TV program. I wanted to save the money for my escape, but somehow the clothes seemed to be a more attainable way of lifting my spirits. The bold outfit filled me with confidence.

I marched into the store and inquired about a job. Fortunately, my interview was with a man, the store manager, Phil Fishman. A woman probably would have seen right through me. Mr. Fishman, who looked like Tyrone Power, seemed taken by my appearance but was skeptical about my age. I was sixteen then, so I lied and told him nineteen. He arched an eyebrow but gave me a job anyway. I was now in charge of arranging the display windows!

Back at the television studio, the star of the program, Mr. Music himself, Morry Twomey, kept pestering me to do promotions for the show. Mr. Twomey was tall and handsome, with thick brown hair and a deep radio announcer's voice. His real love was photography and he was always flashing candid pictures. I was his favorite target. Every time I turned around, there was Morry flashing his camera. He wanted to use me as a professional model, and I wanted to do it, but was terrified that the Man would see a picture. I was taking a big enough risk by appearing on television, but I knew it was unlikely that the Man would ever watch the program. A modeling photo could show up anywhere.

It was fun dancing on the show. They let me do my own choreography, enabling me to gear my dances to the songs. I floated in the shadows draped in a flowing dress for one bluesy number, did a fire dance in which the cameraman somehow superimposed me into the flames, put on a straw skirt and did a hula for some Hawaiian songs, and used a giant air fan for a windswept look during a Russian ballet-style dance performed to a hit love song. One time I even sang the words to "Bahia" in French while doing a tropical free-form dance.

One day while preparing to leave the studio, a number of well-dressed, important-looking men appeared. One of the men, a large, balding, robust man about fifty-five or sixty, introduced himself as James Noe, the station's president, founder, and owner. Noe was also the ex-governor of Louisiana. He said that he had been watching the program and liked the way I danced. He asked me to perform at a big political party they were throwing for VIPs at a ranch somewhere north of Monroe near the Mississippi border. I wanted to say no, but I was intimidated by Mr. Noe and stammered out an acceptance. On the way home I was filled with fear. Could I get away? Who would see me? Would the Man find out? Maybe he would be there.

Despite my misgivings, I had to keep my word; Mr. Noe was the boss. I loved my job and wanted to keep it. Looking back, I probably had no other choice. All the anguished prayers I cried out from upon my knees had finally been heard. In an unexpected way, God answered. The party would change the course of my entire life.

Just how adept Lucy was at hiding her life and juggling her jobs became strikingly apparent when I attempted to trace her steps by traveling to Monroe and interviewing more than a dozen of her former coworkers. The few old timers who remember her at KNOE recall little about her other than her appearance on the *Mr. Music* program. No one there knew she worked in a local store. Those who worked with her at Silverstein's have clearer memories but were surprised to learn that she was a dancer on television. (The show lasted only about six months.) Hardly anyone knew that she was married and had children. Silverstein's has closed, but Phil Fishman still lives in Monroe and remembers Lucy well.

"She was a very beautiful woman, exceptionally beautiful and very petite," Fishman told me. "She was deeper and more intelligent than most girls her age, but extremely quiet and guarded about herself. No one knew much about her."

Mr. Music host Morry Twomey followed his shutterbug fever and moved to Shreveport to become an accomplished photographer of show dogs. Twomey died in 1979, but his partner in Shreveport, Maryetta Jones, clearly remembers the stack of pictures from his TV days that he kept in a box in the back of his office. "He had lots of pictures of that little dancer, Lucy. I distinctly remember them because I thought she looked like Cyd Charisse."

Twomey's widow, Nel, said she only vaguely remembers Lucy, but did recall that she worked in a "clothing store somewhere." Unfortunately, Nel Twomey threw out nearly all of her husband's old pictures after he died.

Gene Milligan, the art director for KNOE at the time, said he and George Lane were probably the other men up in the booth during Lucy's tryout. "We watched a lot of ladies in the studio. It was always me, George, and Pete McCausland." He didn't remember Lucy at first, but did remember the fire dance.

"I probably used that same gimmick a hundred times in my career," he said, explaining how the technique was accomplished. "That must have been the first time I used it. We did a lot of crazy things."

I couldn't jog Milligan's memory about Lucy until I mentioned Twomey's active camera.

"Oh hell yeah, Lucy Ware! Of course. He was always taking pictures of that little gal. He must have taken a thousand. She was a real beauty! I mean a knockout. She was always with Morry. They were just friends though. Yeah, I remember that little gal."

Chapter 3

I FOLLOWED A HOMEMADE MAP TO FIND the ranch were Mr. Noe wanted me to perform. It was about a half-hour drive northeast of Monroe, somewhere close to the Mississippi border. The place was like a scene from *Gone With the Wind.* It was early evening, and the grounds were lit by floodlights that made the weeping willow trees shimmer. Patches of red, white, and pink camellias added color. The white colonial-style house was regal and airy, set off by black shutters and four huge white columns at the front entrance that contrasted with the black roof. A veranda with white rails of delicate latticework wrapped around both sides and led to a screened porch in the back. There was a lake about fifty yards from the front porch. Graceful swans and ducks glided over the water. There was a temporary stage set up between the house and the lake, and a big bonfire was blazing about a hundred yards to the right. People were everywhere, a thousand or more. Some were roasting wieners in the bonfire, while others ate from the tables of prepared food scattered around the area. It was an older crowd of politicians and rich businessmen, the kind of people you'd expect ex-Governor Noe to associate with. I didn't move in those circles, but with so many people, there was a chance of running into someone who knew me. I made myself scarce by walking along the edge of the water.

A young man in a bright blue shirt with big white polka dots was staring at me. He acted as if he wanted to approach me and appeared to be struggling with shyness. I ran back to the house, not wanting to wait until he built up his courage.

I told the woman in charge of the entertainment that I had to leave early. She said I could go on first and told me to put on my costume. My legs were shaking as I took off my red velvet skirt and black décolleté sweater and slipped on my dancing clothes. I wasn't nervous about performing; I was afraid of being recognized and beaten when I got home.

My costume was from the television show. Beth Breece, a talk-show host at KNOE radio, frequently assisted me with my stage outfits. She helped me design the one I wore that evening. It was for a segment that called for a wilderness scene, so we cut up a white sheet in fringes and added slashes and tears to give me a wood nymph look. It was one of my favorite dances and was performed to "Anna," the same song they played at my audition. I heard my cue and climbed onstage to do my number. I instantly became oblivious of the crowd as I withdrew into my dance. It felt wonderful again; the rush of adrenaline when performing is a thrill I'll never forget. When I finished, the applause almost blew me over. I had never danced before a live audience and was accustomed to the silence of the studio. Now people were clapping and whistling and hollering their approval. I bowed a few times, totally flustered, then ducked back into the house.

While I dressed, a haunting voice carried over from the stage area. It sounded like Frank Sinatra. I went to the window to see who was onstage and was surprised to see that it was the same young man with the polka-dot shirt who had been staring at me by the lake. He sang with such depth and richness it was gripping. I figured that the crowd would really go wild, but the applause was only moderate. It was an older audience, and they didn't appreciate him.

I backed away from the window. The young singer's career plight was the least of my worries. Getting out of there as fast as possible was my main concern. I was able to perform because the Man wasn't in town. He could return at any moment. If he found me gone, especially at night, a beating would follow. I made my way down the stairs and rushed out the back door, nearly bumping into someone standing nearby. It was the singer. He was out of breath, and his hair was tousled. He grabbed my arm to steady me. I tried to get by him, but he stood in my way.

"I loved your dance," he said, smiling brightly.

"I enjoyed your song," I mumbled, still trying to get around him.

"You're not leavin', are you?" he asked. "I don't even know your name."

"Lucy," I said. "What's yours?" I immediately regretted asking. I had to leave.

"Elvis Presley."

What a strange name, I thought.

"Will I see you again?" he asked.

"I can't," I said, bowing my head to avoid having him look in my eyes. "Good luck with your singing."

I wanted to stay and talk to him. Normally I would have run away, but he seemed so nice, vulnerable even, and there was something about him that was very attractive. His brown hair was shiny and appeared darker because of the balm he wore.

I walked through the crowd, saying good-bye to people who complimented me on my dance. Something made me turn back. The singer was standing there watching me. Our eyes met and he smiled. I smiled back, then turned and walked away.

In his early days in 1953, Elvis, then eighteen, had not yet formed his own style and therefore imitated other successful singers. Friends and associates were often startled at how well he could mimic Sinatra, Dean Martin, or whomever else he wanted to copy. His audience that afternoon was made up of the same generation that would decry him when he became famous. As one old-timer in Monroe told me, "Nobody who'd a' been at one of James Noe's parties woulda given a damn about Elvis Presley, famous or not. He coulda done his whole Vegas act and he'd a' still been booed off the stage."

THE SINGER'S SMILING FACE KEPT flashing in my mind. It was a brief encounter, a few words and a smile, but he made a lasting impression. I thought he would probably be very successful one day and maybe I would have a chance to see him perform somewhere.

A couple of weeks later Mr. Twomey talked me into modeling for a shoot at the zoo. I thought it might be fun. When the time drew near, Mr. Twomey dropped the other shoe.

"I didn't tell you what zoo," he said, laughing. "It's the Memphis Zoo."

By then the arrangements had been made and it was too late to change. Mr. Twomey wasn't even going. He gave me a phone number and told me he had contacted a photographer in Memphis. The Man was out of town, so I decided to go. It would give me a chance to see my sister Mary, who lived in Memphis. I told Mrs. Fowler that Mary was sick and needed help.

That Friday, I gathered up my daughters, and Mrs. Fowler drove us to the train station. It was a long ride to Memphis, about five hours, and the girls fidgeted the whole way. My sister came to pick us up. Driving to her house, I noticed how lovely Memphis was, full of trees and colorful flowers, and it seemed so large compared to Monroe. After dinner, I called the photographer and he came over with a date. We decided to go out. My sister called a baby-sitter to watch Deborah, Melody, and her own young son. They took me to see a hot new singer in town. We went to a club called the Eagle's Nest, a tacky place with tables covered by red-checkered tablecloths. They wanted to sit right up front, but I was still so afraid of being seen, even in Memphis. I steered us to a table near the middle. A boring western band was playing. No one was singing. I asked my sister which one was the "hot new singer." She said he wasn't part of the band, that he came on when the band took their breaks. If the singer was playing second fiddle to this dull band, how hot could he be?

"Now you'll see him," the photographer's date squealed as the band left the small stage. The house lights dimmed and the solo singer appeared. I was stunned. It was the guy from the party with the funny name. He looked even better than when I had seen him before. He wore a silky white shirt with big billowy sleeves and baggy black pants. It gave him a swashbuckling-pirate look. He moved around more than he did at the party, and his hair flopped down over his face. He gave an energetic performance copying the current hits by Sinatra, Dean Martin, and the other popular singers. He appeared to be staring at me the whole time he sang, which made me uneasy.

When he finished, I was again surprised that there was only polite applause. He had really poured his heart out up there, and except for some girls at a table up front, he didn't excite anyone. It didn't seem to bother him, though.

Instead of retreating backstage, he came out into the audience and began talking with people in the crowd. I watched him and marveled at how polite and courteous he was to everyone, especially after the lukewarm reception. It was almost as if he was thanking them for listening to him.

After talking at some of the tables up front, he started walking straight to our table. He talked to my sister and the other woman, then looked at me and said, "Who's the pretty stranger?" He gave no indication that he remembered me. I was relieved but disappointed. They told him I was this big-time TV star and model from New Orleans, exaggerating of course. They told him about my photo session at the zoo the next day, and he was impressed.

"You'll love Memphis," he said. "It's a great city. Why don't you let me show you around?"

I begged off, saying I'd be working all day and wouldn't be able to get away. We left before he had a chance to give a second performance, if he gave one. When we arrived home, my sister scolded me for refusing the singer's offer.

"Lucy, I know about your marriage, if you can call it that. I know what you've been going through. Some of us have spoken to Archbishop Cushing about it in Boston, and he said you don't have to remain married. You can get out of it. You don't have to feel you belong to that man. You can do whatever you want."

Though my sister chose her husband, her marriage was also bad, so she was sympathetic. I thanked her for her support and promised to consider what Archbishop Cushing had said.

I was up at dawn the next morning preparing for the photo session at the zoo. We had to start early to catch the morning light. I put on a pair of white shorts, an apricot and mint green sleeveless plaid blouse, and white sandals that tied around my ankles. I brought some tennis shoes to wear afterward because the sandals had wedge heels. Brushing my hair, I thought about the singer. It was the first time in my life I began feeling something for a man. I was torn between enjoying it and accepting the hopelessness of it.

The photographer knocked on the door and said it was time to go. It was fun getting in the pens with some of the tamer animals and cavorting with the monkeys. The peacocks screamed at me, but the zebras and llamas were gentle. The photographer wanted me to get near the hippopotamus, but I balked. I especially liked the giraffes because they were so beautiful and graceful. During the shootings I couldn't help feeling sorry for the animals because they were caged. I was no different.

We finished around three o'clock. Since my ride wasn't coming until six, I had some time to wander around. I slipped on my tennis shoes, then walked to the horse stables near the entrance of the zoo. A friend in Chalmette had taught me to ride when I was eight. I wanted to ride the whole three hours, but it cost three dollars an hour and I needed to save my money. When I went to pay, the man at the counter refused to take it.

"You worked hard today," he said. "You'll make us all look good. Go ahead, ride as long as you want."

I steered the horse toward a wooded area bordering the zoo. The wind felt good against my face as the horse galloped across the grass. Turning at the edge of the woods, I noticed another horse and rider coming toward me. That bothered me because I wanted to be alone. When the horse stopped right beside me, I looked up and saw the singer, smiling and sitting proud on the chestnut-colored animal. He was dressed casually but wore a bright scarf around his neck.

"Fancy meetin' you again," he said.

"Why are you following me?" I demanded, trying to sound firm to hide my fear. We were alone and I knew nothing about him other than the fact that he was a singer. My only experience with a man was filled with violence and horror.

"Because I haven't stopped thinkin' of you since I saw you in Monroe," he said.

He did remember! I wanted to know why he didn't say anything at the Eagle's Nest, but it was difficult to talk because the horse kept moving around. The singer grew serious. He politely, almost meekly, said, "I just wanna ride with you a while. Is that okay?"

He was so nice that I couldn't say no. We rode along the edge of the woods, looking at each other and smiling but saying little. We came to a place overlooking a lake. He got off his horse and then helped me off mine. It was the first time I didn't cringe at the touch of a man's hand. He paused, looked in my eyes for a moment, squeezed my waist, then smiled and went to tie the horses to a nearby tree. We sat on the grass.

"I came here today because I wanted to see you," he said. "I didn't think I'd ever see you again."

"Why did you act so strange in the club?"

"I don't know. I just sensed you were uncomfortable. I thought it'd be better 'cause the other girls were around. I saw you the moment I walked out onstage. I didn't forget you, Lucy."

He looked at me in a way that was so unlike the lustful way the Man looked at me. I asked him about his life. He told me that he was poor and wanted to make something of himself so he could help his parents. He didn't want his mother to have to work anymore. He felt the same way I had about my mother. I told him a little about myself and my love for music but omitted the dark side. We must have made a funny pair. Elvis with his distinctive voice and southern twang, and me with my French accent popping out every other word. Riding back to turn in the horses, he asked if he could see me again.

"I don't believe that's possible," I said, fighting to keep from crying. I had finally found someone kind, and he appeared to like me, but I was forced to keep brushing him off. It twisted me up inside. He gently placed his hands on my shoulders and turned me around.

"Lucy, do you believe in miracles?" I nodded. "I wanna tell you somethin'. I've been with a lot of girls, but you have somethin' very special. I saw it from the beginnin'. It's like somethin' I read once. About Lancelot. He kept himself pure and loved only one woman. He was mixed up, I guess, but he could see things others couldn't. I think I'm like that. Does this make any sense?"

It made a lot of sense. I was surprised that he had read about King Arthur and the Knights of the Round Table. Those were some of my favorite stories. Elvis was the kind of man I always dreamed about, only meeting him now seemed cruel. I was better off fantasizing about a prince that didn't exist than being tortured by the knowledge of one who did.

"I really have to go," I insisted.

"Come to the club tonight," he said. "Please. I need to talk to you some more. I have to! We'll go somewhere afterward."

He was so insistent that I relented. He made me promise. We led our horses to the stables and said good-bye.

That evening I told my sister that someone invited me to see Kate Smith. There was an ad in the newspaper that said she was performing in town. That was my excuse. I didn't want to tell her about the singer. She was happy that I was getting out and all but pushed me out the door when it came time to leave. She even let me use her car.

Lucy's sister, Mary de Barbin, had lived on Lauderdale Street in Memphis, a few blocks down from Lauderdale Courts, where the Presleys lived. In his early teens, Elvis used to mow her lawn and often played with her young son. A few years later, Elvis began performing at the Eagle's Nest and although Mary had moved to Peabody Avenue—a mile or so from Lauderdale Courts —she kept in touch with Elvis and was excited about his career. She sometimes went to the Eagle's Nest to cheer him on and lend support.

"When Lucy came up from Monroe for the modeling assignment, I took her to see Elvis's show," Mary told me from her home in Louisiana. "He came over to the table after his performance to say hello as he always did. This time was different. He couldn't take his eyes off Lucy. He was very taken with her. They talked, and he asked her out. The next day Lucy said she was going to a Kate Smith concert or something. I didn't believe that for a second. She went off somewhere with Elvis."

Elvis's infatuation with classic literature played a part in his attraction to Lucy. He was "taken" by her French accent as well as her beauty. Those who have tried to portray him as an ignorant hillbilly overlook the facts that his favorite subject in school was English, and that throughout his life he was a voracious reader who consumed everything from romantic history and the Bible to the complicated religious, philosophical, and spiritual writings of theosophist Madame Blavatsky.

I DROVE TO THE EAGLE'S NEST AND quickly found a table in the back. The boring band played as before, then Elvis came on. He looked so handsome. His hair was shiny and neatly combed in place, and his collar was turned up. He was much more subdued this evening and sang a lot of soft, moody ballads. His singing was nothing like the way it would be later. I tried to pay attention to his performance, but my mind kept wandering to my problems. Being there only complicated them. Elvis did a single set, then came over and said, "Let's get outta here." He walked with his chest held high and expanded, and moved with determination. He led me to an old but well-kept car, apologizing because it wasn't a late model. He opened the door for me, then closed it and went around to his side. Before he started the engine, he reached over and touched my hand.

"I wanna show you my city, the most beautiful city in the world. You don't mind if I'm proud of it, do you?"

Loving one's hometown was nothing to be ashamed of. I wished I could love mine. We drove down a beautiful street lined with large colonial homes.

"I'll have a house like this one day," he said. "It'll take a lot of work. My plan is to make a record. A person can get rich if they can make a good record. What do you think?"

"I think you can do it. Just don't give up. You have to be different to be noticed. I try to be that way when I dance, but I get scared sometimes."

"Yeah, I know," he said. "You never know if the people are gonna like you or not. You can sing the same song the same way, and one crowd loves it and the next doesn't."

He pulled the car into a small lot near a park and asked me if we could walk a bit. I was afraid he was going to ask questions and try to find out more about me. We walked in the cool night for a while, then stopped to sit on a wooden bench. My fears were verified.

"Lucy, tell me about your life. What are your dreams? What do you want to do?"

I told him an abridged version of my story, starting with my father's death and how that affected my family and forced my mother to work. I left out the part about the marriage. Elvis's face became sad. The similarities between our mothers was something we shared.

"My mother never had anythin' pretty," he said. "But I'll

make it right. I'll become a success and buy her everythin' she wants."

He paused for a second, then his face lit up.

"And your momma too, Lucy. I'll take care of her if I make it before you do!"

It was such a warm sentiment. He meant it. He was so sincere. He turned and embraced me. It was a loving embrace between kindred spirits. Slowly, tentatively, my arms rose to squeeze him to me. It felt wonderful.

"You look so pretty in the moonlight," he said, pulling away to take a look. The words were disturbing. I was afraid and suspicious of men. They told girls how beautiful they were just to have their way with them. Elvis was different, but I was so frightened and confused about life, I didn't know how to react.

"Please don't try to flatter me," I said. "I don't like false flattery. You don't know me."

He was hurt. He looked like a little boy.

"I want to know you," he pleaded. "I'm tellin' you the truth, how I feel. Ever since I saw you at that party, I kept hopin' that you were more than just pretty. Now I know. I feel the way you think. You have to believe me."

"I do. I'm sorry. I'm just shy."

We stood up and began walking again. Elvis held my hand.

"Do you have someone?" he asked.

"No."

It wasn't a lie. Not in the sense he meant. We stopped walking and faced each other. I felt so small in his arms. He bent down and gently kissed me. Time stood still.

"Can I see you again?"

"I—I guess so." What was I saying? How could we? This was only going to lead to more trouble. He noticed my hesitance.

"Lucy, I want you to share somethin' with me."

"What?"

"Success. I want you to share my success."

I smiled weakly, knowing that was improbable.

"You seem so distant. What's wrong?"

"I don't mean to, Elvis, really. Just give me time. There are some things I can't speak about right now."

"It's not that you don't like me?"

"No, that's not it. Just personal things. Come on, let's walk some more."

We walked in silence for a while. Elvis stopped and pointed to the sky.

"You see this moon? Remember it. Whenever you see it, think of me and how we will be together again, soon."

"It's getting late," I said. "I've got to leave early tomorrow."

As we drove back to my car, Elvis kept asking me for my address and phone number. I dodged the question, but he persisted. He wouldn't let me out of the car until I answered him. I finally told him that he could reach me at the television station or the department store.

"You'll see me soon," he said. "Don't worry."

It was hard not to. I was certain I'd never see him again, and in a strange way, that hurt as bad as anything I'd ever experienced. The next morning, while waiting to board the train, I was paralyzed with the fear that he would show up at the station and see me clutching my two babies. He could never be mine, but I had to keep the dream alive for a little while longer. I needed it.

I returned to my busy but bleak routine. The only relief was dancing and working at Silverstein's. Elvis didn't call, or if he did, no one told me. Then one Saturday, about two weeks later, someone at the store motioned me to the phone.

"I want to come see you," Elvis said. "I've gotta." I told him he couldn't and gave the excuse that I had to go away on another modeling assignment.

"How 'bout tonight then?" he asked.

I played along, assuming he was calling from Memphis.

"Tonight would be fine. Just fly in like Superman."

"I will!" he exclaimed. "You just wait."

"Actually, I have to work tonight," I said, worrying that he might really show up. "I'm singing at a wedding."

He asked me the name of the church and where it was located, and like a fool, I said St. Matthew's. He couldn't be serious. I promised I'd see him at another time.

That night, I was singing the "Alleluia" from a choir loft behind the pews. Suddenly someone began harmonizing behind me. I turned slightly and saw him—Elvis. What a shock. I was in the middle of the song and had to keep singing. He moved up beside me, still singing along, and gently took my hand. We finished the song together. Elvis sang it beautifully. I sang Gounod's "Ave Maria" next, but it was too Catholic for Elvis's southern Pentecostal background, so he had to let me solo. The minute I finished, we ducked out of the church before anybody saw us and walked around behind the building. Elvis squeezed me tightly.

"You sing really beautiful," he said.

"Thank you. I didn't know you could sing 'Alleluia.' "

"I love church music, especially gospel. I go to church all the time."

"What are you doing here?" I asked, still a bit startled.

"I came to see you! Come on. Are you hungry? Let's go get somethin' to eat."

We went to the Rendezvous Restaurant, an elegant and popular place in the suburban area. We had a wonderful dinner. Elvis wanted to go all out—steaks, champagne, dessert, the works—but I declined the champagne and dessert. I didn't want him to spend his money. As we ate, Elvis kept reaching over and touching my hand. Unfortunately, the evening was almost spoiled when a number of people recognized me from television and came by the table. I was embarrassed. Elvis was impressed.

"You're a star," he said.

I felt something crawling up my leg and jerked back. Looking down, I saw a red rose sitting on my chair. He had reached under the table, tickled my leg with it, then left it there. He laughed when I jumped thinking it was a big bug. The rose was crumbled and wilted, as if he had it in his pocket all day. He signaled the waiter and I was presented with three fresh red roses with long stems. Pointing to each one, he said, "This one is you, this one is me, and this one represents our love.

"I wanna show you what it means to love someone, and what marriage is," he continued. That confused me, but I let it pass. With all the complications, I didn't want to think about anything like that. We left the restaurant, and Elvis asked if there was a pretty place where we could talk. I directed him to a secluded spot on the Bayou Desiard, a large winding lake that weaves through Monroe. We sat on a bank directly across from the Desiard Country Club, talked, laughed, kissed, and watched the lights sparkle in the water. As Elvis leaned over to kiss me, his arm got tangled in the gold chain that held the confirmation cross around my neck. The cross fell into the dark grass. We searched but couldn't find it. Elvis promised to get me another to replace it. We had so much fun, I didn't want the evening to ever end. It was getting late and I was getting worried. He wouldn't take me back until I promised to go to Memphis again soon. He drove to St. Matthew's to drop me off at my car. Before we parked, Elvis looked at me very seriously and said, "When I see you in Memphis, I want you to tell me what's botherin' you. Maybe I can help."

I said I would.

Lucy's knowledge of Elvis comes exclusively from their times together, so she was unable to explain how Elvis came to perform at the party where they met, and why he found it so easy to surprise her in Monroe, a city three hundred miles south of his home in Memphis. My research was more enlightening. In the late summer and fall of 1953 Elvis was almost a fixture in Monroe, Louisiana. Nearly a dozen people told me they saw Elvis then. In fact, it's hard to find an old-timer in Monroe who didn't see him. Some recall seeing him playing in a bar on the west side of town called the Red Coach Club. Others say they saw him at a high school, an outdoor party, or at the fairgrounds. James Noe, Jr., who now heads the family's television and radio empire, said Elvis was spotted playing in the back of a truck in the parking lot of a local shopping center.

This still leaves the question of why. What was it about Monroe that attracted Elvis? Richard Wilcox, a music historian who manages radio station KNOE-AM/FM in Monroe, told me.

"Elvis came to Monroe in 1953 to try to get on the Ouachita Valley Jamboree, a country music show at the Ouachita Valley Fairgrounds," Wilcox said. "I think he came in 1952 also, when he was still in high school. The Jamboree was a pretty big deal at the time and was broadcast live over KNOE-FM. Elvis tried out but he never got to perform. He did get to play at the Red Coach Club and a few other places."

Why did the future King of Rock 'n' Roll fail to make it on the Ouachita Valley Jamboree?

"Because my husband wouldn't let him," Mary Taylor firmly said. Hugh Taylor ran the Jamboree and chose who played. He died in 1975, but his wife Mary recalled the young singer.

"Sure, I remember Elvis," Mrs. Taylor told me. "He came down here a number of times in 1953. Elvis sat in the audience a time or two, checking out the competition, I guess, then asked my husband for a tryout. I was there. He was just a kid then. He didn't have a band or anything, just him and his guitar. He sang okay, but he couldn't stop wiggling that leg of his. That was the problem. He just wiggled around too much when he sang, you know, like he always did. My husband didn't like that at all. We had a family show! There were a lot of children who came. My husband wouldn't let Jerry Lee Lewis perform either the first time he tried because Lewis had this wild, white afro. Jerry cut it off and my husband let him on. But Elvis never stopped shaking his leg.

"The Jamboree was every Saturday night in the exhibit building of the Ouachita Valley Fairgrounds in West Monroe, which is now where the new civic center and city hall is. We had a lot of big stars on the show, Slim Whitman, Faron Young, and one of my favorites, Webb Pierce."

But not Elvis Presley?

"No, not Elvis! Never!" Mrs. Taylor reiterated.

John Birdsong, Jr., whose father ran the fairgrounds, also recalled that Elvis tried out for the Jamboree in the fall of 1953.

Elvis finally did get to play at the Ouachita Fairgrounds a year later as part of Hank Snow's traveling show. That started a series of triumphant returns to the stages or cities where he had once been rejected.

Chapter 4

I TRIED TO PUT ELVIS OUT OF MY MIND, but he called at the store, reminding me of my promise to go to Memphis. Despite my circumstances, I knew I could get away. I told my mother I had to go on a short trip to promote *The Mr. Music Show* and would again stay with Mary. She readily agreed to take care of Deborah and Melody. Being able to get away so easily did little to relieve my conscience. I hated having to lie to anyone, especially my mother. But I had to do something to change my life. The situation was growing worse. The Man had returned briefly. His actions followed the usual pattern. He appeared unannounced from wherever it was he had gone. The first two nights he'd drink and then rape me. When he had satisfied his sexual craving, he became violent and abusive. Shortly before leaving, he knocked me around to make sure I stayed in line while he was away. As I matured, I became less passive and started to rebel, which only led to more severe beatings. Part of his violence was fueled by his knowledge that I still despised him. The years had not tempered my hatred, nor had the children bonded us into a family. I never learned to love him as my relatives promised and never gave up the hope that somehow I could escape. The older I became, the more determined I was to carry out that escape.

Going to Memphis was the boldest move yet. While planning for the trip, I had to pay strict attention to maintaining my composure. The anticipation lifted my spirits, but it couldn't show. Mrs. Fowler was still keeping watch. I caught myself singing a few times and stopped so as not to arouse any suspicion.

I could let my feelings show only when alone. I managed to get away for a short shopping trip the day before leaving. Feeling frivolous, I bought a floor-length batiste cotton gown. It was cream-colored, with long puffed sleeves, snaps down the front, and a fitted bodice. I had never owned anything so sheer. Buying it made me feel young. I was weary of having to be an adult. I wasn't an adult. I had just turned seventeen. I wasn't like other seventeen-year-olds, I knew that, but I wasn't eleven anymore either. There would be no more hiding in the closet.

The next day, I drove to the Monroe airport and left my car. My neighbor, Elizabeth Deville, had taught me how to drive a car before. The Man purchased a dark burgundy, two-door convertible with a black rag top and designated it for emergencies only, like if the children got sick and needed to be rushed to the hospital. I decided this was an emergency. I took a plane because my nerves were too frazzled to deal with the long train ride. The plane was bumpy, but the trip was short. As I waited for my bags at the Memphis airport, another transformation occurred. The anger I drew upon to get there dissolved and was replaced by insecurity. Did Elvis really like me? The thoughts were interrupted by a tap on the shoulder.

"You scared me," I said, catching my breath. Something else frightened me. Elvis wasn't wearing the usual baggy gabardine pants and suit jacket. He wore tight black pants and a bright cowboy shirt unbuttoned halfway down his chest. He looked wild, untamed, and incredibly sexy. He wanted to take off somewhere right away, but I insisted on freshening up at the hotel first. We got into Elvis's car and headed for the city. Along the way he described the conventional roadside sights with such zeal I was uncertain whether he was keyed up by my visit or just devoted to his hometown. Elvis pulled up to the hotel and said he'd be back in an hour. He told me to bring my "sleepin' clothes" and mentioned something about camping. I was wary of his suggestion. He sensed my misgivings and smiled. He gave me a light-hearted kiss and headed back to his car. He stopped, then spun around.

"I have a surprise for you!"

He flashed a mischievous grin and drove away.

I rushed to get ready. The promise of a surprise combined with his boyishness excited and comforted me. Heeding his suggestion to dress casually, I slipped on a pair of white slacks and a light blue blouse. I remembered his comment about the "sleepin' clothes" and eased my new robe from the suitcase. I folded it and laid it inside a small travel bag. As I zipped the top, the phone rang.

"You ready?"

"It hasn't been an hour."

"Sure it has. Memphis time. I can't wait."

I was relieved he had called from downstairs and had not appeared at my door. That showed respect. I lingered only a few more minutes before descending. Elvis immediately escorted me to his car. He was subdued as we drove toward the outskirts of town. It was late afternoon and the drive was pleasant. I quietly admired the arching hillsides and contrasting colors of the trees and vegetation. I also noticed that the backseat was covered with bags and a box.

"Elvis, where are we going?"

"Surprise," he repeated. "You gotta wait for the surprise."

I laughed as we continued deeper into the rolling countryside. The road began to wind. I was afraid he was going to take me to a camp or cabin where there would be other people. I didn't want to be around anyone else. Not with my secret. Finally he slowed down, pulled off the road, and stopped at the foot of a grassy hill. He sprung from the car and dashed around to my side. He opened the door and took my hand. I started to say something, but he put his finger to his lips and made a *shhhh* sound. He didn't say a word until we reached the top of the hill.

"This is the surprise. My gift to you."

Elvis pointed to a breathtaking sunset.

"This is your gift," he repeated. "And you know what? Only God can paint a sunset. Each one is an original. This one is yours, Lucy."

He pulled me to him and kissed me. Instead of frightening me, the kiss drained my fear. I didn't care about anything else. The guilt vanished.

"Come on," he said. "Let's walk."

He took my hand again, and we began to walk along the hill, enjoying the view of the scarlet and golden sky before us. I felt clean and untouched. All the nightmares of the past appeared to be little more than a bad dream. This was what love was supposed to be.

"Lucy, are you happy?"

I stretched up on my toes and kissed him. That was my answer. The devilish glint returned to his eye.

"You know somethin', my girl has to run for her supper!"

He took off in a sprint. I kept in step. We laughed the whole way back to the car. He opened the door and reached for the box and bags in the backseat. Dramatically overemphasizing every move, he spread out a red blanket and dotted it with plates. Elvis was playing the moment to the hilt. "You are to serve the feast," he said, "because you are my lady in waiting." I inspected the first bag and found ham sandwiches, grapes, chips, and deviled eggs.

"Would you like some wine?" he offered.

"What makes you think I want wine?" I replied with mock annoyance.

"Well, you're French, aren't you? Who ever heard of a Frenchman not liking wine?"

When we finished the main course, he reached into the box and pulled out a bag of cherries. We spent the next half hour eating cherries and silently enjoying the deepening colors of the sky.

"I'm glad you came, Lucy."

"Me too. But why did you bring me here? Is this where you bring all your girls?"

"What girls?" he exclaimed. "I don't have any girls. I thought you were my girl."

"I just wondered how you found this place. Have you been here before?"

He grew serious.

"One day I was upset about not doin' anythin' with my life. I just drove into the hills and ended up here. I thought it was the most beautiful place in the world. I come here to talk."

"To talk?"

"To pray," he said. "I feel closer to God here."

I was surprised. I had depended on God so much in my life. Sometimes He was my only hope. Knowing Elvis shared my faith made me believe that God approved of our being together.

"I always wanted to bring someone here with me," he continued. "But it had to be someone special. I could never find the right person. I thought I would always have to come here alone. Now I've found you."

He squeezed my hand. Secure that he had filled one longing in his life, he switched to another, the one that remained unfulfilled. I was glad he continued talking about himself. I didn't want the conversation to shift to me.

"I met some musicians. We seem to have a good mix. They can help me, and I can help them. If we work together, we might have a chance. I recorded somethin' already. Nothin' really. Just a couple of songs for my momma. I'm gonna record some more soon. Now that school's out of the way, I have more time. You wait, Lucy, in a year you'll be real proud of me."

The musicians Elvis referred to were probably Scotty Moore and Bill Black. They would later comprise the nucleus of his band. Elvis was not being modest about his recordings. Anybody who had four dollars could make a record at Memphis Recording Service, a sideline of Sam Phillips's Sun Record Company. According to the book *The Boy Who Dared to Rock,* Elvis paid four dollars and recorded his first two songs, "My Happiness" and "That's When Your Heartaches Begin," in July 1953. (Some accounts place the date a few months earlier.) They were put directly on acetate. Elvis left with the only copy. In January 1954, he paid another four dollars and made a second set, "Casual Love Affair" and "I'll Never Stand in Your Way." Again, he had the only copy.

I WAS IMPRESSED WITH THE MOTIvations behind his determination. His quest for success appeared to be unselfish. He wanted only to please others and to be in a position to help those less fortunate. I was especially heartened by the way he respected his parents.

"I'm gonna make it, Lucy. You believe me, don't you?"

"I know you're going to make it. You're going to be sensational. You have something special."

"You really think so?"

"You're very special. To me, and when you're onstage, to everyone. I know how much this means to you. I've been praying for you every night. God is listening. He always listens."

Elvis was moved by my faith in him.

"I want you to be part of it, Lucy. Help me."

His words jarred me out of my dreamy fog. I couldn't be part of anything. The only future I saw was a miserable attempt to lead a double life, one that relied upon deception at both ends. I thought of telling Elvis the truth but couldn't face losing him. Not yet. I needed these moments more than he realized. I wanted to change the subject, but he was staring at me, waiting for an answer. I had to say something.

"I want to be part of your life, but please, you must listen to me," I said. "Promise me you'll give me time. It has nothing to do with the way I feel. You must always promise never, never, never to talk about us to anyone. What we have is too special. It must remain that way until we're ready to announce it. Please promise me. Just until we know and everything works out."

He seemed confused by my plea and suspected it had to do with my family not accepting him because he was poor. He knew that most grown-ups frowned on his unusual clothes and long hair. He misread my French accent and Boston education as a sign that I came from an upper-class family even though I had told him that after my father died we became poor. I was going to tell him that my family wasn't the problem, but I stopped before I said anything. If he feared my relatives, he wouldn't press to come to my home.

"Sometimes I get the feelin' you're gonna disappear," he said, "that I'll never have you, that our moments together are so great because there aren't gonna be many."

My silence confirmed his suspicions. He looked at me as if I was going to vanish any second.

"I have a feelin' things are gonna start movin' very fast soon," he said. "I don't want the important things to get left behind. That's why I have to tell you how much I love you. I can't let it wait."

For a moment he couldn't find the right words to continue.

Then he said, "Stay here with me for a while. We'll just sit and talk. I have so much I want to say. I want to be with you. Hey! How 'bout if we camp here tonight instead of goin' back to the hotel?"

I knew that was his way of hanging on, but the request made me nervous. I had never willingly allowed a man to touch me. Incredible as it seems, in my mind, I was still a virgin.

"Did you bring somethin' to sleep in?" he said.

I nodded.

"Why don't you change?"

"I really shouldn't," I said, but my heart said differently. I excused myself and walked down the hill to the car. I found my small overnight bag and took out the gown I purchased the day before. It was long, soft, and trimmed with lace. It wasn't really sexy, just feminine. I climbed in the car, slipped off my blouse and slacks, and put it on. I could see the silhouette of Elvis's frame against the dying light as I walked up the hill. He was like a magnet pulling me nearer. He turned, saw me approaching, and extended his hand. When we touched, a soft breeze gently blew through my hair and pushed the gown close to my body. He embraced me with a single arm. The other was hidden behind his back. After a brief pause, he brought up the missing hand and presented a bouquet of wild fall flowers. He gently removed the gold barrette that held my hair, then guided the long, black strands across my shoulders. Silently, he began picking out white frost daisies from the multicolored bouquet and delicately placed them in my hair.

"Lucy, you know what marriage is? It's when two people give themselves to each other and promise to love one another forever. No matter what happens. No matter who tries to stop them, they'll love each other forever."

I'll never know that feeling, I thought to myself. I'll never be able to marry you. I can't.

He was still worried about my family. That's why he said what he did. It was ironic that his attempt to convince me to stick by him made him express the exact strength he would need if he wanted me. He gently touched my face with his fingers, then opened his hands and pressed them to my cheeks, moving them back to my ears. I could hear his heart pounding through his palms.

"Let's be together like this forever. With you at my side, I can do anything. Lucy, honey. Will you marry me?"

I was petrified. It was the best moment of my life, and the worst. The inevitable explosion of contrasting emotions nearly ignited. I thought of a frightened child who once stood next to a stranger and was forced to say "I do." Did that forever chain me to a horrible man who treated me like a caged animal? Did it really count? It couldn't. It wasn't marriage in any form marriage was intended to be.

"In the eyes of God, I love you and will marry you," I said. "You'll be mine forever, no matter what comes between us. I'll always love you."

It was a strange, revealing acceptance, but Elvis let it pass.

"I accept you as my wife," he said formally as if a church full of people were listening. "I'll love you and only you. No matter what happens. I'll love you forever."

The wind picked up and began blowing the flowers out of my hair. They fell upon my shoulders and rolled down my back, landing in a ring around my feet.

"I can't have a bride without flowers in her hair!" Elvis said, reaching for the bouquet I still held at my side. He picked out small purple and lavender vernonias and set them in a new wreath around my head. I dropped what remained of the bouquet and slipped my hand under Elvis's shirt. I needed to feel the warmth of his body.

"Darlin', close your eyes," he said. "Now open them."

Elvis was holding a single red rose. I had no idea where it came from, but it was crumbled and wilted like the one he gave me in the restaurant. That didn't matter. It was still beautiful. I sighed deeply when he presented it, and that pleased him.

"This rose contains all the love we've promised," he said. "It stands for the love I'll have for you forever. Whatever happens and wherever you are, when you see a rose, let it remind you of me."

We knelt together on the blanket. Elvis appeared unsure of himself.

"What's wrong?" I asked.

"May I have you for my very own?"

I'll never forget the way he looked at me, with eyes so gentle and loving. The time had come to offer myself freely to a man I loved, a man I had chosen. I answered him with the first passionate kiss I had ever given. My sudden forwardness frightened me for an instant. I backed away.

"Don't be afraid," Elvis whispered. "I won't let anything bad happen. I won't never let anything bad happen to you."

We lay down facing each other with our bodies together. Slowly Elvis began caressing each part of my body. He playfully nibbled my lips as he stroked my face, neck, and breasts with his hands. Under the bright stars of a cool Memphis night, we consummated our love. It was more than just making love. Elvis's body washed away all the shame and dirtiness I had known before. He elevated me from a degraded child to a woman who knew the ecstasy of submission.

"Our love is written on the wind in heaven," Elvis said as we lay on our backs, looking up at the stars. "Do you believe this?"

I believed.

The night grew chilly. We abandoned our plan to camp out and gathered our things. We reluctantly walked back to the car. Neither of us wanted the moment to end. We stood at the car and embraced, glancing up at the dark outline of the hill. Our vows of marriage had been unofficial but had a lasting effect. Our love would carry us over the tremendous obstacles of the next twenty-four years.

Chapter 5

B ACK AT THE HOTEL WE TALKED LATE
into the night. Elvis continued to outline his plan for success. He
was obsessive about it.

"I won't let anybody stop me. If they knock me down, I'll get
right back up. That's the only way to do it," he said. "I know what
it's like to have nothin'. I want to prove to you what I can do."

"You don't have to prove anything to me," I said. "I know how
wonderful you are, not only because I love you, but because you
have a special gift. Just remember. Don't ever leave God out of
your life. He will always guide you. Please promise me you'll do
that."

"I will if you promise not to let anythin' separate us."

I froze with fear. That was a promise I could never make. Elvis
gently stroked my face and cupped his hands over my ears as he
had before. It felt as if he was sending his love through his palms.

"From now on I'll put my hand over my ear when I'm performin' to remind me that you love me," he said.

He went to the phone and called home, telling his mother he
was all right and would be staying over with a friend. He spoke
to her gently and lovingly. She seemed so concerned about him,
but he was able to convince her that he was okay. After speaking
to her, he went to the window and opened the curtains to let in
the moonlight.

"We can't shut out our old friend," he said. He turned, then
came to me again. He slowly loosened my gown and let it drop
to the floor.

"Your breasts are like ripe peaches covered with dew in the
mornin'," he said. "Soft and beautiful." After that, he always
wanted me to wear peach-colored clothes. He asked how I felt

about him. I was too shy to say that everything about him was perfect. His lean, young body was so different from the repulsive horror of the Man.

I woke up early the next morning. He was next to me, lying face down, one leg sprawled out across the bed. I lay there for a few minutes feeling the warmth of his body, recalling our night together. I didn't want to wake him because he'd try to keep me from going. I slipped out of bed, went into the bathroom, and quietly gathered up my things. I slid off my batiste gown, put on white slacks, and fished a fresh red knit blouse out of my travel bag.

I tiptoed into the bedroom, glancing over at him to make sure he was still asleep. He was. He had drifted into the center of the bed, and his leg was all twisted up in the yellow bedspread. He was clutching his pillow so tightly it made me think he slept with a teddy bear when he was younger. I sat down at a small, wooden table that wobbled, looked in the drawer, and found a few sheets of hotel stationery. I also found a pen with the name of a Memphis restaurant stamped on it in gold letters. I read the inscription on the pen and began visualizing what the restaurant might look like, doing everything but writing the note. What could I write? I couldn't give him my home phone number or address. I couldn't even say I'd call him because I wasn't sure where to reach him. I stared down at the stationery and realized that the best twenty-four hours of my life were coming to an end, and that they might never be repeated.

I heard him stir and was afraid he was going to wake up. He shifted again and his light brown hair fell down over his forehead. He looked better that way than with his hair slicked back, which was how he wore it. I noticed again how dark his eyebrows were and the strange way his upper lip dipped down in the center like a heart. I wanted to kiss him but couldn't risk waking him. Maybe I could just creep over and touch his face one last time. I tried to write, but the pen wouldn't work. I turned the paper over and scribbled some lines on the bottom until the blue ink finally flowed. I thought about the restaurant again—was the food as bad as its pen? Silly thought, but I was trying hard to keep from writing what could be my last good-bye.

I never wrote the note. Elvis, the sneak, had been awake all along, watching me tiptoeing around. He leaped out of bed totally naked, scaring me to death, then roared out a laugh. He took me in his arms and kissed me, and then began to tickle me.

"Where are you goin'?" he asked. "Why'd you get dressed?" He held me away and looked at me. "You're as pretty in the mornin' as you were last night."

I loved his compliment but was embarrassed by being caught trying to slip away. I fumbled for an explanation, finally blaming the plane schedules.

"I'm going to drive you to the airport, honey," he said. "But first, I've got to go home. I'll be right back." He pulled on his pants and his black and white buckskin loafers, and slid his arms into his blue cowboy shirt, leaving it unbuttoned. He rushed out the door.

He was gone less than thirty minutes. I hadn't even finished gathering my things before he blew back into the room. He was wearing a jacket and a different shirt, a red one, but it was still unbuttoned. The whole way to the airport, Elvis talked excitedly about our future. I was his official girlfriend and that was that. I would soon be his wife. He would become a famous singer like Frank Sinatra, Dean Martin, or gospel singer Jake Hess. We would live like royalty. I let myself accept the wonderful picture he was painting. We got to the airport much too soon. Our parting was brief and happy, a beginning instead of an ending, at least in his eyes.

"Can you come back next weekend?"

"I don't think so. It's hard for me to get away."

"That's okay. I'll be in Monroe again soon. There's a country music show down there. I'm tryin' to get 'em to let me sing."

"I'm sure they'd let you perform. You'd be good."

"You should tell 'em that. But don't worry, I'll be around Monroe a lot," he said. "We'll see each other."

Climbing up the dimpled metal stairs into the steel-gray airplane was like walking to the gallows. I looked back and saw Elvis standing at the gate. He was smiling and waving, and his shirt was still unbuttoned. At eighteen he was a vibrant, happy boy becoming a man. It's an image I'll never forget. I waved back, then turned and entered the plane. Inside, the cabin and seats were dull gray. The plane was as dismal as the life to which I was returning.

I'd been so happy, and now this airplane with the black-tipped propellers was taking me away.

The walkway to my house on Jackson Drive in Monroe was dotted with freshly fallen acorns. The cement path led to three concrete steps with a whitewashed wood banister lining each side. I had insisted on the railing for the children's safety. Framing the windows were dark gray shutters I had painted myself. It was a beautiful house. I hated every part of it.

I stood in the front hall and listened. The quiet was unsettling. Mother and the children should have been there. I put down my bag and called out for them, but there was no reply. I walked into the master bedroom, and my heart froze, as it always did when I entered that room. No matter what I did to make the room pretty and cheerful, it always chilled me because of what happened to me there. There were six windows. The white lace curtains were pulled tightly to let the maximum amount of light inside. The dark oak floor was brightened by a woven white rug. The bed was covered with a white and powder blue chintz spread, matching dust ruffles, and a half dozen blue and white throw pillows. I'd decorated the walls with my own artwork, knitted designs of brightly colored trees and flowers. There were no picture frames because of the sharp edges. I usually kept fresh flowers on the small night table to the left of the bed, along with a blue porcelain pitcher and bowl. In the corner was a dark prayer bench I'd found in a flea market. I'd worked for weeks sanding and varnishing it until it shone like new.

Over the bed was a picture of Christ encased in a bubble of glass. Dried red and blue flowers were trapped inside the bubble. I put it there thinking that the Man wouldn't be so mean with Jesus looking down at him.

The Man suddenly walked out of the bathroom. That explained why the children were gone. He'd come back home unexpectedly while I was in Memphis. He was in his sleeveless undershirt and his face was red and twisted with rage. His thinning red hair hung down over his eyes in a V-shaped clump, making him look even more horrible. I braced myself for what was coming. I wouldn't break no matter how much he beat me. I'd die before confessing anything.

"Where have you been?"

"I had to go away—"

I felt the familiar pain as his fist crashed into my face, only this time the blow was harder and hurt more than ever before. The force of the punch knocked me back into the plaster wall, but I stayed on my feet. Staying up was crucial. It was the only dignity I had.

"I know you've been dancing with your sinful body! Luring men to lust for you through this wicked dancing!"

He talked like the fire-and-brimstone preacher he listened to in Mississippi. The meaning, however, was clear. He had found out about the television show. I'd dreaded this moment but expected it and had my answer prepared. The purpose of the awful marriage was to help my career. I never got the chance to say it. He punched me again, then grabbed my shoulders and threw me against the wall. He paused for a moment, assessing the damage. He stormed over and slapped me, back and forth, again and again. Then, in an instant, it was over. He was gone.

I stood in the corner, fighting to remain on my feet. It wasn't his blows that now weakened my legs, it was the humiliation. I saw blood on my blouse just above my left breast and realized why he had stopped. My blood had become a ritual signal that he had accomplished his task. I reached up to determine where I was bleeding and discovered that both my mouth and nose had given him his satisfaction. I remained rigid against the wall, searching my mind for some peg to hold on to. There was one. It had an immediate calming effect. The pain eased. The tension left my body as I walked over to the shining prayer bench and slowly knelt down. I clasped my hands together and brought them to my face.

"Dear God. Thank you for not letting him find out about Elvis. That's all I ask. Allow me this one secret."

With renewed courage, I got up from the bench and walked to the long, narrow bathroom to deal with my injuries. I lifted both hands to open the white-shuttered doors of the medicine cabinet. All the bandages and medicines were neatly in place. A trace of dried blood was on the edge of the gauze roll, a reminder of my last beating. The orange iodine stung as it touched my nose, but I was used to it. I had played this scene so many times before.

The Man left the next day. I went to see a lawyer about a divorce. He was a pleasant young man named Billye Adams, tall and thin, with thick sandy blond hair. I explained little about why I wanted a divorce, only that my husband wasn't around. I think "desertion" was listed as the official grounds. I was too afraid to put anything about physical and mental cruelty into writing. Mr. Adams informed me that if the Man didn't contest, it would cost about $380. I didn't have anything close to that, but he said it wouldn't have to be paid until the divorce was final. He also told me to be patient. Divorces weren't easy in the 1950s. Especially for a seventeen-year-old. After he finished explaining, Mr. Adams offered me a part-time job in his office. I thanked him and declined.

Billye Adams, a colorful sort who pulls no punches, continues to practice law in Monroe.

"I remember Lucy like it was yesterday," he said. "It was one of my very first divorce cases. I'm sitting in my office, and in walks one of the best-looking women I've ever seen in my life. What she told me about the guy never being around shocked me plumb out of my chair. You had to see her to understand what I'm saying. She had it all, everything a man would dream about in a woman —beauty, body, brains, poise, personality, bearing, class, the works. It defied reason that anyone would desert her."

Adams arranged a separation based on Louisiana's "bed and board" law, meaning the couple was no longer living together. They had to continue on that basis for a year in order to pass the law's "no reconciliation" condition.

I KNEW THAT I HAD TO DO MORE THAN file some papers to save myself—and soon. The contrast was too much. Elvis was heaven. Home was hell.

Two weeks later I received another phone call at Silverstein's. It upset me when I was motioned to the phone. *The Mr. Music Show* had been on the air a few months now, and men who'd seen me dancing sometimes recognized me in the store. The bolder ones would call. When I politely turned them down, a few became abusive. The phone was out in the open and the salesladies could hear both sides of the conversation if they strained, which they usually did.

"He has a real nice voice," the woman said as she handed me the receiver. I hesitated, then took the phone.

"Is it okay to keep calling you here?" It was Elvis.

It wasn't okay. It was too risky. But I wanted to talk to him.

"It's okay for now. For a little while."

"Could you meet me in Shreveport next Saturday? I'm goin' to the Louisiana Hayride. I'm tryin' to get on."

Shreveport was only 105 miles from Monroe. I had to go and tell him the truth. It wasn't fair to lead him on. Elvis told me to go directly to the motel where he was planning to stay. He said it was easy to find, just off the main highway near a military base. I couldn't miss it. I arranged to have Mother take care of my daughters and told her I had another modeling assignment. Driving the burgundy convertible, I left for Shreveport in the early afternoon dressed in black Jantzen pants with a matching knit sweater.

The motel was easy to find. It had a glaring red and blue neon sign out front that said IDA MOTEL or something similar, probably the name of the owner's long-lost love. It was a seedy place, about thirty rooms, with flaking white paint trimmed in peeling pea green. Ida couldn't have been too impressed. Elvis was standing outside in the parking lot when I arrived. He was also dressed in black, including a cowboy shirt with a bright red neckerchief, a must for any aspiring country singer in those days. His pants were baggy and his shoes were white. His hair looped down across his forehead, the way I liked it, and his sideburns were thicker than when I had seen him in Memphis. He was standing with another man, a stocky, dark-blond fellow who was smoking a cigarette. As I got out of the car, the blond man let out a shrill wolf whistle. It unnerved me so much I jumped back in.

"Get out of here!" Elvis shouted at the man, pushing him away. "Don't you have any respect?"

I didn't get out of the car until the man was out of sight. Elvis ran over, hugged me, and apologized about the whistle. I stiffened when he embraced me, and he sensed something was wrong. He took my hand and led me to a semi-secluded spot behind the motel.

"I guess I should check into a room," I said.

"I already have a room for us." The edge in his voice told me he was offended that I hadn't assumed we'd stay together. That bothered me because meeting in a tacky motel made me feel cheap. A beautiful hilltop was one thing, but Ida's palace wasn't exactly Tara.

"Just meet me there," he said, handing me a plastic keyholder. "You go first. I'll come a few minutes later."

I walked down the rows of doors until I found the right one. The key didn't seem to fit. I double-checked the key against the fading number on the door. It matched. I tried the key again and it finally worked. The first thing that hit me was the smell. It was the rug. Years of humid Louisiana summers had given it an unpleasant musty odor. The double bed was covered with a flimsy brown spread that was threadbare from washing.

Elvis came in about fifteen seconds later, hardly discreet. His presence changed the entire room. It was as if a warm light flashed on, softening all the hard edges. He held me, and I inhaled his nice clean smell. I didn't know if it was his soap or the hair tonic he carried in a tall, skinny bottle with a shiny silver top, but it was enough to drown out the rug.

I fought to keep my emotions in check. I didn't want him to know what I'd gone through since the last time we were together, but I was determined to tell him the truth. When he pulled back to kiss me, he stopped, startled by my tears.

"Hey, what's all this? Did you miss me that much?"

When I didn't smile, he realized I was serious.

"What? What's the matter?"

His blue eyes were wide, demanding, and full of fear. He hated rejection. Rejection was something he was constantly forced to face. He'd pour out his soul performing, come bounding off the stage, and then have some bored booking agent tell him he lacked talent. He braced himself for a rejection from me.

"Honey, come here," he said, hugging me. "I love you. Nothin' can change that."

Instead of comforting me, the words stirred my guilt. I could handle pain—my life was full of it. But to inflict pain on this sweet person would be awful. I was trapped, forced to hurt the only man I ever loved.

He sensed my concern and kissed me gently. My lips, my whole body trembled.

"What is it?" he whispered.

"I have a story to tell you," I said, choking with tears. "Once there was a very young girl who lived in a convent. One day her grandmother came and said the girl was to be someone's wife. A deal had been made. It was all agreed upon and settled. The girl couldn't do anything about it . . ."

He was silent for a moment. Confused. Then suddenly, he understood. He started to say something, but nothing came out.

"I've wanted to tell you so many times," I said. "I didn't know if you would understand, if you would hate me."

Elvis turned and walked over to the bed. It creaked as he sat down. He buried his face in his hands.

"I never saw the man before they made me marry him," I continued. "I was only eleven . . . it was all arranged. I don't love him, I never have. He's awful . . ."

I couldn't go on. Through my tears, I caught a glimpse of his face. The lamp reflected in his watery eyes. His breathing became quick as the hurt and confusion built into anger. He shot up off the bed and slammed his fist into the wall.

"No, no, no!" he shouted, hitting it again and again. "Who is this bastard?"

I couldn't bear to talk about my ugly life. "Elvis, you're the only man I gave myself to willingly. He'll never have that."

He grabbed and hugged me close in his arms. We both cried as we held on to each other. "You belong to me," he said, holding me tighter.

"I've tried to get away. After I was married, I went to a priest. I couldn't stand it anymore. I begged him to help me. But the priest wouldn't listen. He told me I was immature. He told me to go home and be a good wife."

Elvis broke away and began pacing the room.

"Things are startin' to go well for me," he lied. "I want you out of there. I'll take care of you. This hasn't changed anything. I love you! I want you with me. Nothin' else matters."

I was comforted by his words but knew Elvis really was struggling. He was in no position to support a family, and I hadn't even told him about my two children. If he was to have any chance at success, he had to be free to go after it. I couldn't burden him with children when he needed to pour his money and energy into his career.

He stopped pacing and sat on the bed beside me. He kissed me softly. It was his signal that our love had survived my shocking revelation. It was something for me to hold on to, a spark of promise. I reminded him of our marriage vows on the hilltop in Memphis and told him that I still meant every word. I smiled for the first time in hours.

"You have your career to go after," I said. "You mustn't let anything stop you. Don't worry. It'll work out between us."

We talked for the rest of the day and late into the night. I told him more about my life, starting again with my father's unexpected death and the trouble it caused my family, and how my grandmother believed that the only way out was to barter me. Elvis was understanding for the most part but became furious whenever he thought of me with the older man. He threatened to kill the Man, but he was just expressing his anger. He wanted me out of the marriage. Spent and exhausted, we fell asleep on the thin brown bedspread, still dressed in our matching black outfits.

Shreveport was the pivotal city in Elvis's career. The Louisiana Hayride was second only to the Grand Ole Opry as the most important country-and-western music showcase in America. It was just five years old at the time and was already dubbed "The Cradle of the Stars" because it had launched the careers of Hank Williams, Webb Pierce, Slim Whitman, Jim Reeves, Faron Young, and dozens of others. The biggest career the Louisiana Hayride would launch was that of Elvis Aron Presley, but that was still a year away.

In the summer and fall of 1953, Elvis was even more of a fixture in Shreveport than he was in Monroe. Richard Wilcox, the current station manager of KNOE radio in Monroe, was the sales manager of KWKA in Shreveport at the time. KWKA was the station that produced the Hayride and broadcast it to Texas, Arkansas, and Louisiana.

"The Hayride bands would rehearse at the big studio we had

at KWKA, and Elvis would ride the bus from Memphis all night so he could watch them jam on Saturday mornings," Wilcox explained. "I think he started coming as early as 1952. I saw him hanging around the station dozens of times."

Billie Jean Horton, the salty widow of Hank Williams and Johnny Horton, was a friend of Elvis's then. She still lives in Shreveport.

"Hell, Elvis was just wanderin' around Shreveport all the time, 1952, '53, sometime 'round then, I can't remember, but it was long before they let him go on," Billie Jean told me. "He was drivin' back and forth from Memphis for years, beggin', borrowin', and pleadin'. We were about the same age, so we were friends. I used to give Elvis a dollar that I couldn't afford so he could have his white pants cleaned. I gave him lots of dollars, and it was usually my last dollar. I wasn't sweet on him. I was a damn good-lookin' lady, I had my pick of the Hayride litter. But if I had a buck, I'd give it to him. That's what you did back then. You helped people."

Elvis's cousin, Eugene Smith, sometimes traveled with Elvis to Shreveport in the early days.

"I remember he had a little gal somewhere along the road, in Louisiana, but not in Shreveport," Smith said. "I think her name was Lucy. Yeah, I definitely remember a Lucy. Never got to see her, though. No one did. Elvis wouldn't talk much about her."

Chapter 6

I LEFT SHREVEPORT EARLY THE NEXT morning. Despite my shocking confession, Elvis said he still wanted to see me. He asked me to go to Memphis the following weekend. Now that he knew everything, there was no reason to run. He called that Wednesday and reminded me of my promise. I didn't know how long it would take his romantic idealism to fade, but it had to be soon. I wanted to enjoy him while I could. I wasn't using him as an escape or a respite from my life, I truly loved him. He was the life I would have had under different circumstances. The life I should have had.

He met me at the airport and we headed out of town. He said he wanted to take me to Mississippi to see where he used to live. He was nice and loving as before, but he was worried about my situation and how that would affect us. Along the way I dropped another bomb.

"Elvis, I haven't told you everything."

"There's more?"

He said it with such incredulity. If I wasn't so upset, I probably would have laughed.

"It's not real bad, or at least not to me. I don't know what you'll think."

"What?"

"I, uh, Elvis, I have two daughters."

Elvis closed his eyes as if in pain. The pain I felt seeing his expression cut deeper.

"Wow. Two, huh?"

We were silent for a while. Elvis was considering the matter carefully. Suddenly he brightened.

"That's okay! I love kids! How old are they?"

That was a terrible question. I've danced around it all my life. I thought of lying but decided I should tell him the truth.

"Deborah is five. Melody is almost two. They're beautiful girls. I love them dearly."

He frowned. I could almost hear the wheels spinning in his head as he did the arithmetic.

"How, ah, how old are you?"

"I told you before. Seventeen. My birthday was last month." I knew what he was thinking but kept silent. Maybe he would drop it. He wrinkled his forehead and thought some more.

"Can—can people do that?"

"I'm certainly a testament to it."

Elvis was quiet again. Tears welled up in his eyes.

"It musta been awful."

"It was."

"What kind of damn sick person would do that?"

"Elvis, please. Let's not talk about it. It's in the past. Don't be upset. I'm okay. Really."

He turned and looked at me lovingly and put his hand on mine. "I'm sorry, Lucy."

That put a damper on the mood for a while, but he quickly recovered. He said it still didn't change the way he felt. He offered all kinds of suggestions about what to do—get a divorce, run away, leave town—he even suggested that we get married so he would have just as much a legal right to me as the Man. He grew weary of the ride and decided to stop in a town named Holly Springs. Elvis didn't feel like going on to Tupelo anymore. It wasn't the time to retrace birthplaces. We decided to check into a room at a quaint village inn.

"Nothing is gonna change, is it?" he asked when we got inside.

"Not on my part," I said.

"I won't change either," he said. "I'll always love you. You're part of me no matter where I go or what I do. I'll have you soon so you'll never have to leave. I need you close to me. I want you to be part of my family. I want you to meet my momma and daddy. You'll like them."

"I'd love to, Elvis. I know how much you love them. But let's hold off until things get better. I'd like you to meet my mother one day, too. She's a little hard to understand because she speaks only French, but you'll love her. And I know she'd like you."

We spent a quiet evening together planning my escape and our future. We playfully talked about building our own family.

"If we had a girl, I know she would be so precious," Elvis said. "She would have green eyes, and say 'really' and 'actually.'" I pinched him for making fun of the way I talked. I was embarrassed enough about my accent.

"If we had a boy," I said, "he would be the most handsome child in the world. He would have a lot of hair, an impish grin, and he would say 'you know,' 'you know,' all the time."

Now it was his turn to pretend to be upset. He tickled me, and we fell into each other's arms, laughing.

"I tell you what," he said. "I'll trade you a double dozen 'you knows' for a basketful of 'reallys' and 'actuallys.'"

"It's a deal!"

"You know, Elvis—" I started, then caught myself and laughed. "Well, that's one I've used. Only twenty-three left."

"Really?"

"Oh, be quiet," I said, hitting him with a pillow. "Now listen! I've got something important to say. Remember when you called me your 'lady in waiting'? Well, I've decided that you are my El Lancelot. The 'E.L.' stands for 'everlasting love.' Remember that."

We stayed in the room the rest of the evening, talking, laughing, and making love. The next morning we drove back to Memphis. Elvis took me to the airport, and with a heavy heart, I left.

Two days after I'd returned home, the Man reappeared. I was alone in the house. Mrs. Fowler had taken the children to a nearby park to play. I wished they were home. I didn't want to be alone with him. He was drunk. He rushed toward me and waved the divorce papers in my face.

"Do you think this is all it takes?" he screamed. "You'll belong to me until I decide differently."

He slapped me across the face with the papers, then grabbed me, picked me up, and carried me into the bedroom. This was worse than being beaten. I fought as hard as I could, but he was too strong. He threw me on the bed and began violently ripping off my clothes. It was like the first night all over again. Dear God, I prayed. No more. No more.

I slipped out of his grasp and started to run, but he caught me by the hair and almost ripped my head off. The pain was unbearable. He hit me in the face four or five times, then pushed me on the bed and raped me. I hated him with all my being. I wanted to kill him. He made me feel so dirty and lifeless. I just lay there stunned on the bed. He put on his clothes and was walking out the door when he stopped.

"Oh, and about that kook with the sideburns you were seen with. I'm going to kill 'im. Kill 'im dead."

Instead of walking out, he ran back over to the bed. But he wasn't after me this time. He reached up and grabbed the picture of Jesus that hung over the bed. He held it in both hands, then smashed it on the floor. The glass from the bubblelike covering shattered into tiny pieces. The Man looked up and waved his finger in my face.

"He can't help you. Don't think He can. He doesn't even exist!" He laughed hideously and walked out of the room. I went into the shower and scrubbed my skin until it was raw, trying to wash him off me. I couldn't stop crying. I came back out and began sweeping up the glass, bending down to recover the picture of Jesus. The broken glass had ripped His face.

The next few weeks were a daze. I didn't take any more calls at work. If Mr. Twomey took any pictures of me then, he would have captured a sad portrait. One night at the studio I became dizzy and fainted. I had lost a lot of weight and hadn't been feeling well, but brushed it off as stress. I fainted again a month later. Mr. Twomey made me see a doctor, something I dreaded. It wasn't that Dr. Gallaspy was mean. The problem was he asked too many questions. He suspected something was wrong from the beginning. I finally gave in and went to see him. He examined me and became really upset this time, madder than ever before. He said I had a damaged cervix and ovary and needed immediate surgery.

"I'd like to talk with your husband," he demanded.

"I don't think that's possible."

"Lucy, what's going on? I'm your doctor. Tell me about your husband. How old is he? What is he doing to you?"

I didn't say a word. That confirmed what Dr. Gallaspy already suspected.

"This can't go on, Lucy. You won't survive."

"I've filed for divorce. I'm taking care of it. Please, can we talk about something else?"

"I'm tired of this, Lucy. I've been taking care of you for what, six years now? You said you were seventeen when you first came. Lucy, are you even seventeen now?"

I started crying. Dr. Gallaspy eased up.

"I'm sorry. I don't mean to pry. I'm just concerned about you. Listen, if you want me to testify in court, I'll be glad to."

I dried my eyes and tried to change the subject back to my condition. That hardly helped. It was bad. Not only was I chewed up inside, I was pregnant. I nearly collapsed on the floor when he told me. Dear God, what more could happen? Was this my punishment for being with Elvis? I was so confused. Depressed, shocked, sick, and confused.

Dr. Gallaspy scheduled the operation for the next day. One of his associates, Dr. Roy Robertson, was going to perform the surgery. The operation, performed at St. Francis Hospital, was a success. They removed half of my ovary and managed to save the child. I had mixed feelings about that. I loved my children but despised their father.

That night in the hospital I walked to the window and opened it. The pain was so bad it nearly doubled me over. My mind still foggy from the anesthetic, I considered jumping. As I stood near the window, Deborah's and Melody's smiling faces came to mind. They were so beautiful. They needed me. What would happen to them?

My neighbors, Tom and Janet Miller, came rushing into the room. They quickly grabbed me and closed the window. I broke down and cried. In a moment of weakness I blurted out the story. Mr. Miller, an animated Polish man who was usually cheery, became enraged. He didn't like the Man, and now he was ready to kill him. Janet calmed him down. She convinced him to talk to my doctor instead of confronting the Man.

I don't know what Mr. Miller or Dr. Gallaspy did, but they must have stirred up something. When I was released from the hospital, I received a call from Mr. Adams, my attorney. He said he had arranged to have the Man provide me with a larger home, one that held no memories. Even better, I learned that my friends had filed for a legal order that prevented the Man from coming there. It happened so fast. I had to temper my elation because I couldn't believe it would stop the Man. A month later I moved into a beautiful one-story, four-bedroom house in an exclusive neighborhood on Azalea Drive. It had huge glass windows across the front, and the yard was full of willow trees.

Best of all, I could walk inside without feeling nauseated . . .

As for reuniting with Elvis, that was hopeless. I couldn't see him now. I was pregnant. It wasn't his child. We had always taken precautions. Elvis would feel betrayed. Even if he did understand, my shame was unbearable. After recovering from the operation I danced one more time, then had to quit. The show went off the air a month or so later. I was depressed for the next nine months, both mentally and financially. The Man was not paying any support, and I had informed Mrs. Fowler that her services were no longer needed. That forced me to hire a succession of baby-sitters in order to work. I kept my job at the store as long as possible, then took a leave when I started showing. I didn't want anyone to know. Elvis kept calling at both the store and the television station, but I didn't have the strength to accept the calls. I knew that the moment I heard his voice I would break down and cry. He might then come to Monroe, and the Man had threatened to kill him. I couldn't risk that.

My third daughter, Denise, was born at the end of July 1954. After her birth, I started thinking about Elvis. Maybe we could start back up. He had left me a phone number, a neighbor who was a priest or preacher of some sort. Elvis was embarrassed to admit that he didn't have a phone. I dialed the number and a woman answered. I asked her about him, but she was more interested in taking my name and number than updating people about Elvis's life. I said I'd call back, too afraid to leave my name.

It soon became much easier to find out about him. His voice started coming out of the radio. I remember how shocked and happy I was to hear the first song. Denise was only a few weeks old. I was feeding her one afternoon and listening to the radio. Suddenly, I heard Elvis. He was singing "That's All Right

(Mama)." It sent chills through my body. I was so happy for him I started to cry.

The tears soon came for real. It hurt so bad not being able to see him and enjoy his success. He must have been thrilled. His dream was coming true! More songs followed. Something about a "Blue Moon," and "Good Rockin' Tonight." The newspapers said Elvis finally got on the Louisiana Hayride and was creating a sensation. All the girls were supposed to be crazy about him. That was hardly comforting, but it was good he was so busy. That way he wouldn't have time to look for me, that is, if he even wanted to. I didn't want him to try. It was best that I never see him again.

The couple who fielded Elvis's calls in those days was Rabbi Alfred Fruchter and his wife, Jeanette. They lived upstairs from the Presleys on Alabama Street in Memphis. Lucy probably spoke with Jeanette.

Elvis recorded "That's All Right (Mama)" and "Blue Moon over Kentucky" at Sun Records in Memphis on July 6, 1954. They were released on July 19, and by August "That's All Right" was the number-three song on the Memphis country-and-western chart. On July 30, the night Lucy was having her baby in Monroe's Riverside Hospital, Elvis was making his first public appearance of consequence. He was a last-minute addition to a country-music show at the Overton Park Shell in Memphis. Slim Whitman was the headliner, but Elvis stole the show. His "wiggling" leg evoked screams for the very first time.

It wasn't a rocket to the top, at least not yet. A huge tumble followed. His recording success enabled him to get a shot at the big time. On September 25, 1954, Elvis performed at the Grand Ole Opry. Although the crowd liked him, Opry manager Jim Denny practically kicked Elvis off the stage, uttering the now immortal line "If I were you, I'd go back to driving a truck." Elvis cried the whole way back to Memphis. A few weeks later his luck turned. Instead of being jealous, Whitman was extremely generous and went to the Louisiana Hayride officials and told them that they had to sign this "sensational kid from Memphis." With his song getting increasing airplay, and Whitman's enthusiastic endorsement, Elvis was finally allowed to step out of the Hayride audience. He was a smash and was quickly signed to a one-year contract that called for forty-eight weekend performances. The King was born.

Some versions of the Elvis legend say his appearance at the

Hayride in October 1954 was the first time he had ever been to Shreveport, and that he saw the famous Hayride stage for the first time that night. That version is vigorously repeated by Horace Logan, one of the Hayride emcees. It originated with Elvis himself. When his big moment came, Elvis told Logan he had never been there before. Elvis no doubt wanted to disassociate the newfound "Memphis sensation" from the wide-eyed kid who hung around watching rehearsals and scrounging bucks from Billie Jean Horton. Like much of the Presley legend, the Elvis-first-night-in-Shreveport story caught the fancy of biographers and lives on.

"They said that same foolish thing about Hank Williams and the Grand Ole Opry," Billie Jean chides. "The legend says Hank came outta the sticks, got to play on the Opry, and became an overnight sensation. Truth is, he was workin' around Nashville for years tryin' to get on. Same with Elvis and the Hayride. He knew where he had to be to make it, and he damn well was down here tryin'."

In the spring of 1955 Elvis was playing at the Hayride and touring the surrounding area in package shows spinned off the Hayride. One of the shows was headed by Hank Snow and was booked by Snow's high-profile manager, Thomas Parker, a former carnival huckster who had previously orchestrated Eddy Arnold's success. Parker had been alerted about Elvis and was watching his career closely, but had yet to take control.

Elvis's latest songs, "Milkcow Blues Boogie" and "You're a Heartbreaker," sold well regionally, but he had yet to crack the national charts. At this point he was still just a local phenomenon.

M R. SILVERSTEIN GAVE ME MY OLD job back in September. The work had become more than a diversion. I needed the money to feed my children. I lived quietly, refusing all phone calls, trying to avoid the Man. The winter was uneventful. I kept up with Elvis through the newspapers and listened to the radio for new songs. One Sunday in late spring, I decided to take Denise out to a local park. She had just started walking and wanted to run around outside. Deborah and Melody were at the movies with a nice Italian woman who had become their regular sitter. Some weekends she took them out on her own time, which was a great relief. I took Denise to Forsythe Park. I especially liked it because it was next to the Ouachita River and near a large levee. Denise ran around, stumbling frequently, always getting back up and going on. I sat in the grass and watched her. She was so happy, just the opposite of the way I felt. I sat and stared in space, reliving my short time with Elvis. We hadn't been together in more than a year. He had come through town as part of a Hank Snow show, but I hid in my house, not wanting to take a chance that he would see me and find out about the baby. Suddenly my eyes focused on a figure approaching. It scared me. I tried to round up Denise, but she playfully ran from me. By the time I got her, the person had reached us. It was Elvis! He was wearing a brown fedora and a big sloppy jacket with the collar rolled up. It was a peculiar outfit for him.

"Hello Lucy," he said. I just stood there with my mouth open. I wanted to run to him and kiss him but didn't know how he would react.

"Aren't you glad to see me?" he said, stretching out his arms. I put Denise down and ran to him. We kissed passionately and frantically, laughing and crying at the same time. It felt so wonderful again.

"Why didn't you trust me?" he asked. "Didn't you think I'd try to find you?"

"You can't imagine all I've been through."

"Baby, I know."

He couldn't know, how? I wanted him to explain, but didn't want to press. We always had an unspoken trust. We each seemed to know when the other was hurting, and maybe that was what he meant.

"I kept callin', but no one would tell me anything. I didn't give up," he continued. "I was driving home from Shreveport and I kept seeing your face in front of me the whole way. I knew I'd find you today. I knew it."

Denise had run over and was clutching my leg. Elvis crouched down to play with her.

"Is she mine?"

"No."

"I wish she was. Tell me all about it."

"Oh, Elvis, it's the same old thing. You don't need to hear it again."

"I want to. Please tell me." We sat down in the grass and I told him the whole sordid story. I felt bad about telling him. His life was going well. He was on the way to achieving his dream. He didn't need me dragging him down into my dark pit.

"Elvis, you don't have to be here for me. I understand. Things just weren't meant to be. It was wonderful, and I'll never forget you, but I think you should go on with your life."

"Don't be foolish," he said. "I wouldn't have hunted you down if it was just to say good-bye. That's kinda stupid. Our love is forever, Lucy. Nothin' matters. Don't you remember?"

"I remember. I just thought you might have changed."

"I'd like to put that Man out of his misery. Where is he?" Elvis said angrily.

"No, please. That would harm you. I would lose you. Your life is too important for that. Just let it go. It's over. This is where we begin. You're doing so well! I hear your songs on the radio and see stories about you in the newspapers!"

"I'm travelin' around everywhere. I lose track of where I am sometimes. Why don't you come with me?"

"I'd love to, Elvis, but not yet. You still have a long way to go. One day, when you've reached your goal, when you've climbed all the mountains there are to climb, then I'll come to you. If you still want me."

"I'll always want you, baby. Always. I keep meetin' new girls, but none have come close to you. No matter how badly I need a woman, I still can't stop thinkin' of you. Women are so loose. They come on to me all the time just because I can sing. I don't like that, so don't believe all that stuff you read about me and women. You're the only one that knows the truth."

"You don't have to explain," I said. "It's all part of your image. It will draw the people to your concerts. That's what's important. Don't worry how I'll feel. I understand."

"I've got a big tour coming up with Hank Snow," he said. "We're goin' through Texas, Louisiana, and Florida. There's a new man that's interested in promoting me. Some Colonel guy. I don't know what to do. I hate changin' people. Mr. Neal has been good to me. What do you think?"

I asked him if he felt the new man could help him, if he could take him further than Bob Neal.

"I dunno. He sure talks bigger. He says within the year I'll be doin' records, television, and even the movies! I'd like to do movies."

It sounded so good. I could tell Elvis wanted it.

"Then do it, Elvis. It's not like you're betraying Mr. Neal. He's part of it, right?"

"Yeah, they all seem to be in it together somehow."

"Well, what's stopping you? I'd love to see you up on the giant screen playing romantic parts. You can play El Lancelot, the Memphis Knight." We both laughed at that. Elvis was intrigued. I didn't know much about the music business but had hung around the television station long enough to hear the people talk about contracts and managers and all. The TV people talked about little else.

"If you sign with him, just don't make it too long. One or two years at the most. Then when you're a success, you can regain control of your life."

"How 'bout you, Lucy? Are you doing all right? Have you got enough money?"

"I'm okay. Don't worry about that. I'm fine," I lied. I was really broke and struggling, but didn't want to tell him. Elvis would have given me his last dollar.

We weren't together very long that afternoon. Elvis said he was on his way back to Memphis. Some people—his band, I guess— were waiting for him in town. He made me promise to accept his calls and see him in Memphis again. We kissed deeply, then he left.

I didn't hear from Elvis for over a week. Then one day at the store a man came and handed me a dozen red roses. The card read, "Love Is Forever—El Lancelot."

He called the next day and said he was in Lubbock, Texas. He was touring, playing in a country-and-western roadshow. "You remember when you told me to look right at the audience and give them all I have. Well it's workin', baby!"

His call lifted my spirits. I was on the outside—way on the outside—but he made me feel a tiny bit part of it. I was finally able to give him my home phone number, and that enabled him to call more often. He'd call from small towns with names like Conroe, Greenville, and Wichita Falls. He professed his love and said how anxious he was to see me.

I managed to get some work at the television studio once in a while, singing and doing a live commercial now and then, not much, but keeping my feet wet. The cerebral palsy telethons were big then. I helped out with them at KNOE and even got to sing. Michael Ansara, Forrest Tucker, and singer Charlie Applewhite were some of the hosts. I thought of becoming a singer and trying to record something myself but realized it would be difficult.

In August 1955 Silverstein's was having a sales promotion for the winter furs. Actress Gloria Swanson had a fashion line then and it was getting a big push. As part of the promotion, Swanson's people were bringing in a famous designer from France, a woman named Gabrielle Chanel. I was dressing a mannequin in the window when someone said Mr. Silverstein wanted me.

Dave Silverstein was the store owner. He was a short, bald, energetic, and immaculately dressed man who wore the finest silk suits and chewed on a cigar. He was abrupt and gruff with most people but friendly to me. Still I was petrified about being summoned to his office.

He greeted me warmly and told me to sit down. He started telling me how important the promotion was for the store. Fine, but why was he telling me? He said that everyone in town would be there, including ex-Governor Noe, and even Jack Dempsey from New York. I pretended to know who he was, suspecting it was a fashion designer. I met him later and thought he didn't look anything like a fashion designer. He was big and brawny, a tough-looking character. No wonder: He turned out to be a famous fighter.

"Lucy, you speak French, right? I always see you talking to that man across the street. We need you to translate for Miss Chanel."

I said I'd be glad to. The "man across the street" was Sam Rubin. He was an older man who owned a nearby jewelry store. He had been educated in France and would come by and chat with me in French. Figuring the translation request was all Mr. Silverstein wanted, I got up to leave. He told me to sit back down and continued talking.

"There'll be a lot of important men at this affair," he said. "The kind of men you should meet." I begged him not to start introducing me to people.

"Lucy, can I ask you something personal?"

"No!"

"Why do you run from everyone who wants to meet you?"

"I'm just not interested."

"I know you think you're in love with that singer. That kind of person is bad for you."

I was dumbfounded. How did he know? I hadn't told a soul, not even my friends. Mr. Silverstein was the nosiest man in town. If he knew, how many others did?

"He isn't what everyone thinks," I said, defending Elvis. "And I'm not seeing him. He's just a friend. My life is too mixed up."

"Is your divorce final yet?"

"I haven't got enough money to pay for it. It's taking longer, since I can't afford it." Mr. Silverstein offered to lend me the money, but I declined. I didn't want to take anything from anyone.

"Listen, little Lucy, consider this carefully. There's a man coming to the promotion who used to watch you on television and has seen you here. He has fallen in love with you from afar. He really wants you. He owns a large manufacturing company and is rich. He has all the money you'll ever need. He asked me to introduce him."

I tried to keep calm. This was the same thing that happened to me before. Someone I never met had been watching me from a distance and wanted me. Instead of coming himself, he went to Mr. Silverstein. It was supposed to be okay because he was rich. He wanted to buy me all over again. I couldn't believe it. Why are men like this? Don't they realize women want to be loved, not owned? I had already been owned in every sense of the word. It didn't matter if this man was Rockefeller himself and Elvis fell flat on his face. Elvis gave me love. Nothing else mattered. I wanted to stand up and tell Mr. Silverstein this, tell him off, but good sense prevailed. There were three mouths to feed at home.

"That's very kind of you, Mr. Silverstein," I said diplomatically. "I appreciate your thinking of me. But please don't put me on the spot. I need to recover a little longer."

"Well, don't wait too long. You're too beautiful and alive to be alone."

I wasn't in the mood to continue arguing. How could he understand? He got up to escort me out of his office, then stopped and said, "You know, of course, he's coming to town."

"Who?"

"Your singer. And let me tell you this: If he hurts you, he'll never find a hole deep enough to hide in."

Why couldn't everybody stay out of my life? Mr. Silverstein put his arms around my shoulders and told me everything would be fine. I left the office angry and confused, but mostly thinking about Elvis. Was he in town? I hurried and finished the windows, then rushed from the store. Turning past the second entrance, I stopped—there stood Elvis! He was holding a single wilted red rose.

Ginger Coats, who now lives in Texas, ran the millinery concession at Silverstein's. She is a few years older than Lucy.

"Lucy was adorable. She had a big beautiful smile and a great figure. She was also very mysterious. She had a secret life and a secret boyfriend who kept calling her at the store. I never knew who it was. She wouldn't say."

If Lucy had known the real story behind the rich "secret admirer" Dave Silverstein was trying to foist on her, she would have been even more upset. The man, Joseph Durrett, owned a chain of furniture stores across Louisiana and had a bedding manufacturing plant in Monroe. He was in his late fifties or early sixties at the time, and was very married.

Dave Silverstein died in 1965. Joseph Durrett died in 1972.

Elvis performed in Monroe, Louisiana, in February 1955 on a bill featuring Hank Snow, and again in August 1955, as part of a package tour that featured him, Snow's son, Jimmy Rodgers Snow, and the Carter Family (June Carter, her mother Maybelle, and assorted other sisters and aunts). The second performance in Monroe, when he reunited with Lucy, was one of the most significant points in his career. The tour was put together by Thomas Parker for one purpose—to take a final look at Elvis in action before he wrangled his way into getting him under contract. Parker, known as Colonel Parker in the southern tradition, joined the tour in Monroe and rehearsed his fast-talking assault on Elvis's parents, Vernon and Gladys, during the ride to the next and final stop, Little Rock, Arkansas. After the Little Rock show, the Colonel was introduced to the Presleys and poured on the carny charm. On August 15, 1955, the Colonel signed his first contract with Elvis, a multifaceted deal that included Elvis's previous manager, Bob Neal, along with Hank Snow acting in a management capacity. By March 1956 Colonel Thomas Parker would rid himself of all the other names on the contract and sign a new deal making him the exclusive manager, agent, and iron-fisted ruler of Elvis Aron Presley.

Chapter 7

"WOULD YOU DO ME THE HONOR of walking with me?"

Walking was a good idea, and fast. I didn't want anyone to see us together. As we crossed the street I almost bumped into my friend Mr. Rubin, the jeweler. He just looked at me, then at Elvis, and smiled his approval. I smiled back weakly and hurried away.

"I love you, lady," Elvis said as we ducked around a corner.

"You're crazy. Why didn't you call?"

"It's better this way. I get to see your face light up when I surprise you."

"What you're seeing is fear," I said, only half kidding.

"Come on. I have a room. I'm stayin' here for a while. I have to perform." Elvis had checked into an old hotel only a few blocks from the store. I hated the idea of going immediately to his room, but we had to get out of sight. Elvis dropped behind me as we walked.

"I just wanna see the view from the back," he cooed.

We spent the rest of the afternoon in each other's arms.

"Hey, there's still one thing we've never done together," he said, jumping out of bed. "We haven't gone to the movies! I saw the sign sayin' that a Brando movie was playin' here. Let's go!"

We dressed and walked to the Paramount Theater, about a half block away. The movie was *Desirée* and starred Elvis's hero, Marlon Brando. Jean Simmons played Desirée. It was an incredible coincidence. The movie seemed to be all about us. Desirée was Napoleon Bonaparte's lost love. His career and great ambition forced them apart, but their love never died. It was a moving story that held us spellbound. We held hands the whole time. When an especially tender scene came on, Elvis squeezed my hand. He chattered during the movie, offering his opinion on everything from history to the clothes.

"Do you think I look like Brando?"

"No! You look like Elvis Presley."

"I wish I could act like that."

"I'm sure you can," I whispered. "And you're better than Brando. He can't sing." He really liked hearing that.

"Lucy, you saw how he loved her forever," he said after the movie ended. "That's how our love is. You'll always be my Desirée. Napoleon was a fool to let her go. I won't make that mistake. I promise."

The next evening I saw Elvis perform onstage for the first time since the Eagle's Nest two years before. I arrived early and got a seat up front. It was a smart move. The performance attracted a large crowd, practically everybody in town. There were many different acts in the show, including a bunch of hillbilly bands and a man who sang corny songs. It was clear that everyone had come for one reason—to see Elvis. The instant he appeared the woman next to me screamed so loud I thought someone had been murdered. That started it. The whole crowd started screaming. I'd never seen women, grown women, act so stupid. They were jumping up and yelling at the top of their lungs. I was happy for Elvis though. This kind of reaction would enhance his career. I wasn't jealous. I was proud that I knew him. Right after he came on he looked through the audience until he found me. After that, it seemed like he was playing the whole concert for me. He was sensational. His voice, what little that could be heard over the screams, was richer and more practiced. His movements were smooth and sensuous. My only complaint was his outfit. He wore a shiny black satin shirt with gold braiding around the collar and front, and gold buttons. It was tacky. Baggy black pants and two-tone black and white shoes completed the picture. He did a short show, only three or four songs, then left them begging for more. I can't even remember what he sang. The show was more action, image, and audience reaction than music.

We had arranged to meet at Forsythe Park after the show. I waited in the darkness, afraid of being there alone, wondering if he was going to appear. Someone grabbed my shoulder. I heard his laugh before I saw him. I scolded him for scaring me.

"So what'd you think?"

"You were great. I can't imagine why the women were carrying on so."

"That's my bread and butter."

"Well, they can yell all they want just as long as they don't touch."

"I'll save that for you," he said, hugging me. "What did you think of my singin'?"

"Much better. You've improved so much it's almost unbelievable."

"Do you think I'm too sexy or anythin'? Should I calm down?"

"No! You just keep doing what you're doing. That's why they were screaming."

"Did you notice the makeup?"

"The eyeliner? Who gave you that idea?"

"I saw some actors in a play wearin' it. It's okay, isn't it? Marlon Brando uses makeup. He isn't a sissy."

"No, he's not a sissy."

"What about my hair? It's so straight hangin' down in my face. Do you think I should curl it or somethin'?"

"It looks good just the way it is. Don't mess with it. It looks sexy when it flops down in your face. It excites me."

Elvis immediately shook his head so his hair fell down.

"Like this," he said, smiling. We kissed and cuddled. He told me that he didn't know what lay ahead, but it looked good. "This Colonel guy is pushing me in every direction. I dunno what's gonna happen. Don't forget me, Lucy. Even if I'm gone for a while, I'll be back. I gotta run, baby. I wish I could stay out here all night, but we gotta go to Arkansas."

He didn't call as often during the next six months. His career had taken off. This Colonel certainly was making things happen. The newspaper said that Elvis signed a big recording contract with RCA and was paid some astronomical figure. He called me from Nashville a month or so later, in January 1956, and told me he was preparing to make his first recordings for RCA. He said the Colonel also lined up a television appearance. A month or so later he called and told me he had signed exclusively with Colonel Parker. Then, before the ink had dried, he was off to Hollywood for a screen test.

In April 1956 Elvis's career rocketed. There were articles about him everywhere, in *Time, Newsweek, Life,* all the major magazines. Everyone was talking about this rock 'n' roll star with the great voice. His fame kept growing and growing. "Heartbreak Hotel" had reached number one, and he followed that with the equally big hits "Don't Be Cruel" and "Blue Suede Shoes." Milton Berle had him on his television show and made a big deal about it. Then that summer he was on Steve Allen's show and sang "Hound Dog" to a hound dog in a silly skit. Elvis was enraged.

"Did you see what they made me do?" he said when he called. "I can't believe it. You work so hard to make it, to get on television, then they make you sing to a damn dog! How do stupid people like that get such big jobs?" Fortunately, that appearance was quickly forgotten.

Somehow he managed to squeeze in filming a movie. He called and told me about how much fun it was. I was so happy for him, but I wondered if it was changing him. Was he taken in by all the fast fame? Did he still care? He called me more frequently, assuring me of his love and asking me to come see him. I told him I would later, when things cooled down. I didn't want to enter his life then. It would be hard for us to be alone, and I didn't want anyone to see us. I was still legally married with three children. The media was following Elvis's every move. Many of the stories were unflattering. The older generation, including some newspaper editors, viewed rock 'n' roll as sinful and Elvis as its demonic leader. They were resentful of his fame and would have loved to bring him down with a scandal.

In early September he called from Los Angeles and told me he was going to be on *The Ed Sullivan Show.*

"Can you fly here and be with me?"

"I'd love to, but I have to work. I'll be with you in spirit," I said. "This is a great opportunity for you. Getting on *The Ed Sullivan Show* means you've arrived."

"Yeah, but they want me to tone down. They said I'm too

'suggestive.' 'Suggestive of what?' I asked them. But they wouldn't say."

"Don't change anything," I said. "Be as you are. That's what everyone wants to see."

"I'll send you a signal. I'll cover my ear. Watch for it," he said.

It was obvious that what they said had bothered him. He was stiff and uncomfortable, nothing like he was in concert. He had been bridled. He looked great, though, and I was proud of him. He brought his hand over his ear a number of times. That was what we did in our tender moments to hear our heartbeats through our hands. Elvis said he did that onstage whenever he needed inspiration and wanted to remember my love. I was surprised that with all the nervousness he must have felt that he remembered the signal. He called the next day and asked me how his performance was.

"You looked sensational, Elvis. But they got to you, didn't they? You toned down."

"Yeah. I had to. So many people tellin' me what to do. I don't know. They're messin' with my head. The newspapers sayin' I'm obscene. People protestin' the concerts. I'm not obscene. Why are they sayin' that?"

"It's just the older generation. They say that about everyone. They said the same thing about Frank Sinatra. Don't worry. It will make you even more famous. Just don't change. Be yourself. When you try to be something else, it's not as good."

"Was it that bad?"

"Oh no. Don't worry about it, mon chéri. Most of the audience never saw you in concert. To them, you were sensational. You were all everyone was talking about at the store today."

"You're right!" he exclaimed. "They don't know better, so I musta been okay. I never thought of that."

"When's your movie coming out, *The Reno Brothers*?"

"I dunno. Soon, I think. I'm supposed to start filming some more. I may be on the third before the first comes out. Movies are too slow!"

Life certainly was speeding up for him. I worried that he soon would find me "too slow." After fame and Hollywood, would he still enjoy the simplicity of our love, especially now that half the women in the world wanted him?

His first movie came out that November. The title was changed to *Love Me Tender,* which was Elvis's song. That was another sign of just how big Elvis was becoming. They had changed the focus of the whole movie to showcase him. I went to see it at the Paramount, the same theater where we saw *Desirée* together the year before. I started crying the minute he came on the screen. I missed him so much, and he seemed so real. They captured him well in that movie. Elvis appeared at ease and looked like he was just being himself.

The ladies at work had also seen the movie and were talking about him. "Isn't he the kid that played out at the fairgrounds?" someone said. "Can't be," someone else said. I guess people feel movie stars drop from heaven or something. My friend Ginger Coats asked me why I wasn't excited like the others. "Hey, Lucy, this is one guy who would even excite you," she said. Little did she know.

Elvis appeared on *Ed Sullivan* a few more times. The last time, in January 1957, was the time they showed him only from the waist up. I liked it because they showed more close-ups of his face. I wanted to reach out and touch him. Elvis wasn't too happy about it, but he had come to expect that sort of thing from television. "I don't think I was meant for TV," he told me when he called. "This stuff gets crazier and crazier. I like the movies better."

Video buffs can see Elvis signaling Lucy during these *Ed Sullivan* performances. In the first appearance, a remote from Hollywood on September 9, 1956, Elvis brings his hand to his ear four times while singing "Ready Teddy." At his second appearance, October 28, he signals her once during "Love Me Tender" and twice during "Love Me." (He can also be seen struggling to tone down his movements during "Hound Dog.") In his third appearance, January 6, 1957, he signals Lucy once during "Too Much."

I READ SOMEWHERE THAT HE MIGHT have to go into the army and asked him about it. He said he didn't know what was going on. He seemed afraid. I missed him so much.

Seeing him on television and hearing his voice practically every second on the radio only made it harder. Another movie, *Loving You,* came out, and I naturally went to see it. "Listen to the words of the title song," he told me. "I'm singin' it to you."

"You probably tell that to everyone," I said. "I keep reading about all your girlfriends. You seem to be having a good time." There was a slight trace of resentment in my voice. I had no right to say anything, but it still bothered me. Instead of getting upset, Elvis assured me that it wasn't true. He was always like that, and frankly, I was a little surprised. He never once told me to mind my own business. He always made me feel that I was the only one.

"Baby, you're all I want. Tell me you know that. The Colonel wants me to have this Romeo image. All this stuff you read is phony. They set up dates and romances like you're still playin' a scene in a movie. Man, it's crazy. They make a date for you, then call all the reporters and photographers to go along. Some date! Hollywood is a crazy place, baby. I'll be glad to get outta here."

The next week I got a letter in the mail from California. I knew it was from him and eagerly opened it. He had never sent me a letter before, not even a scribbled note. I don't think he wrote anybody. He always said he'd rather hear my voice than see "writin'." When I opened it, I was disappointed and insulted. He had sent me a money order for $5,000. The short note just said, "Buy something pretty." The money order was signed "John Jones." The next time he called I expressed my dismay.

"Elvis, I don't need or want your money."

"Baby, all I have is yours. It's not for you. It's for me. I want you to buy somethin' for me. I want you to buy yourself a whole wardrobe of peach-colored clothes."

I had to laugh at that, but I still made him promise never to send me money. That was important. I didn't want to take anything from him, especially money. I had pride in myself and making it on my own. In a way, that sort of gift made me feel as if I was being bought again. Elvis wasn't like that, but I was overly sensitive about material things being used in place of love. I should have been more specific with him. A few days later a box arrived containing two expensive dresses. The first was gray wool with a cowl collar and buttons down the front. It was cut in sharply at the waistline and each silver button had a rhinestone in it. The second dress was an extravagant foam-colored silk chiffon. It had a bodice shirred across the bustline down to the waist, and velvet straps. The skirt was a full bias cut, and the dress came with a long draped chiffon scarf.

"They're lovely, Elvis, but no more dresses either," I said when he called the next day. "No money, no clothes, no candy, no nothing. If you send me anything else, I'm going to send it back. Except one thing. There is one thing I want."

"Just name it. It's yours."

"You. I want to see you again. Not in a movie or on television. In person."

"I will, baby. The first chance I get. I promise. Hey, why don't you come here?"

"You know I can't. There are too many people there. I want it to be just us again."

"It will be. Soon. I have to play in Canada, then I'm goin' to Hawaii, but after that I'll come see you. Did I tell you about my house?"

"The new one in Memphis?"

"Yeah, they finally got it ready. It's beautiful. I can't wait to show you. Maybe we can live there together one day."

"That would be wonderful," I said, trying to sound convincing. Elvis was sincere, but the circumstances of my life made such a move unlikely.

I didn't push him to come see me because he was so busy. Ever since Colonel Parker came into his life, Elvis didn't have a moment to spare. Sometimes he sounded out of breath when he called, like he had run from someplace and had only a minute or two to talk.

I thought again of developing my own career. I was taking singing lessons and got involved in a small theater group. I pondered moving to California, where my chances might be better. While I was planning that move, the Man inexplicably began taking an interest in the children, or so he pretended. He forbade me to move and take them away. He had never showed them the least concern before. He wasn't paying a dime for their support. It was just a way of trying to get at me. I still hadn't finalized the divorce. The legal proceedings kept him away, and I was content with that. My bitterness also played a part in the long delay. It wasn't fair that it was so hard to end such a phony marriage.

Mr. Silverstein approached me at the store with another one of his promotional schemes—a local beauty contest sponsored by KNOE that was a preliminary step leading to the Miss Universe pageant. He wanted me to compete, but I told him no. Then Beth Breece, whom I knew from working at KNOE, came into the store and tried to convince me to enter. I still refused. Mr. Silverstein argued that it was too good an opportunity to publicize the store not to take full advantage. He told me it was important to the business and he would pay for my time. He pestered me until I relented.

"Listen, no one's got to know you're married," he whispered after Beth left. "If you have any problems, I'll take care of it."

The contest was worse than I imagined. The contestants had to ride in a parade of convertibles through town. There was secretive me, sitting on top of a convertible in the middle of town, waving to the crowd, wearing the chiffon dress Elvis had sent. I could imagine someone thinking, Hey, wait a minute. I know her. She has three children! How'd she get in the contest? Then going to the judges and exposing me. I would be run out of town.

The contest was even more traumatic. Mr. Silverstein presented me with a hot pink one-piece bathing suit with a plunging back. It plunged all right—almost to my rear end.

"I can't wear this!" I exclaimed. "This is insane."

Guess what I wore? The hot pink bathing suit. Mr. Silverstein made a big deal about it being the new rage and unless I wore it he would be stuck with a whole load at the store. He always had the answers. For the formal-wear competition the ever-ready Mr. Silverstein provided a bright red strapless gown. My bust was too large to wear a strapless gown, but such subtleties were lost on him. I endured the evening and to my shock finished second. Thank God I didn't win. What a scandal it would have created. I was twenty years old with an eight-year-old daughter and two other children.

At least the embarrassment paid off in one respect. Mr. Silverstein was so delighted with my pageant performance he gave me a promotion. I became a cosmetics buyer and got to travel to New York. That was a thrill. When I told Elvis about it, instead of being happy, he became upset.

"New York's a horrible place. There's all kinds of lunatics there. Don't go. Please."

His reaction baffled me. He even offered to give me money so I wouldn't have to work. I explained, for the umpteenth time, that I didn't want his money. I had to do things on my own.

"I miss you so much," he kept saying. For some reason, my promotion and pending trip made him start pouring on the affection. It was such a strange reaction.

"Tell me you still love me," he begged. I was confused, but it was nice to hear. I assured him my love was the same.

"It's you I'm wondering about, Elvis. I read rumors about you and Natalie Wood and some others. Are they true?"

"I told you about this sleazy town," Elvis said, his voice rising. "It's the Colonel. He makes it all up. I told you that. That Natalie Wood stuff is all just publicity. You gotta believe me."

"Darling, you don't have to explain," I said. "Nothing has changed. I'll always be here for you."

Elvis's unusual reaction to Lucy's New York trip and career is typical of his behavior. He wanted anyone important to him to gear their lives around his. Detective John O'Grady, a Los Angeles supercop turned private eye, became close to Elvis in the 1970s. He knows the syndrome well and offers a keen insight into both it and Elvis's relationship with Lucy.

"If Elvis met someone who gave him something—security, comfort, encouragement, whatever—he wouldn't let go of that person. He would hold on to them even if he had to buy them, which he often did."

Of all the people in Elvis's life, the only one known to have refused his largesse was his beloved mother, Gladys. If his mother refused his gifts, then, in his eyes, that was the ultimate quality a woman could possess. It proved that the woman loved him for himself, not for his fame or wealth. Lucy reflected his mother's attitude, and thus must have been placed upon the same pedestal.

Chapter 8

Elvis went on a concert tour in September that included performances in Canada and Hawaii. I followed it in the newspapers. He was drawing large crowds and attracting lots of attention. When the tour ended, things slowed down a hair. He called and said he would come see me soon. I didn't get my hopes up. He was the hottest entertainer in America, maybe even the hottest of all time. In October his third movie, *Jailhouse Rock,* came out and the title song was number one. His fame kept growing and growing. How could he spare the time to spend a few moments with me?

He called in late November and said he was back in Memphis. He asked me to come and made all the arrangements. I flew in the next day and took a cab to a hotel near the airport. Elvis had the room registered under Lucy Barbin.

I washed my face, reapplied some light makeup, and tussled with my hair. That was a problem and I was extremely apprehensive. Someone had talked me into going to a beauty salon in Monroe, and the beautician cut my hair to my shoulder and lightened it. I cried. Elvis loved my hair long and black. He told me never to cut it. I was worried that he was going to be mad. To distract him, I put on my sexiest dress. It was a one-piece, form-fitting gray and gold knit with a gray leather belt that made my waist look tiny and my bust impressive. Maybe he wouldn't notice my hair.

There were other things troubling me. We were both growing up. I had just turned twenty-one. Elvis would be twenty-three in January. Had we outgrown our teenage love? Then there was Elvis's fame. I would be meeting a different Elvis. Instead of the unknown country boy I fell in love with, he was now a wildly adored movie star with a number-one song who wowed the nation on the *The Ed Sullivan Show*. Had it changed him? Had it gone to his head? Would he be a stranger who was so full of himself I wouldn't know him?

The qualities that made him so special—his meekness, kindness, respect for elders, deep love of family, and tender heart— are qualities that appeared most vulnerable to his fame. I'd already noticed some changes. Everything was "baby this, baby that." Was that just the beginning? On top of all this, there was the question of other women. There had been so many rumors. Every week he seemed to be dating a different movie star. He said they were just for publicity, but it still made me jealous.

My heart nearly stopped when I heard the tapping at the door. I knew the pattern of his knocks. I took a deep breath, took one final swipe with the brush at my horrible hair, then opened the door. He stood looking at me for what must have been twenty seconds. He didn't say a word. Oh no, he hates my hair, I thought. Slowly, he started smiling, then broke into a laugh. He dashed over, picked me up, and twirled me around.

"How do I look?" he asked. That was just like Elvis. Here I had been so worried, and he was just as worried about his own appearance. He looked good. Actually, he looked magnificent. He wore a dark open-neck shirt with mother-of-pearl buttons, and a brown tweed sport coat a size too large. Some things never change. He also wore those baggy pants that were in fashion and he liked so much, but I never did. I could overlook that. His hair was tinted black and his Hollywood haircut made it look fuller. His sideburns weren't as long as before. Other than that, he looked pretty much the same. The only signs of his new wealth were a gold chain or two around his neck and a weird-looking pinkie ring. The major difference was in his diction and attitude. He was starting to lose his Deep South accent. I attributed it to his acting and his move to Los Angeles. Elvis adapted to his surroundings. Changing his environment had taken some of the twang out of him. (And put the "baby"s in.) He was also more self-assured and assertive. The doubts brought on by rejection and failure were gone.

"You look great, Elvis. Like the big, famous movie star you are!"

"Yeah, can you believe it? Not bad for a hick from Memphis."

"Are you feeling all right?"

"I'm okay. Just a bit tired. I don't have time to think. The Colonel says we got to strike while the iron's hot. That's the business."

We didn't talk for a long time after that. He held me tightly and kissed me on each side of the neck. I kissed his chest. The eighteen-month separation built our desire to a fever pitch. It was exciting to rediscover each other again. Instead of the changes pulling us apart, it was better than it had ever been. We were so intent on being together, Elvis didn't take the usual precautions. I was too enraptured by the moment to protest. We made love freely several times.

Afterward Elvis relaxed. He could be himself with me. He didn't have any image to maintain. I knew him before all that.

"I remember the first time I saw you, Lucy. Man, were you beautiful, standin' on that stage in that torn jungle dress. Then you did that sexy dance. I love the way you dance. But I want you to dance only for me."

He put his hands over my ears just as he used to, then kissed me deeply.

"If I couldn't keep seein' you I think I'd die. Even when you're not with me, I feel you with me and that keeps me going. Why can't you come and be with me?"

We both knew the answer. It didn't need discussion.

"If I didn't have you, I'd be so frightened out there. I'd drown the earth with my tears. You're what keeps me alive," he repeated.

"We must never let tears be for sadness, Elvis, only for joy."

Whenever I tried to talk after that, he would kiss me in midsentence and stifle my words. He was so playful. We sat yoga-style in front of each other and Elvis stretched his arm out to the side. When he did that I would lightly run my fingers up and down his arm and over his hand. He loved it and said he could feel the love through my fingers.

"Remember when I said I would cover my ear when I performed as a sign that I'm thinkin' of you?" he said. "Well, I've decided that's not good enough. From now on, I'll stretch out my arm in the air. Whenever you see that, Lucy, even if it's a hundred years from now, it'll be my signal to you, to show you that I'll never forget. Remember that. You won't forget, will you?"

"I won't forget. Even if it's a hundred years from now, mon amour."

"My ears are cold," he said. That meant he wanted me to put my hands over them. I did. Making love to Elvis was full of moments like this. He was so romantic. He never forgot anything from the past. Each little gesture carried a deep meaning. It was one of the most beautiful things about him. He also put the most important things first. Aside from my few inquiries, he hadn't said a word about his career. He didn't want that part of his life to intrude upon our special moments. I had to ask him before he talked about it. Once I let him know it was time, he talked freely. Naturally, I wanted to know about the women.

"Do you ever feel like being with someone else?"

"There could be a thousand women around and you would be the only one," he insisted. "Always believe that, Lucy. You will forever be number one."

I didn't miss the "non-denial" despite how well he put it.

"Would you ever let anyone destroy our love?" I asked. He held my face between his hands and eased it toward his. He looked deep into my eyes.

"Desirée, do you remember our vows and how special they were?" That's all he needed to say. He kissed me and said, "Let's go hear the earth speak." That was his way of saying he wanted to go outside and feel the grass under his feet. He told me to meet him at the side of the hotel by the atrium. He had to sneak out a back way so he wouldn't attract a crowd. Outside it was late afternoon and a bit chilly. He quickly pulled up and I jumped in his car. Elvis was car crazy and bought all sorts of fancy vehicles, but it was lost on me. I never paid any attention to his cars. This one was large and dark. He drove and talked about his new home.

"Remember how I always told you that one day I'd have one of those rich folks' houses we used to drive by? Well, baby, I got it. My momma really loves it. My daddy's got a big garden going out back already. I want it to be your home, too. Wherever I live will be your home. Come on. I'll show it to you."

I tensed up. He read my fear.

"Don't worry. We won't go in. We'll just drive by."

When we got there he parked a short distance from the gate. "Isn't it beautiful? It used to be a church or something. They called it Graceland. I like the name. I'm gonna keep it. And look," he said, pointing to a street sign. "It's on Bellevue Road, just like your middle name! When I saw that, I knew I had to buy it!"

His voice became low and deep, as it always did when he grew serious. "I know, I promised not to tell anyone about us, and I haven't. I haven't told a soul. I want to tell my momma. I want to tell her everything. Maybe she'll know what to do. Is that okay?"

Fear gripped me. Elvis was close to his mother and loved her deeply. I wasn't anything close to the kind of woman she would want for him. I was in spirit and character. It was just my past —my ugly past. No one could overlook that.

"No, Elvis, please. Not even her. Not yet. You promised me. Don't break your vow."

"If it still means that much to you, then okay. But don't keep me to this forever. I've got to tell Momma. She wants me to find a nice girl and settle down. I'd like to tell her I have. Lucy, we should get married. We've got to get married before all this Hollywood stuff gets too crazy."

My eyes filled with tears. What could I say? I couldn't marry him. Not at the height of his fame. Elvis was so naïve. He had no idea what this kind of scandal would do to his career. My concern was for him, but I was also afraid for myself. Could I handle the scrutiny? Hiding was my life. How could I suddenly expose myself to the world? I told him we would marry, but not for a while.

"I think I'm gonna have to go in the army," he said. "I'd like to marry you before I go."

"We'll see. We'll talk about it later."

He started the car and we went driving in the hills. I thought we were going to our hill, but he found a new spot. It was a small grassy incline overlooking a river, possibly the Mississippi. It was a nice place, but it was late in the season and that made a big difference. The trees were bare and the river looked angry. We walked for a while, then Elvis stopped and reached into his coat pocket.

"I have a present for you."

He pulled out a crumpled rose. It warmed me to see he hadn't changed. The rose was semi-wilted, as usual, and even that was comforting.

"That isn't it," he said, grinning widely. "I have something else."

He took a small box out of his pocket and opened it. That's what pressed against me when we hugged. The box contained a tiny gold cross. Real tiny. It couldn't have cost ten dollars.

"You told me just to give you little things," he said, laughing. "This is the littlest thing I could find."

"You remembered," I said, recalling when he broke my chain and caused me to lose my confirmation cross in the grass. I reached for it. He pulled it away. Elvis presented all his gifts with a speech.

"This cross symbolizes our love crossed with God's love," he said. "Until you wear my ring, wear this close to your heart." With that, he took it out of the box and put it around my neck. "I love you forever, baby. You won't let me give you anything expensive, so I put all the love I could squeeze into this."

It was the perfect gift. I embraced him and gave him a deep kiss. Unfortunately, Elvis didn't grasp the beauty of the moment. He pulled another box out of his pocket.

"Now for the real gift," he said. He opened the box and showed me a stunning bracelet covered with huge sapphires, emeralds, and diamonds. I couldn't let him give me something like that.

"It's beautiful, Elvis, and the thought is so nice, but I can't accept it. I've never had anything so expensive. Please do me a favor. Give it to your mother. She deserves it more than me. Someday I'll let you give me things like this, but only when we are together permanently."

His face twisted up in anger.

"You think I can't afford it! Well, watch this!" He ripped the bracelet out of the box and threw it into the river. It was the first time I had ever seen Elvis's legendary temper. "If you won't wear it, no one will!" he snarled.

I was shocked. It frightened me. "I'm sorry," I said. "I didn't realize how important it was to you. I've never been given anything like that before. I guess I just don't feel worthy."

"If I give 'em to you, that means you're worthy," he growled.

"What I want is you. That's all. I miss you."

His anger drained as fast as it erupted.

"You're some lady, Desirée," he said tenderly. "Don't ever change." He pulled me to him and kissed me. "I want you with me. Forever. No more being apart. As soon as this army thing is over, we'll get married. Do you still want to marry me?"

"Yes, yes, mon chéri. I'll be here waiting. Two years or twenty. I'll be here. Don't ever forget." I was relieved that he wasn't pushing me to marry him before he went into the army. I still wasn't officially divorced.

"I don't want to forget," he said, suddenly looking tired. "Sometimes I think the only true friends I have are you and my momma and daddy. All these people I'm meetin' now, these Hollywood types, they're not my friends. It's hard to explain, but it's not the same."

"Hey, what about God? You haven't forgotten Him, have you? He's still your biggest friend. God is the most important one of all."

He smiled a slow, weary smile.

"You keep reminding me, baby. That's why I love you so much. You keep it real. No matter where I go, I feel you're with me. When I'm away, it's like I'm only half alive. You're my other half."

We hugged again.

"Baby, I've been worrying about something. When I made love to you before—"

"When we made love," I corrected.

"Yeah, when we made love. And I forgot, you know, the protection—"

"Don't worry," I interrupted. "Nothing's going to happen. It'll be all right."

The sun set and it became cold. We returned to the car and

drove back to the hotel. He dropped me near the atrium and went around to park. Although I understood it, I was uncomfortable with all this sneaking around. It made me feel like an infidel. I went into the room and began combing my hair. He knocked, and I let him in, still holding the brush. He looked angry.

"Is there something wrong?"

"As a matter of fact, there is," he firmly stated. "Why did you cut your hair?"

Oh no, the brush! Why was I holding the stupid brush! He hadn't said a word about my hair. Now I go and practically flaunt it. I could have killed myself.

"It wasn't my fault," I whimpered.

"Who has control of your hair?"

I stuttered out the explanation about the beauty shop. He came over and brusquely ran his hand through my hair, emphasizing how quickly it took.

"See what I mean? It's not the same," he said. "I want it to always be the same. I want your hair long, black, and I want you to use that same shampoo. It has to smell the same. Everything has to be the same. That means a lot to me, Lucy. You know that."

He wasn't ordering me or anything, he was expressing what was important to him. Familiarity was everything. He wanted to remember and relive things with all his senses. I understood. That's why I always washed my hair with Drene shampoo. He loved the smell. If I didn't, he noticed it right away. I thought I had gotten away with my haircut, but I should have known better. He was too aware of the smallest things to let something as important as that go by. It was kind of him to wait so long before mentioning it. I promised I would never cut my hair that short again. He came over and held me close.

"And you have to speak French. I love that more than anything."

"Pour toujours, mon chéri, mon coeur est pour toi. Je t'aime, El Lancelot. Je t'aime beaucoup."

"I got the 'El Lancelot.' What's the rest of it mean?"

"For always, my love, my heart is yours. I love you, El Lancelot. I love you very much!"

He had me teach him each word in French so he could repeat it back to me, substituting "Desirée" for "El Lancelot." His accent was so funny it made me laugh. I put my mouth close to his and we spoke the words together. He sighed deeply and clutched me tighter.

"Your hair has changed, but you still have the same beautiful body. I love to look at your body. Please let me see it again." I obeyed, lifting my knit dress over my head. "Don't ever let anyone else see your body." I started to say something, but he put his finger to my lip. "There is never enough time to soak in all your love, Desirée. I try, but it doesn't last. I need to be with you more often."

He left late that night. Elvis preferred moving in the darkness so he wouldn't be noticed. I had an early flight to catch, and he didn't want to leave in the morning. What he really didn't want to do was wake up in the morning. He never had much use for mornings.

The hotel room was empty and lonely when he left. I had a horrible feeling that I wouldn't see him again. His fame and career would make it harder to hide our love. It went beyond that. I felt there was a force at work keeping us apart. It's hard to explain, but the feeling was strong. I worried about how this Colonel man was using him. I warned Elvis to be wary and not to be so trusting. Maybe I was thinking only of myself. This manager would view me with the same horror as Elvis's parents, maybe even more so. Unlike Elvis, he had to know how damaging I would be to Elvis's career. If Elvis didn't see the problems I presented, his manager would waste no time explaining it. And Elvis said the Colonel was close to his father. That would do it for sure. Despite the beauty of my day with Elvis, I fell into a troubled sleep.

It was cold and misty the next morning. The flight home was gloomy. Seeing my children cheered me up. They were my whole life. They were all I had. Elvis called a few days before Christmas. He said he'd received his notice to go into the army. He didn't appear to be upset. The Colonel had him convinced it would help his career. I couldn't see how, but I was glad Elvis was taking it well. He said he didn't have to leave for a while because the Colonel had gotten a delay so he could make another movie, *King*

Creole. I marveled at how his manager could pull so many strings, even with the army.

"Yeah, he's somethin'. There ain't nothin' that man can't do," Elvis said. "I just wonder if what he's doin' is right."

Albert Goldman's investigation into the Colonel's control of Elvis, detailed in the book *Elvis,* is by far the most penetrating. Goldman reported that Elvis believed Colonel Parker set up the army stint. First, a story was planted in *Billboard* magazine that accused the army of preparing to give Elvis a sweet deal. At the time, the army hadn't given a thought to drafting the singer. When the story came out, the Colonel told his boy that there was a lot of criticism from veterans' groups and Elvis would have to do the right thing. According to Goldman, the reason behind this madness might have been that the Colonel was afraid Elvis had become too big for him to control and he wanted to knock Elvis down a few pegs. Nothing like two years in the service to make Elvis totally dependent upon his master manager again.

I DIDN'T HEAR FROM HIM FOR A WHILE after that and spent an unhappy New Year's Eve. There wasn't much hope for the future. Elvis was off filming another movie, and when it was completed he would go directly into the army. I probably wouldn't see him the whole two years. Could his love survive that long a separation? With all the women after him, what chance did I have?

I occupied my time working and rehearsing a play staged by the theater group in Monroe. We did *Dracula* and *Affairs of State.* I wanted to stay backstage and work behind the scenes, but they kept giving me parts. I got to be one of Dracula's victims.

One night after rehearsal, a bunch of us went out to have a snack at a nearby coffee shop. We were joined by a group from KNOE. The conversation got around to "this sexy new singer" that everyone was talking about. They started mentioning the women who threw themselves at him and speculated on the hundreds he must have caught. "He must have a different one every night," someone said. I kept sinking lower and lower into my chair. I wanted to defend him but didn't want to be challenged about how I knew differently. On the way home I worried about what they said. I was painfully lonely and hearing talk like that didn't help.

At home I changed for bed and was in the living room drinking a glass of warm milk, reading, and listening to a Roger Williams record. My children were all in bed. I heard the milk bottles on the front stoop scatter. I figured it was a neighbor's dog or something and went back to reading. A minute later I was startled by a frightening noise coming from the kitchen. I got up to check it out, and just as I entered, I saw the door leading to the garage splinter as someone kicked it in. A few more kicks and it burst apart. In walked the Man. He was ugly and angry. His face was flushed and his eyes were bulging. His mouth was so tight I could see veins in his neck. He lunged at me and almost ripped my nightgown off.

"You bitch! You little whore!" he screamed.

I tried to make it to the bedroom, but he grabbed the end of my gown, causing me to fall hard on my face. He dragged me into the kitchen, where he lifted me up, punched me in the face, then threw me through the shuttered pass-through above the kitchen table. I crashed onto the record player in the living room. My hand went through the plastic top and was badly cut. I got back up and ran toward the picture window.

"Go ahead! Jump out, you bitch whore!" he said. I was thinking of doing just that, but he didn't give me the chance. He grabbed me around the waist and carried me into the kitchen. He dug his hand in his pocket and pulled out a thin object. Suddenly a silver knife blade snapped into place. This was it: I was going to die. I screamed. He threw me back against the sink, grabbed me around the neck, and put the knife to my throat. Dear God, I prayed, don't let him kill me.

"How does it feel to know you are going to die? How does it feel? Tell me, whore. I know you're seein' that son of a bitch. I'm gonna kill you, then I'm gonna kill 'im. No, I got a better idea. I want you to watch me kill 'im. You'll see him nailed to a cross. You want to see that, don't you?

"I suppose you're gonna tell me you love 'im? Go ahead, tell me. Make it easier for me to kill you both."

I didn't move, not wanting to incite him further. If I could just stay calm, maybe I'd survive. He eased the knife from my neck. For an instant I thought he had stopped. Instead he put the knife up against my face.

"I'm gonna cut your damn face up to see if he'll love you then. You think he loves you? You? Who the hell you think you are? He has all kinds of whores. He doesn't love you. You know what he is."

I heard screaming and became terrified about what might happen next. Debbie and Melody came running into the room and started beating on his legs and trying to pull him off me. "Please don't hurt Mommy," Debbie cried. I was so afraid he was going to kill me with my daughters watching.

"You two go to bed," he demanded. "Git outta here."

They refused to move. He kicked at Debbie with his leg, but that only made her scream louder. Finally he let me go.

I kneeled down to comfort my children.

"Everything will be okay. Please go to bed. I'll be there in a minute." I wanted them out of there before he turned on them. When they left, I faced him and calmly said, "Leave this house."

"Leave the house I own? The one I pay for?" he said.

"Just leave this house."

"You don't deserve to have children. I'm gonna take them away because I know what you really are."

"Don't you ever touch my children."

"If I can't take them away I'll do something else. I won't let them live around you. I won't let them live at all," he said.

"Leave this house."

He moved toward the broken door. Just before he walked out, he turned and looked at me again.

"I'll let you go this time. But if I ever see that son of a bitch in this town again, I'm gonna kill 'im. I don't care how famous he is. You tell 'im that. You tell 'im he's gonna be singin' in hell soon. That's where he belongs anyway."

I went into the bedroom to calm the children. We all cried, but I stopped as quickly as possible because it was scaring them. I told them that the Man wasn't serious, he just had a bad temper. It wasn't true. I could see in his eyes that he was capable of murder. Me, Elvis, the kids, anybody. The next time we wouldn't be so lucky.

"Mommy, you promised me he wouldn't come here. You promised," Melody said, wiping her tears.

"I know I did, honey. I'm sorry. I promise you'll never see him again."

I stayed in their room until they fell asleep, then went to check Denise. Mercifully, she had slept through it all. I went to the bathroom to treat my injuries. My hand was badly cut. My neck was bruised black where he had grabbed me. It hurt so bad I could hardly swallow. After I cleaned and bandaged my hand, I moved Denise into Debbie and Melody's room, locked the door, and slept on the floor between their beds.

The following day, I went searching for another place to live. I found a small house across the street from Northeast Louisiana State College and quickly made arrangements to rent it. I spent the next day moving a few necessities. That evening we moved in. My plans were to leave Monroe as soon as possible and not tell anyone where I was going. Not even Elvis. He wouldn't take the threats seriously and might get hurt or killed. I told Mr. Silverstein at work that I would be leaving soon. He was upset and wanted to know why. People didn't leave town much in Monroe. You were born, raised, and died there. I told him about what happened, omitting the part about the threat against Elvis. He told me that running wasn't the answer and offered his help. "I'll protect you. I have a lot of influence." I had heard that before and had been fooled into thinking that the legal proceedings would keep the Man away. What's a trespassing charge to a man who wants to kill someone? Nothing could stop him anymore. The only way to save my children was to hide and never let anyone see me again. Elvis would be better off without me. My life with him had been an impossible dream to begin with. The darkness of my past prevented us from making a life together. I let it go too far. I couldn't allow it to ruin his life. He would be okay. The papers were full of stories about his girlfriends. It broke my heart, but I was happy for him. Elvis was the kind of man who needed someone all the time.

On my last day at the store I remained after closing, gathering up my things. I noticed that no one had left, which was unusual. Mr. Silverstein appeared and said, "We have something for you." Then everybody gathered around and started giving me gifts. It made me nervous. I wanted to vanish from town without anyone knowing. My friends asked me to stay and offered their help. I didn't know what Mr. Silverstein had told them. He called me into his office and after much discussion, convinced me to stay two more weeks.

I sold practically everything we had and gave away whatever remained. I was at the store the following week when the phone rang. I answered it myself and was startled to hear Elvis's voice asking for me. He was in Hollywood making that final movie before entering the army. I put on an act and pretended everything was okay, fighting not to let on that I was about to move and never would speak to him again. It was so hard. I almost broke down.

"I'm gonna be seein' you real soon, baby. Real soon," he said.

I didn't say anything.

"Are you okay? What's the matter?"

"I've been a little sick, that's all. Everything is fine," I lied.

"Lucy, when I go into the army, I think I'm gonna train in Texas. I'd like you to move down there and be with me. I'll pay for everything. Will you do that?"

That made me feel worse. How could I have doubted his love? I held on to every word he said, trying not to show my pain. "I love you, Elvis. No matter what happens. You've got to remember that. I'll love you forever."

"Nothin's gonna happen. I'll do my army thing and be out in no time. Don't worry. When I get out, I won't be so famous anymore. All this craziness will be over. Hell, nobody'll probably give a damn about me. Then it'll be just you and me again, like it used to be. You'll have no excuse not to marry me. But we'll talk about that when I see you. I'll be there in a couple of weeks."

I didn't want Elvis to lose his fame. That would hurt him more than he was letting on. But if he did lose it, he wouldn't lose me. I didn't care anything about his fame or money. Maybe it would calm down someday. Maybe he could perform and be happy, but the cameras and reporters wouldn't be around. Then we could be together. It was a tiny spark of hope, something to hold on to so I wouldn't have to exist without dreams. That cheered me up for a while. I couldn't let him see me though. I had to be gone before he came. If I was still here, the Man would try to kill him.

The stress of moving and my fear that the Man lurked behind every corner was twisting me up inside, making me feel really sick. An older woman at Silverstein's said it was the flu and gave me two capsules and told me to take them. She said they contained quinine and it would make me feel better. I swallowed them. For the next two hours I was doubled over in pain. My stomach felt like it was going to explode. Fortunately, my mother was in town and rushed me to the hospital. The doctors became alarmed when they found out about the pills. In my delirium, I heard a nurse say, "I believe she's pregnant." That sent shock waves through me. A doctor later confirmed it.

"Do you know you're pregnant?"

"No."

"Well, that quinine could have killed you. You're not supposed to be treated by store clerks. That's what we doctors are for." He continued to scold me, but my mind drifted. All I could think about was being pregnant and what a cruel twist it was. This was the one child I should have been happy about. A child born out of love, fathered by a man I loved. Instead, Elvis's life was in danger and he would soon be entering the army. His career was at a critical stage. He couldn't survive the scandal of my pregnancy. I was still legally married. To protect him, I had to leave town without a trace and without letting him know I was pregnant.

The next day, though I still felt queasy, I packed the car. There was no time to spare. The phone rang just before we left. Who was it? The Man or Elvis? Something prompted me to take a chance.

"You're gettin' slow, baby. I almost hung up," Elvis said.

"I was outside."

"I just got the urge to tell you I love you. You don't mind, do ya?"

"I never mind. You know that."

Hearing his voice made me weak. I thought of telling him the truth.

"I have something to tell you." The minute the words left my lips, the Man's threat rang in my head: *"You tell 'im he's gonna be singin' in hell soon."*

"I'm going away for a short time," I said.

"Where? Why? Give me a number!"

"It'll only be a while. Don't worry. I'm just visiting some relatives."

"You sound so sad. You'll be back, won't you?"

I desperately struggled to maintain my composure.

"I'm just visiting some relatives. My aunt is sick."

"Don't run away again, Lucy. I'm comin' to see you soon. Remember. You gotta be there. That's all I ask. I'm beggin' you, baby. Don't leave me again."

"I won't."

I hung up the phone and cried my eyes out.

As Lucy knew, Elvis did need someone with him all the time, especially when he was under stress. Thus, it would be Anita Wood, not the pregnant Lucy, who would comfort Elvis in Texas during his basic training. Wood was a budding singer/actress who had a television dance show in Memphis. Elvis dated her periodically. For a time, she was referred to in the fan magazines as "his number-one gal."

Chapter 9

I T WAS COLD AND RAINING WHEN I pulled out of the driveway and steered my gray Oldsmobile out of Monroe for the last time. My brain was numb and running on pure instinct. I had no idea what to do or where to settle. My sister Mary had moved from Memphis to Denver and said we could stay with her until deciding upon a permanent location. Just before leaving, I gave in to despair and cashed Elvis's five-thousand-dollar check. I wanted to send the check back but was desperate for money. It was humiliating when the teller handed me the bills, a death blow to my pride. I vowed to pay him back as soon as possible.

My children were overjoyed about leaving. They associated leaving Monroe with leaving the memory of their father brutalizing me. Deborah asked if we could find a new daddy. I couldn't promise that but did promise them a better life free of nightmares. For the first time since the scene in the kitchen, they were laughing and playing and having a great time. Thank goodness they couldn't see the pain in my heart. Driving through northern Texas reminded me of what Elvis had said about wanting me with him during his army training. Wouldn't that have been wonderful? Wouldn't it have been impossible? "Good-bye, my love," I quietly said, fighting back tears.

It began to snow outside of Texas. The farther north we went, the harder it snowed. I knew nothing about driving in snow or putting chains on the tires and didn't realize the danger. When I stopped for gas in Gunnison, Colorado, the attendant warned me not to continue. I didn't listen. We felt like the Man was right on our heels. The car stalled halfway up the Continental Divide. The wind blew our suitcases off the roof and they disappeared down into a gully. That left us with little more than the shirts on our backs. A stranger pulled over and offered to take us to a nearby inn. God was watching over me.

The snow really began coming down. I tried to call Mary, but the phone lines were down. We were trapped at the inn for two days, waiting for the storm to pass. When I finally called Mary, she was frantic. She said the police had found my car and thought we had frozen to death trying to find help. They found the registration papers in the car and called Monroe to get information. I later learned this started the rumor there that we had perished in the storm. I cried when I heard that the nice man who had given us a lift to the inn had died in an accident just a mile up the road. Then I realized we could have easily died with him.

I told my sister not to tell anyone we survived. It was a perfect escape. If the Man thought we were dead, he wouldn't try to find us. That plan had one major flaw—there was a strong chance that Elvis would hear the same rumor. Maybe it was best that he too believed it. He could go on with his life. That was cruel, but I felt in my heart he would know it wasn't true. He could sense I was alive. When the time was right, I'd call or write. Yes, that was best. Let everyone in Monroe think I was dead. I could close that door forever.

My sister drove down and together we found my car. It had been towed to a nearby gas station. The mechanic got it started for me, and we followed Mary to Denver.

Traveling to Denver from Monroe, Lucy shouldn't have been anywhere near Gunnison, Colorado. Relying on bad directions, she overshot Denver by almost two hundred miles and was heading toward Utah when the storm stopped her. Apprised of this thirty years later, she said her anguish clouded her thinking. Mary de Barbin said she was aware that her sister had been lost, but she never mentioned it. "She was upset enough as it was."

W E STAYED WITH MARY FOR ABOUT a week, then found a rustic cabin for rent near Grand Junction. I wanted to get away from everyone and figured the mountains would be a good hiding place. It wasn't much, but at least we were safe. We quickly regretted moving to the "safety" of the Colorado mountains. It was a bitterly cold winter. I was ill and exhausted. The only comfort was my daughters and my memories of Elvis.

It's hard to express the depth of my love for my children. I never once associated them with their father. They were beautiful, gentle, and strong. We were more than just a family. I was so young when they were born we had actually grown up together. We were children together. We shared the pain of the past and survived. We would continue to survive. When they were tucked away in bed, I turned to my memories of Elvis. I endured the long, dark nights reliving our moments, remembering every word we said, recalling every embrace, every kiss.

We lived in constant fear that the Man would find us. My sister said he was searching for me and was trying to determine if I was with some other man. I knew he suspected Elvis, and I was relieved that the gossip filtering to my sister didn't name him. I was afraid he would discover our location and try to kill the unborn child. I tried to concentrate on other things. My days were spent teaching my children so they wouldn't get behind in their schooling. I was hiding and too afraid to register them in a local school. I wore out my knees praying for guidance about what to do next. My plan was to have the baby and wait for Elvis to return from the army. Or maybe I'd get his address from someone at Graceland and contact him by letter or phone. I'd explain what happened, about the threats and my need to run. I'd also tell him about our baby. He would understand and forgive me. He'd be happy about the baby. Or would he? Maybe he had already found someone else. My plans were slowly melting. My courage draining. If he hated me for what I'd done, then he shouldn't know. If he rejected me, it would be unbearable. I wouldn't blame him. If he was happy without me, that was my punishment for what I'd done. So many questions. The anguish was so strong I couldn't eat or sleep. I was only twenty-one yet felt so old. The only hope was my faith in God. He would show me the way. He wouldn't desert me.

Spring finally arrived and the cherry trees at the foot of the mountains blossomed more beautifully with each day. They reminded me of Elvis; everything reminded me of Elvis. "Mountains are God's special creations," he told me once. "Whenever you have problems, God will meet you on the mountain and take care of them." Here I was, weighed down with problems and surrounded by mountains. One day in early summer, I walked to the top of a mountain near my house and stood with the wind blowing through my hair. It was longer, the way Elvis wanted it. "I love you, Elvis," I shouted down to the cherry trees. I once told him that when I was overcome with loneliness, I'd sing to him. No matter where he was, he'd hear me. I started singing "Answer Me Oh My Love," a Nat "King" Cole song we both liked. Then I sang "Darling Je Vous Aime Beaucoup," another Cole song Elvis always asked me to sing because he loved hearing the French. I thought back to the first time we had been intimate, on the hill in Memphis. It seemed so long ago. Where was he? It was June, and I had no idea where the army had taken him.

I was seven months pregnant. Our child was alive, moving and kicking inside my body. It comforted me. I tried to send Elvis messages through my mind, hoping he could somehow sense me calling. "Please know I love you. Forgive me for running away." His music was everywhere. His songs sounded like they were speaking directly to me. "I'll never let you go," he sang. "Don't leave me now" and "Wear my ring around your neck." Hadn't he told me the cross around my neck signified our love crossed with God's love, and that I should wear it until he gave me a ring?

A radio story finally informed me that he was still in Texas but soon would be going to Germany. That meant he couldn't see his child born even if I changed my mind. I wouldn't have. If he was going to resurrect his career when he was released from the army, he couldn't have any scandals. I loved him too much to ruin his life. Or maybe I was just using this to justify my own guilt. An old saying came to mind. "There are no ambitions noble enough to justify breaking someone's heart." It was so confusing. What to do? Tell him? Protect him by not telling? Until a clear answer came, I would remain silently in hiding.

My sister Louise called and said that our mother had suffered a heart attack and might die. She wanted me to come at once. She was at England Air Force Base in Alexandria, Louisiana. Louise's husband was a captain, stationed in Germany. I quickly packed our things, gathered up the children and headed for Louisiana, driving straight through without stopping. I didn't want my mother to die before we got there. Although exhausted, we immediately went to the hospital to see her. She had improved, and the doctors said she would survive. I was overjoyed. Louise told me that Mother had been asking for me and the children. She wanted me to stay with her, or at least stay until my baby was born.

"You don't have to tell me anything," Louise said. "I don't care. You just stay here and let me help you."

Louise was sweet, but she didn't know much about me. She was five or six years older and had lived a whirlwind military life, traveling around the world with her husband, spending long periods in Germany and Panama. I agreed to stay, mainly for my mother. I watched Louise's young son while she worked, which kept me from feeling like a burden.

One night, while lying outside on a hammock and going over everything, I began feeling dizzy. I stumbled and collapsed trying to get up. My sister rushed over and insisted on taking me to a doctor. "It's okay, really. I'm just seven months along." She couldn't believe it because it barely showed. We went into the living room and she gently asked me about the child's father. I broke down and told her part of the story, everything except the father's name. He was, and would be, the only man I ever loved.

The next day I went to see an obstetrician, Dr. Thomas Easterling, under the name Lucy Presley. I wanted my child to have its right name. Presley was a common name in that area and wouldn't arouse any suspicion, or so I thought. The doctor asked embarrassing questions. How old was I? I told him twenty-four instead of twenty-one. It wasn't that I was too young, I just knew what the next question would be. "How old are your children?" My oldest was ten. The other questions were harder to dodge. "Why haven't you been under a doctor's care until now? Where's the child's father? What's his name?" I had nothing prepared and just blurted out the first thing that came to mind. My sister had been talking about Randolph Air Force Base in San Antonio, Texas, earlier that morning, so "Randolph Presley" became the father. Dr. Easterling said I was anemic and needed iron supplements and rest. Then he looked at my chart and asked, "Is your husband related to Elvis Presley?" It stopped me cold.

"I'm not sure. It's possible."

The next two months were spent living at my sister's, visiting my mother, and trying to plan my uncertain future. My sister lived on the base in a lovely, rambling ranch-style house surrounded by acres of forest. I spent hours walking through the woods and thinking about Elvis. I talked to God and asked Him to forgive me for having a child out of wedlock, eventually feeling assured that God understood and would bless the child despite the circumstances. In return, I promised that I'd never tell anyone who the father was until I first told Elvis. That included the child itself. I thought about my promise and realized it meant that no one might ever know. How could Elvis believe me? A woman who ran away from him after promising she wouldn't. How could I explain why without telling him about the child? If I told him and he came to me, would the Man find out and try to kill him? What if Elvis didn't come to me? What if he no longer cared? Didn't he have every woman in the world at his feet? The doubts always made me cry. Not out of fear that Elvis had forgotten but because I knew in my heart he hadn't. Doubting his love to cover my guilt was unfair.

I was home late one afternoon with my sister's young son on my lap. We were playing and my thoughts turned to my unborn child. What would Elvis want, a boy or a girl? What should its name be if it was a boy, a little boy with Elvis's face and his crooked grin? The last time we were together, Elvis was worried about our having made love without any protection. Did he suspect? We once talked about having a family together.

"If we have a boy, he'll have to have a title, not just a name," he said. "How about 'El Lancelot Aron de Barbin Presley'?"

"That's too long to put on a poor baby."

"You're the one who likes those long French names," he said, then began messing up my hair and tickling me.

"And if it's a girl—"

I knew he was going to tease me again and interrupted him. We wrestled and he pinned me down and started kissing me. I started speaking to him in French. We forgot about everything else. He never did tell me what name he liked for a girl.

The doorbell interrupted my reminiscing. I was alone and didn't want to answer it, choosing instead to peer out the peephole. A uniformed guard stood at attention outside the door. Afraid something had happened, I immediately opened it.

"There is someone at the gate who insists on speaking to a Mrs. Presley at this address."

Who knew me by that name?

The guard said it was a "Mr. Durrett" and said the man insisted it was urgent. "He wouldn't leave without seeing you, ma'am." I told the MP to get a telephone number.

I vaguely remembered the man from the fur promotion at Silverstein's in Monroe. He was a well-dressed older man, nearly sixty, who kept staring at me and later asked me to have dinner. I declined. Why was he here and what did he want? The MP brought me the number. I wasn't going to call, but curiosity got the best of me. He said he had traced me here, knew what had happened, and wanted to help. His detective work was so good he even discovered the name I was using. That was upsetting. Was someone trying to hurt Elvis by exposing me?

"What right do you have to trace me? And for what reason?"

"Lucy, I've been in love with you for years. When Dave Silverstein introduced us at the store, you showed no interest in me. But I still care."

"What are you saying? You don't know me. I'm not interested in discussing my life with anyone."

"I know it's hard for you to believe. And I know I'm not as handsome as Elvis Presley, but I've been obsessed with you for a long time. I watched you on television, and I watched you at the store. You never noticed. I like the kind of lady you are. When I saw you at the ranch long ago, I felt that someday you might need me. Will you please at least see me? I've come a long way."

The ranch he mentioned was the same place I first met Elvis. What irony. How dare this man tarnish that memory and follow me across the state!

"Look, thanks for the compliment, but I have to live my own life. What you've heard is gossip. I'm just visiting here. I'll be gone soon."

"Please hear me out," he pleaded. "I know you are under stress and financially in need. I can give you anything in the world you want. I'm a very wealthy man. I know you are expecting, and I still want you."

I was in hiding. How did this man know so much? It made me tremble with fear.

"I'm sorry, that is not possible."

He urged me to think about it and said he'd contact me later. I begged him not to try to find me again, but he refused. He said he wouldn't give up. That put me on edge for weeks. I was afraid to go out of the gates of the base, thinking this man would be waiting. Unfortunately, another doctor's appointment had been scheduled for the first week of August. The doctor had already dressed me down, so skipping it was impossible.

The day was hot and humid. I wore a summery voile dress that concealed my condition. My spirits were low. I was driving along a winding road and noticed a large, white limousine following me. My fear eased when it turned and headed in another direction. I thought nothing more of it and went to the doctor. He fussed at me, as usual, for not resting or eating properly. As I was walking back to the car, my heart skipped a beat when the white limousine appeared. I started walking faster, trying to get to my car. Suddenly, a figure got out and blocked my path.

"Hello, Lucy, do you remember me?" It was Mr. Durrett from Monroe. He was perfectly dressed in a silk suit with a burgundy tie and matching handkerchief. He wore a fedora over his thick gray hair and cut a rather handsome figure. He also had a kind face and manner. He reached for my arm. "Will you please just let me talk to you? We can sit in the car." He must have seen the fear on my face because he added, "I won't hurt you. I just want to talk. Please. Do this for me."

"What do you want with me?"

"Please, just sit with me for a moment and I'll explain everything."

He appeared unthreatening, so I reluctantly entered the car. The car was beautiful, luxurious. It was almost like a small room. He handed me a bottle of Coke from a bar in front of us. I had never seen anything like that in a car. I declined, accepting a glass of water instead.

"Why are you following me?"

"Lucy, I want to make certain that you are all right. And I want you to know that if you ever need anything, or get into any trouble, I'll be there for you." He handed me an envelope with an address and phone number on it. I refused to take it. I didn't want charity. I didn't need anyone.

"You have to understand. I desire you. I'm a patient man. I'm willing to wait. I know you will get over this Presley fellow. When you do, I want to be there. I can give you the kind of life a beautiful woman like you deserves."

His words made me feel small and unloved. I needed to hear these words from the right person—Elvis.

"You can't really believe he loves you. He has the world. He doesn't need you."

"Don't you see I'm carrying his child? How can you say that? Don't you have any feelings? What right do you have to pursue me? Please leave me alone." I began sobbing uncontrollably. Why did everyone doubt Elvis? He wasn't like they thought.

Mr. Durrett took my hand and closed the envelope inside. He took me to my car. "Call me," he said.

The envelope contained an inch-thick wad of hundred-dollar bills. There must have been a few dozen or more. The minute I got home I stuffed the money into another envelope, wrote a brief note, "Thank you, but I can't accept this," and mailed it back.

The only bright spot during that time was my mother's continued recovery. She was released from the hospital and was resting at my sister's house. One night my mother and sister decided they wanted to take me out to dinner at the officers' club. I didn't want to go, but they talked me into it. To my surprise, the evening went well. I felt good and enjoyed myself. I should have known better. Suddenly, a low haunting voice came over the restaurant speakers. I could barely hear it, but it cut through me like a knife. It was Elvis singing "Loving You." My mind spun back in time. "Honey, this is your song. Listen to it. I tell you I love you in my songs." I had been so happy back then. I was so miserable now. Tears began spilling on my plate. I excused myself. My mother and sister understood and let me go.

Instead of going to the ladies' room, I darted out the door to get out into the night. The first thing I saw was the moon. It was bright and full. There was no respite. "Whenever you see the moon, think of me and how we'll be together again soon." Did he ever look at the moon and remember me? Why didn't the memories fade? They were so clear. I could almost feel him touching me, feel his lips kissing mine. I wrapped my arms around myself to try and ease the loneliness. Turning back toward the restaurant, I noticed a soldier staring at me. I was embarrassed and became conscious of the tears streaking through my makeup. I started to walk past him on the narrow sidewalk. He didn't move. He appeared rooted to the ground. "Excuse me, please."

"Are you all right, miss?" he asked. I looked up and saw his face. He was very young and looked as if he too was separated from someone he loved. "I don't mean to intrude, but I heard you crying. It's not that bad, is it?"

"I'm fine. Thank you for your concern. I'll be fine."

He didn't move. "I saw you inside the restaurant. I'm sorry to pry, but is there anything I can do?"

"No, thank you," I said. "Is she beautiful?"

"Yeah!" he said sheepishly. "But how did you know?"

"There is something you can do for me. Go home and write her a beautiful letter. Tell her how much you love her. Tell her you think of her whenever you see the moon. She'll like that. Will you do that for me? That would make me very happy."

"I will," he said. "Right now. Thank you."

He dashed away and disappeared into the night.

Inside, my mother and sister said nothing. They were so wise. Louise advised me to get out more. "I'll send you on some errands around the base," she said. "Maybe you should go to the pool more and get some sun." I promised I'd try.

The days dragged. Those last few weeks before a child is born are the worst. I felt bloated and uncomfortable, and wanted only to get it over with. One night I had a horrible dream. I was in labor and a group of scary-looking people dressed in black-hooded tunics carried my bed into the center of an arena. The crowd was waiting for my child to be born. When it was, the people came running out of the stands onto the field, clamoring to claim the child. I fought them off. "No, go away. It's my child. Mine. You can't have it." Someone pulled out a sword and stuck it into my side. I began peacefully slipping into darkness. Then I heard Elvis's voice. "Desirée. Desirée. Come back. I love you. Don't leave me." I could see him so clearly. He was running in slow motion through a fog to reach me. I rose up from the bed to greet him. I was so happy. He had finally come for me. "I'm here. Elvis, I'm here." But he never reached me and I felt myself dying. I looked down and saw my side covered with blood. I screamed.

I woke up screaming, covered with sweat, and my side really did hurt. Was Elvis looking for me? Was he near?

The next day I took my sister's son to the base pool. A tall officer who lived nearby approached me. He wore a white band on his uniform hat, which must have signified something. He said hello and tried to strike up a conversation. He was nice, but I didn't want to talk to anyone.

"I see you alone all the time. I think maybe you've lost someone you care about. I know you're not married. I asked your sister." He was trying so hard to be friendly, but that wasn't the right thing to say to anyone in my condition.

"I have lost someone. I prefer not to talk about it. Please understand."

"I understand. I just want to be your friend."

"That's nice of you. I'm not going to be here much longer, though." I smiled and said good-bye. He stood and watched me walk away. After that, every time we went to the pool he came out in his yard or would be standing on his terrace, watching me. It made me uncomfortable. My sister told me that he approached her and asked about me. He wanted to get to know me. She assured him I wouldn't be interested. I wondered what everyone must have thought of me.

After that I left the house only at night, mostly to sit on the porch and think of Elvis. One night I got a strong premonition that something was wrong. I went inside and turned on the television news. The first thing the announcer said was that Elvis Presley's mother had died. I watched in horror. He was so close to his mother. I wanted to run to him. The next day they showed Elvis on the news. He looked alone and brokenhearted, and was surrounded by a gang of men. What would happen if I went to him? Could I get by all those bodyguards? That night I shared the pain he was feeling and cried myself to sleep.

Nine days later, on August 23, I felt the first contraction and took half a bottle of castor oil to help my labor along. I left my sister a note, got in my car, and drove off the base to Baptist Hospital in Alexandria. It was 10:30 P.M. At the hospital I wrote Elvis a letter, telling him about our child and expressing my love. I put it in an envelope and wrote down the address of Graceland he had given me. I clipped a note to it saying it was to be mailed only if I died in labor, then stuck it into the top drawer of the dresser by my bed. Shortly after midnight, the doctor gave me some kind of gas. A nurse said, "Mrs. Presley, don't pass out. You've got to push." I must have passed out anyway because the next thing I remember is someone saying, "It's a girl. Look at all that dark hair."

Through the years, Lucy has kept in her Bible the unmailed letter she wrote to Elvis that night. It remains in the original envelope, now yellowed and torn, and is addressed to Mr. Elvis Presley, Graceland, Hywy. 51 So., Memphis, Tennessee. In the right corner she wrote "Personal" and underlined it. Inside, the letter has aged a little better than the envelope. The ink has faded, but the writing remains clear. This is what she wrote:

My Dearest El—My love—

I suppose by now you must think nothing else but that I deserted you, or perhaps that I don't care for you. How it pains me to have gone from you.

My darling, I want to first say the very reason I went away is because I love you so very much. You see, darling, I can't detail it completely right now because my time is running out. I'm at this very moment going to have your baby—our baby. I'm writing because I'm afraid, El, afraid I may die and our baby will have no one. There is no reason to go on if I can't be with you. I wanted to tell you so many times. Oh, I need you so badly this moment to hold me. El, I'm so afraid. I don't know if I will ever see you again. But remember, I love you more than I can ever tell you.

The reason I left is because I didn't want you to be killed by this awful man. He promised to destroy you and kill me if I'd see you again.

My Everlasting Love, I can't live knowing I hurt you. Will you please forgive me and please understand I do love you with all my heart? I can't see beyond this moment because it's hard to think right now. El, my darling, I'm so very sorry about your mother. I wanted to come to you and hold you so badly, but I was so afraid.

Please take care of our baby and know I love you, El Lancelot, with all my heart.

> Pour toujours
> mon amour,
>
> Your Desirée

Chapter 10

"MRS. PRESLEY, MRS. PRESLEY, wake up."

I opened my eyes groggily and saw a nurse standing over my bed. It was daylight. I was in labor most of the evening and must have fallen asleep.

"My baby?"

"She's fine. Don't worry. We'd like to notify your husband. Where can we reach him?"

"No!" I said, much too forcefully. "My family will do that. Thank you. Will you bring me my baby?"

"The doctor said you should rest. You're very weak. You can see the baby later."

"I want to see her now. I must see my baby." The nurse continued to put me off. The more she did, the more I suspected something was wrong. I became adamant. They finally brought her to me. She was so beautiful. Her hair was long, almost to her shoulders, and dark. She opened her eyes. In that brief instant where lifetime impressions are made, I could see his eyes clearly in hers. Her little face, chin, cheekbones, curled lip—she was every inch her father. How Elvis would have loved her. She was as beautiful a child as we had talked about long ago. I cried and held her in my arms.

I tried to leave the hospital that day. They wouldn't release me. They still needed more information about the father. The nurse was a Gestapo type. Her mouth was hard and tight, and she appeared devoid of lips. Her dark hair was short. She had no breasts and looked like a man. Worse, her hands were cold as ice, like a corpse. I recoiled each time she touched me. She came in, pointed to the dresser, and said, "Do you want me to mail your letter?" She looked at me strangely.

"No. That won't be necessary."

"Should I list Elvis Presley as the father?" she intoned. I couldn't believe the gall.

"No!" I shouted. "He's just a relative. A distant relative."

The wicked nurse finally left. I held my baby in my arms and thought again of Elvis. "I have to tell him. She's too beautiful to keep from him." The doubts returned. His life had changed. Maybe he had fallen in love with someone else. Or was he perhaps lonely?

The next day, I chose her name. Our child would be Desirée Romaine Presley, though she might not know the last name for a long time. Desirée was a perfect first name. Elvis loved it. It's what he called me ever since we saw the movie in 1955. It symbolized our love and means "desired one." She was conceived out of the greatest love. I chose Romaine as her middle name because I read a story once about a beautiful young girl who died just before she was to be married. Her name was Romaine.

Miss Cold Hands came in to file the papers. She peered at me suspiciously when we got to the father's name. Without looking up from her writing, she asked again, "Any relation to Elvis Presley?"

"Distantly," I said.

The doctors let me leave that afternoon. I bundled up Desirée and drove back to the base. Louise was so excited. She cuddled the baby and told me how beautiful she was. Louise was also happy because her husband was coming home. I begged her to help me find a place of my own to stay. Her husband would ask questions. "Do you have enough money?" she asked. All I had left was eighty dollars and was behind in my car payment. I couldn't tell her that. I had to find a job as soon as possible. If I asked Mr. Durrett for help, he would never leave me alone. Dave Silverstein had offered to help. I called. He was beside himself.

"Lucy! Where are you? Who are you with? Did you know how many people were trying to find you?"

"I know."

"This one guy, John Jones, kept calling and calling. I told him the last we heard was that you were missing in a snowstorm. We thought you were dead. Why didn't you call me?"

John Jones was Elvis. Thank God Mr. Silverstein hadn't figured that out. Or had he? He knew everything else.

"I've been through a lot," I said. "I need your help. Will you loan me five hundred dollars? I'll pay you back soon. I promise." It was so humiliating having to beg.

"Sure, Lucy, anything you want. But I have to know where you are and why. You're such a fool," he scolded. Begging for money was bad enough. The insult made me cry.

"Are you okay, Lucy?"

"I'll be all right. Please don't tell anyone where I am."

"Why do you want to hide?"

I answered that I'd explain later. He wired the money the next day. I immediately found a gray and white colonial house, fully furnished, that was available in two days. I did all this running around, and Desirée was still only four days old. The next afternoon I took Desirée outside with me and told her stories about her father. "He'll love you just as much as I do. You'll see. One day you'll know him." I sensed that someone was watching me. I looked up and saw Louise's husband, Vernon, staring at me from the doorway. I waved and said hello. He didn't reply, appearing distant. He was tall, six feet five, and I was always uneasy in his presence.

"The baby," he said. "Who's the father?" No greeting. No hello.

"I don't want to discuss it," I said.

"You don't have to. I know. It's Presley, isn't it?"

"Don't be ridiculous," I said, brushing past him to retreat to the bedroom.

Vernon had arrived early, and when Louise came home, she was delighted to see him. I told her I'd move out that night. I packed my things, rounded up the children, and left. Louise called the next day and said a courier had brought a message for me. The message said that Dave Silverstein had recommended me for a job setting up a promotion at a local clothing store for Alfred Shaheen, a designer of Hawaiian clothes.

I was thankful for the work, and also thankful that chemise

dresses were in style. No one would know I just had a baby. Unfortunately, my body did. I began feeling dizzy and started hemorrhaging. It didn't matter. I had to keep working. There were four children to clothe and feed, plus the five-hundred-dollar debt to Mr. Silverstein to repay. When I showed up at the clothing store, Ginsberg's, they put me to work full-time as a sales clerk and a window dresser. That helped. My mother had moved in with me to assist with the children. I loved Desirée so much. She never left my sight. My weight quickly dropped to my normal 105 pounds because I wasn't eating much, mostly vegetable soup and Jell-O, in order to stretch the dollars.

A well-dressed, older gentleman came to the door of the house one night and said he was the owner. He told me his name was Walter Melson and wanted to make sure everything was satisfactory. He was an intelligent man, about fifty, with a radio announcer's voice, a big smile that revealed perfect teeth, and sandy brown hair. He said he owned a television station and a radio station and asked me to drop by his office to discuss the lease. I was curious about why he wanted to meet me and asked the people at the store about him. Turns out he was a well-known playboy. Did he know about my work on KNOE? It didn't seem possible because there hadn't been that much. Still, it was too much of a coincidence.

A couple of days later I happened to be in town and decided to go to Mr. Melson's office. He was pleased to see me. "I have only a few minutes," I said. He got right to the point.

"Haven't I seen you on KNOE?" he asked. I doubted it. Someone must have tipped him off. It was incredible how quickly my cover in Alexandria was disappearing. I nodded and changed the subject. He told me he was planning to redecorate the house, insisting that "such a nice tenant" deserved better. I said it wasn't necessary and left.

I went outside to window-shop and have a leisurely stroll in the afternoon sun. In the reflection of a store window I noticed that a big white car had pulled up to the curb behind me. I started to walk away and heard a deep voice calling me. It was Mr. Melson. "Come on. I'll take you to your car," he beckoned. I backed away and explained that I had taken a bus. That was a mistake. Now he insisted that he take me home. He was beginning to attract attention, which made me nervous, so I finally relented. On the way home, Mr. Melson told me he was trying to promote his radio station, KALB, and wanted to sponsor a performer's concert.

"I know you worked on the *P.M. Panorama* show at KNOE," he said. "Could you handle this for me? I'll pay you well." That was an offer that was hard to refuse. The extra money would help.

"Now, who should we bring in?" he continued. "What about that hot rock 'n' roll singer—what's his name? The guy in the army?" This started getting increasingly suspicious. Was he using me to try to get Elvis? Or was I just paranoid?

"I don't think he's available," I said without any revealing emotion. "I think it would be better to have someone like Roger Williams, the pianist, or David Whitfield, the English singer."

"Maybe you're right. I'll leave it up to you."

I considered refusing the job, then decided to take it. Mr. Melson didn't appear to be dangerous. Things got busy after that, working on the promotion and at the clothing store, and taking care of the children. It was strange that I ended up working for a man who owned a television station, and at a clothing store, just like back in Monroe.

Late at night, when the house was quiet, I'd sit and remember. A magazine had a picture of Elvis in Germany with women hanging all over him. His army duty didn't appear to be strenuous. One night a radio station was playing his songs. I was drawn to it even though each one made me sadder and sadder. When they got to "Loving You," the tears flowed. My mother must have heard me whimpering because she placed her hand on my shoulder and asked in French, "Ma chérie, do you really love him that much?" She held me for a long time.

Fall came and I remained active. Both the concert promotion and the store promotion were nearing completion. I decided on Roger Williams for the concert and the tickets were selling briskly. At the store I put a hula girl in the display window to promote Shaheen's clothes. I met the woman on the base. Her name was Nancy Smith and she was Hawaiian, married to a soldier. The promotion was a big success. Every time she danced, lines of people gathered out front. The men from Mobil Oil, whose office building was nearby, kept sneaking away from work and coming back to watch. We practically sold out the entire line.

The following week, while changing the display window, I noticed some hustle and bustle going on at the huge Hotel Bentley across the street. The hotel was a curious structure. It was a luxurious monstrosity that took up the entire block and had large white columns at the entrance. That led to a white marble-and-tile lobby with a domed ceiling. The building had more than three hundred rooms. It was so out of place for Alexandria, a city with a population of about thirty-seven thousand then. The locals referred to it as the "Biltmore of the Bayous."

I asked someone what was going on, and he told me they were filming a John Wayne movie around town and the crew was staying at the hotel. It made me remember a conversation I'd had with Elvis about John Wayne. "He works constantly, like me. Only difference is, he can grow old. I can't."

"Sure you can," I told him. "You'll be a brilliant businessman at fifty and still give special concerts. And you'll be the most handsome and debonair man alive. A touch of gray here and there will make you look distinguished."

"I love the way you talk, baby," he said. "Will you still talk like that when I'm an old man?" I assured him I would. Then we kissed and stretched our hands in the air . . .

"Lucy, Lucy, wake up," one of my coworkers said. "Boy, whatever you were thinking about must have been nice. You were a million miles away." I blushed, then went on with my work. A few days later an Oriental-looking man walked into the store and came directly to me. He handed me a set of keys and pointed to a brand-new, snow-white Thunderbird convertible parked out front. Then he gave me an envelope and left. Everybody in the store was staring. I was petrified. Was it from Elvis? I opened the envelope. The note said, "At your disposal until the project is over —Walter." I immediately returned it to him.

Mr. Melson kept sending his valet by the store to ask for dates. It was so absurd it got to be a joke. I did agree to go to a society function at the country club with him. I said I'd meet him there. He said the party was important for business, and even though I abhorred being his "date," the kind of people who would be at the country club were the same people who would go to Roger Williams's concert. I wore a dress I had made myself, a black crepe de chine gown with four inches of black lace at the shoulders and neck, and more lace gathered at the calf-length hem. It was pulled off the shoulders in a Latin style. I threw on an inexpensive but acceptable set of cultured pearls.

It was a miserable day. A storm hit in the early afternoon and lasted into the evening. I waited in the store as long as possible. When the last person closed up, I ran across the street to the hotel. I frequently had lunch in the hotel restaurant and had subsequently made friends with the assistant manager, Sylvia Knigh. The hotel was a madhouse that evening. The crew of the John Wayne movie, *Horse Soldiers,* was scattered about the lobby. They couldn't work because of the rain, so they had nothing to do but drink, carry on, and hang around. I walked in and was startled by a number of shrill whistles directed at me. Sylvia rescued me and found a corner table away from the bar. As we left, the whistles were louder than before. It upset me so, I was near tears and ran outside.

I saw a taxi in front of the hotel and ran down the steps through the pouring rain and jumped in. The cab was already occupied. I apologized and was about to get out when the man in the cab reached over and said, "Hold it." He turned to the driver and said, "We can't let the lady get out in the storm." I couldn't see him but the voice was unmistakable. A flash of lightning lit up his face for an instant and confirmed it. What a way to meet the star of the movie. What a cliché—jumping in a cab in the rain.

"I'm sorry, Mr. Wayne," I said, recovering from the initial shock. "I won't bother you." I tried again to leave, but he grabbed my arm a second time.

"We got time, little one. With this rain, I got nothing but time. Where you going?"

I told him Effie's Restaurant.

"Well, you're in luck. That's just where we're headed." Before I could say anything, he motioned the driver to start.

"Are you going to meet someone there?" he asked.

"It's a business function," I answered.

"As a matter of fact, so is mine," he said. I explained that my

affair was a chamber of commerce—sponsored gathering to promote business for the area. He smiled and said, "Looks like we're
attending the same party." I thought of the last movie I had seen
him in, *Reap the Wild Wind.* I enjoyed it and always admired him.
He was more handsome in person than in the movies. He was
dressed in a black tux and a white shirt. His eyes were kind and
he kept grinning. My flustered, wet-rat appearance must have
greatly amused him.

After a short ride, the taxi pulled up under a brightly colored,
striped canopy. There was a flurry of doormen opening doors and
a horde of photographers waiting to snap pictures of Mr. Wayne.
I quickly shook his hand, thanked him for the lift, and slipped out
the opposite door of the cab. Mr. Melson spotted me within
minutes and came running over. He kissed my hand formally. Mr.
Wayne noticed, wandered by, and said, "Lucky man." I could
have died.

The evening was a stifling bore. Fortunately, Mr. Melson was
playing the social butterfly and was busy socializing. I sat alone
in the back at a small table near a window, playing with my food
and thinking of a graceful way to sneak out. I was looking out the
window watching the rain drops roll down the glass when someone
touched my arm. It was John Wayne again.

"You're right. It's boring. Let's get outta here." We both
laughed and I readily agreed. What better excuse than to leave
with John Wayne? I felt safe with him. Who wouldn't feel safe
with John Wayne?

It was still raining when we walked outside. A cab pulled up
immediately, and we jumped in.

"Mr. Wayne."

"Hold it," he interrupted. "My friends call me Duke. If you're
my friend, that's what you call me."

That was difficult. I was too shy to call him by a personal
nickname.

"Where to?" he said. I answered that he could take me back
to the hotel. I planned on taking another taxi home from there.
He asked if I was staying in the hotel. When I told him no, he said,
"Driver, the lady will give you her address." I couldn't believe this
was happening.

"You know, this is a small town. And the motel room is even smaller," he said.

"I thought you were staying at the hotel?"

"Nah, I stay off by myself. I have to get some privacy. The fans and all. Hey, how about some supper tomorrow after we finish shooting?"

I thanked him and declined.

"How about a drink later?"

"I don't drink."

"Good, little one," he laughed, patting my hand. We were nearing my home and I began directing the driver. My rented house looked impressive from the outside, like a typical southern mansion. And here I was with only twenty dollars in my pocket. Mr. Wayne got out and took my hand.

"I'll see you tomorrow. Thank you for letting me take you home."

Meeting John Wayne made me miss Elvis more. I was broke, lonely, and confused about what to do with my life. I took comfort in my daughters. They were a welcome spark of life. Tiny Desirée was a good baby. She hardly ever cried, unlike her mother. It was almost as if she was being strong because she knew I needed help. I tried to be the perfect parent and fought to put on a happy face when my daughters were around. I dedicated my life to them, thanking God for placing the children in my care and promising that their needs would always take precedence over my own. Melody, now seven, caught me crying one day and came over and gave me a big hug. "Mommy, don't be sad. I love you and so does Jesus." That touched my heart, but it also made me worry. Was my unhappiness affecting my children?

"Mother is extremely emotional and was always crying," Melody recalls today. "We knew she was heartbroken over something. It was really sad. She never got over it. It was the same as long as I can remember, and it continues even now. She just couldn't get over it. And she never told us why. To this day, she hasn't told us. It wasn't hard to guess. Every time an Elvis song came on the radio, or a movie came to town, or he was on television, she would look very sad and put her hand over one ear, a funny habit she has always had. Then she'd walk out of the room. At first we thought that maybe his songs reminded her of someone. As we grew older, we could see it was Elvis himself."

T HE NEXT DAY AT THE STORE, MY friend Max Hatter handed me a note. He said someone had called. The note read: "Since you don't eat or drink, how about just talking?—Duke." I smiled and dismissed it. Mr. Wayne called in the late afternoon, following up on his note. He was surprised when I made an excuse and refused his invitation. He remained polite and vowed to try again later. Max came over again a short time later and asked me to come to his area, the men's department, the first chance I got. I did about ten minutes later and found him talking to a customer. Max saw me and rushed over.

"I want you to meet a friend."

I was furious. Max had promised he wouldn't do that to me.

"How do you do," I offered icily to the stranger, then turned and walked away. Max later apologized and said the man was persistent and he had no choice.

That night after work I heard on the radio that Elvis had sent an engagement ring to a girl in Memphis. I couldn't expect him to be faithful to me, especially if he thought I had died. Still, I was shattered. His words repeated in my mind. "It's all just publicity. Always trust me."

I came in to work one morning and caught a glimpse of myself in the full-length store mirror. I was shocked at how dreadful I looked. The "beautiful girl with the laughing eyes" that Elvis knew was gone. She was replaced by a sullen stranger. One of the salesclerks, Neva, took me aside. She was a kindhearted woman about ten years older.

"Lucy, I don't want to intrude into your personal life, but whatever it is, it can't be that bad." I thought this was going to be another one of those busybodies telling me how to live. Instead, she talked about how much she loved her husband and how he had been killed in the war. It took her a long time, but she got over it and was dating a fine man from Wales.

"Time heals. You have to go on," she said. "And the best way to start is to talk to this man who keeps calling you. If you don't, I will." I asked her who the caller was, hoping she would say "Mr. Jones." She said it was a Mr. Morrison. I had no idea who that was and had no desire to find out. The next morning Neva called me to the phone. She made me answer.

"Is this Lucy? This is your good friend Mr. Morrison." The man had an unpleasant voice and a deep southern accent. Whoever he was, he gave me the creeps.

"Look, I have no friends here and I really don't want to speak to you."

"Wait," he said in another voice. "This is Duke, kid. I'll be in front of your place at six-thirty. I need to talk to someone." Before I could protest, he hung up. I spent the rest of the day nervous about him actually showing up. I walked out of the store at six-thirty and was immediately met by a bearded stranger. I knew he was one of the movie people because just about everybody over there had a beard. It was some kind of Civil War movie.

"Lucy, there's a car out front for you."

"Who's in it?"

"Mr. Morrison."

Chapter 11

T HE BEARDED MAN WAS POINTING TO a double-parked car. Mr. Wayne was inside, smiling and waving me in. I hesitated, and he beeped the horn, startling me. He was creating a scene, so I had no choice but to go over. He explained that he just wanted someone to talk to. He was completely in charge and it was appealing. "We'll have some supper. You certainly look like you need it."

He took me to a cozy country inn somewhere outside the city. It was a functional place with wall lamps, the typical candle-in-amber-glass on the table, old-fashioned ladder-back wooden chairs, and plastic glasses. If one was going to dine with Hollywood's finest, one would expect crystal and accept glass. But plastic? There was a stir at the other tables when he sat down. He didn't mind. He was totally at ease with his fame, an attitude Elvis never mastered. Soon people in the restaurant came over to shake his hand or ask for an autograph. He attracted so much attention I was uncomfortable. This was not the place for someone in hiding. When he ordered, he sounded as if he was reading a line from one of his cowboy movies.

"Bring us two of the biggest Louisiana steaks you got," he bellowed. "The finest wine for the lady and whiskey for me."

Halfway through the meal, a middle-aged lady wandered over and asked for his autograph. He readily agreed and used the moment to embarrass me further.

"Sure, ma'am. But she's prettier than me," he said, pointing at me. He scribbled something and handed it to the lady. She was puzzled when she looked at it, then walked away. "I wrote Marion Morrison," he said, then laughed heartily.

"I want to show you where I'm living," he said afterward. I stayed quiet, not wanting him to notice my nervousness. We talked about the countryside, climate—everything and nothing. He asked me what I was doing in Alexandria, and I said I was just passing through doing some promotions for a former boss.

We drove for more than a half hour, toward Baton Rouge, and finally pulled up to a small motel. Mr. Wayne announced that this was his temporary home. He asked me in for a drink. I balked. "I just want to talk. Please. I have something I want to tell you." I couldn't tell if it was a line or what, but he was persistent and I was curious.

The only sign of life in the typical motel room was a few liquor bottles on the dresser. He grabbed one of his bottles and poured me a drink. I didn't want it but took a sip to be polite. It was strong, burned my mouth, and briefly brought back bad memories of the Man.

"Tell me about yourself," he said. "You look like a lady with a story to tell."

"There's nothing to tell," I said, quickly changing the subject. "What did you want to talk to me about?"

"Right to the point. I like that. I wanted to know why you resist men."

"What are you talking about?"

"I watched you that night at the country club. I can tell you're anguished over someone. Who hurt you? I've got to leave soon, so let's hear it. Get it off your chest."

"Please, no," I murmured.

"Are you in love?"

"No," I said. "Is this what you wanted to tell me? You haven't told me anything. You're just asking lots of personal questions."

He walked straight toward me. I was scared to death. He stopped in front of me and said, "Don't be afraid of me. I won't hurt you. I like you. But that's not why we came here. I can see how scared you are about everything, little one. Sit down."

I sat down without a word.

"Since I've been here I've been lonely. I want to finish this picture and get away. My wife and I are separated."

"I'm sorry," I said, not knowing what else to say.

"I'm not. You can't take a person and mold them into what you want. Love is accepting a person and trusting and growing with them."

I wasn't sure what he was saying, but I wasn't going to ask him to elaborate. His marital problems were none of my business.

"You've heard my problems, now tell me yours. And don't say you don't have any, because I can see it in your eyes." So that was it. We were to trade heartaches. Instead of being angry, I suddenly felt like opening up a crack. I had kept everything inside for so long. John Wayne wasn't the type who would gossip about something like that. He was above it all.

"There is someone I love very much," I began. "Now it's over. It's simple as that." To me, that was exposing myself to the world. To anyone else, of course, that was saying nothing.

"Little one, you're lying. There's a whole lot more to your story than that. You better get it out before it eats you up."

I was beginning to break. He was so firm and authoritative.

"The man I love is far away," I said. "I hurt him because I love him. I had to. But I can't forget. When do you stop loving someone? Is it when they aren't there to reassure you? Or never?" I couldn't finish. As usual, my emotions took over.

My tears disarmed him. He got up and said, "You know, if you tell me everything now, I won't have an excuse to see you again. Let's go."

I apologized for breaking down. "Thanks for wanting to help. No one can. You've been very kind." He came over, hugged me, took my hand, and led me out of the room. I could think of nothing but Elvis as we drove back to my house. Elvis liked John Wayne. He was one of his heroes. Elvis was so famous, and I was a nobody, and here I had met Mr. Wayne before he had. Life is strange.

"I'll see you soon," Mr. Wayne said as we pulled up to my house. "We'll go for a ride in the country. Stay sweet, little one."

"Good-bye, Duke," I said, using his nickname for the first time. I felt I had made a friend.

I didn't hear from him for three or four days and was relieved. I had no desire to finish my story.

After work one day I noticed a man following me as I walked

to the bus station. He caught up and began walking in step with me. I recognized him from somewhere but couldn't place it. He introduced himself and said he had met me through Max at the store. He was the man I had snubbed. He was six feet tall, slender, had short black hair, and looked like a typical businessman in his dark suit and tie. In a thick Texas accent he asked if he could drive me home. I was taking the bus everywhere now because I had gotten behind in my car payments, fought with the finance company, and told them to take it back. I declined the Texan's offer, and he responded by asking me out to dinner.

"I don't go out," I responded bluntly. "I have four children at home that I have to take care of, along with my mother, who is ill." He was stunned enough for me to hop on the bus. Men, movie stars, dates, fancy restaurants, and expensive cars—I had no desire for any of it. I just wanted to take care of my children and get my life on some normal course. I asked God to give me a sign that would lead me in the right direction of what to do and where to go next.

Mr. Wayne called the following day and asked me to meet him after work on a quiet back street a block or so from the store. I wasn't too pleased with the idea of hanging around on a back street. I threw on a black cape I had sewn and headed down the block. I imagined he would drive up and collect me off the street like a prostitute, an image I found disturbing. To my surprise, he was standing there big as day in a tan overcoat. I didn't think movie stars could hang out alone on a corner like that.

"You look like you're standing in a hole, little one," he said, laughing, making fun of my five-foot, two-inch stature. He was about six feet four.

"It's just because you're so big."

"Let's walk," he said.

It was a pretty street and, thankfully, deserted. The leaves were falling and the colors were beautiful in the dying light. It reminded me of Memphis and walking with Elvis. Everything reminded me of Elvis.

We came to a corner where there was a park bench under a large oak tree.

"Lucy, we're going to finish shooting in a few days. I want to see you again if you can. I want to hear the rest of your story."

"My life is really over. I've lived so many years since I was eleven."

"What's hurt you?"

"I have to make my own decisions. I'm so afraid." He just stared into my face, waiting for an answer. I felt I could trust him.

"I've had a very difficult life. I don't want to go into it, but I met someone who took all the pain away. We became very close and the nightmares of the past didn't matter anymore. Then he became famous and the nightmares returned. He couldn't save me anymore. I had to save him. I had to save him from me and my past. I know you can't understand this, but please try. I had to run away from the only light I've ever had in a very dark life."

"Who is it, Lucy? Let me help. Maybe it's not as absolute as you think. Tell me who it is."

"Elvis Presley."

"Damn," he said. "No wonder you're so afraid of everything."

I covered my face in shame. Elvis promised never to tell anyone about me, now here I had told someone. Mr. Wayne wanted to know exactly what happened. I gave him a brief version of the story. He told me to move to Los Angeles and wait for Elvis to return. He said that my family could stay at a place he had in Newport and he'd get a job for me. I told him it was a generous offer and I'd consider it. We walked back down the street. All I could think about was how I had betrayed Elvis.

"If you need help, I'll be there. I have a big heart and an even bigger shoulder," he said.

"I need your friendship," I said. "Thank you for being my friend." When we got home, he scribbled a number on a card and told me to call him in Los Angeles if he didn't see me before he left. The next time I saw him was at a rosary service for a movie crew member who was killed on the last day of filming. It was a sad occasion and a solemn end to what had been a nice friendship.

Stuntman Fred Kennedy was killed during a freak accident while filming the last scene of *The Horse Soldiers.* He broke his neck during a scripted fall from a horse and died the following day at Natchitoches Hospital.

DECEMBER WAS A DEPRESSING month. My children had gone to stay with one of my sisters, and mother was in Denver visiting another. I was alone with Desirée. A week before Christmas there was a knock at the door. I opened it and saw two men. They were gruesome-looking and one seemed vaguely familiar. He had a round face and his hair was slicked straight back. The other man was tall, with dark hair, and was wearing a brown overcoat. I asked them if I could help them, and the tall one said, "I sure hope so. May we come in?" I wasn't about to let these characters in. "I think you should hear me out, lady," the man said. "Do the initials E.P. mean anything to you?"

I walked out on the porch and closed the door. They knew something and I wanted to know what.

"How's your baby?" the second man asked. A chill cut through me. What did they want?

"Get to the point," I said to the one that was familiar. "What's your name?"

"That's not important," his associate cut in. "What is important is there are people looking for you. On both sides, if you catch my drift."

"What do you want?"

"How much is it worth to you for us to keep quiet?"

"Please leave."

"Look, just give me what money you have, and we'll forget we ever saw you. We don't want to get you hurt, lady."

I looked at them with disgust and said I'd be back with the money in a minute. I went to my bureau drawer and took all the money I had, twenty-five dollars, and gave it to them.

"Feel proud that you've taken food from a baby's mouth."

This was the final blow. Is that what it had come to? Being blackmailed by small-time crooks? The only thing that tempered my depression was trying to place where I had seen one of the men before. It started coming back. When I was in Monroe, a stranger came to the door one day and said the Man had told him to see if I needed anything. He said he was a friend. He pushed his way inside and just stood there. Then he said, "I came to see what you looked like in person. I've seen you dancing on TV. I just wanted to see if you were as beautiful up close."

"Please get out!" I had shouted, showing him to the door. He appeared to be the same man as the one with the slicked-back hair. That meant more people knew where I was. I was about ready to give in to despair when Desirée started to cry. I lifted her out of the crib and held her, thanking her for reminding me of the beautiful things I still had. Elvis, Desirée, and I were a family. We would be bound no matter what happened. I thought of something he said during one of our conversations. "If we're ever separated, just listen to my songs. I choose songs that tell you how I'm feelin'. Listen to the words. I talk to you in my songs."

On the surface, Elvis's promise about talking to Lucy in his songs appears to be a pretty but empty line. He wasn't a songwriter, so he couldn't have crafted any songs for Lucy. Furthermore, he's been harshly criticized for not caring about his music and letting others dictate what he sang. Elvis often told interviewers that the words meant nothing. He just sang songs. But when one digs deeper into the Elvis legend, a different portrait emerges.

Charlie Hodge, Elvis's army buddy turned guitar player and one of his closest associates, sat in on several RCA recording sessions. In his book *Me and Elvis* he describes Elvis as a master artist who would tape a song fifty to sixty times to get it perfect, then tell the startled technicians that the thirty-sixth was best. Hodge also shatters the myth that Elvis sang whatever was put in front of him. The truth, according to Hodge and other insiders, is that prior to recording, Elvis was brought scores of demo songs. He and his boys would sit in the studio and listen to them. Elvis chose the songs he liked.

From the time he lost Lucy in 1954, continuing through the second separation in 1957, Elvis gave the thumbs-up to an inordinate number of songs about lost love, heartache, and despair. Granted, those are the themes of many a country-and-western tune, but Elvis was relentless. Some of his choices became hits— "Heartbreak Hotel," "Don't Be Cruel," "Are You Lonesome Tonight?," "Return to Sender," and "Kentucky Rain." The bulk, however, were the flip sides of his singles or album fillers, throwaways that could only have been chosen for their words and not their mediocre arrangements. Check the B sides in the Elvis collection and you'll find songs like "You're a Heartbreaker," "My Baby Left Me," "I'm Gonna Sit Right Down and Cry (Over You)," "Trying to Get to You," "That's When Your Heartaches Begin," "I Beg of You," "A Mess of Blues," "Lonely Man," "They Remind Me Too Much of You," "It Hurts Me," "Always on My Mind," and on and on.

Did Elvis know what he was singing?

"Elvis could get into a song better than anyone I've ever seen," Hodge said. "That means he understood what the songwriter was saying and he could feel it. He had the rare ability to believe a song and make you believe it. To do that, you have to find something in your life that ties in to what the song is saying. That's what Elvis always did. He'd really get emotional sometimes. He never told us what he was thinking. Those things you don't talk about. You just do it."

Chapter 12

I WENT TO SLEEP EARLY ON NEW YEAR'S
Eve so I wouldn't have to face the pain of entering 1959 alone.
Fall, lonely holidays, and memories of Elvis—they would forever
be intertwined. My mother returned from Denver after New
Year's to give me a hand with the girls. They were growing up fast.
Deborah was ten, Melody, seven, Denise, four, and Desirée was
six months. Quite a family for a twenty-two-year-old working
woman with no husband. I continued to decorate the windows of
Ginsberg's but stopped working for Mr. Melson. My goal was to
save enough money to leave Alexandria. I wasn't having much
luck.

Jack, the Texan, approached me about helping him open a
boutique he had purchased. I thought it strange that a man in the
oil business would suddenly want to sell clothes. He offered a good
salary, about a hundred dollars a week, and a chance to travel to
Dallas and New York to purchase the lines. I didn't accept at first.
I eventually caved in to necessity and agreed. My plan was to
work long enough to save the money needed to move to California
and become a singer. Still dreaming. Surprisingly enough, Mr.
Wayne called a few times and reiterated his offer to help me get
established on the coast. I told him my plans but said it would
take time.

Opening a new store was hard work. I hired a woman from
Ginsberg's, Delphia Price, to help me. The trips to the fashion
shows in Dallas and New York were fun. Meeting the top design-
ers and selecting the best numbers was exciting. Desirée was at my
side almost everywhere I went, even at work. I was afraid someone
would kidnap or harm her. She was a most unusual child. Her

black hair hung past her shoulders, which was not normal for a baby. Her hazel eyes followed me everywhere. Her face was a miniature of Elvis's.

"I can't believe this baby," the housekeeper said. "She's perfect."

That's because she was born of love, I thought.

The store was coming along nicely. Civic leaders and Jaycee types visited. Jack was respected in those circles. One day he announced that he was resigning from the oil company to go into the clothing trade full-time. That upset me. He was depending heavily upon me for all the decisions, and I viewed the job as temporary. We should have been training someone to take over for me, but he wouldn't listen.

Opening day arrived and we put on a beautiful show of luxurious silk organzas and black capes sprinkled with rhinestones. My sense of fashion came from Dave Silverstein in Monroe and out of the necessity to make clothes for my daughters. Sales were good and the store was doing well. I became even more detached, longing to go away and prepare for Elvis's return.

One day a group of about eight men entered the store. Delphia walked upstairs to the office and said they wanted to see me. None were recognizable.

"You're the same person who used to dance on KNOE, aren't you?" one of them said. "We saw your picture in the paper. You're a great dancer."

My photo had been used in some of the store's advertisements. I objected but was talked into it. This was the reaction I sought to avoid. I thanked him and changed the subject. Jack was standing off to the side frowning. We both waited for the men to get to the point, but there wasn't one. They just wanted to gawk. All this because of a tiny television show in a small town five years ago?

Things were peaceful for a month or so, too peaceful. Louise called and told me that she had heard from the Man and he wanted to see me and the children. She assured me that she and her husband would be there the whole time. I dreaded it but agreed. The divorce wasn't final because I still couldn't spare the money. They were his children. If he was prevented from seeing them, the divorce proceedings might be inhibited. After work Louise and her husband drove me to the hotel where he was staying. He was waiting downstairs when we arrived. He looked the same as before—same smirk, same arrogance, hell revisited. It was stupid of me to agree to this. Louise's husband, Vernon, suggested we go to a restaurant and talk later. We ate in silence. Vernon broke the ice by chattering about his stay in Germany.

"There was this hillbilly singer there that was really pissed off about being in the army and how it was messing up his career," Vernon said. I don't know if he was doing it intentionally or what. It was cruel. Louise noticed and steered the stillborn conversation to another topic. It had always been my policy not to intrude upon other people's lives. Why couldn't people show me the same respect?

"You two should forget your past and get back together," Vernon said. The Man agreed. I couldn't believe these two. We left without further discussion. Back at the car, I tried to maneuver so Louise would sit in back with me, with the two men up front, the way we had come. The Man changed that when he jumped in the back. Just being across a seat from him made my skin crawl. All those horrible nights. A scared little girl all alone. I hated this man. What was I doing here? Wasn't he the reason my life was so messed up to begin with? This was insane. He started pleading with me to go back to him. My head began ringing.

"Maybe if you knew he wasn't going to come back to you, you'd come back to me. You know you won't see him again," the Man said.

"Who are you talking about?"

"That Presley idiot."

"Don't mention his name. I don't want to ever hear his name on your lips. And as far as I'm concerned, you don't deserve to see your children. You don't care if they starve. And don't you ever come near me again. Just the thought of being in the same city with you repulses me. You're a criminal. You should be in jail for what you did."

The hate boiled in his eyes. That same murderous hate I saw so many times before. Only we weren't alone anymore. What could he do? I underestimated his sickness. He grabbed my arm and twisted it behind my back.

"Stop the car!" I screamed. Vernon kept driving. I screamed louder, and my sister begged her husband to stop. He ignored her. I hated him for it.

"Stop or I'll jump out!" I screamed.

"Just do as you're told," Vernon said.

My head felt like it was going to explode. I had to get out. I pushed the door handle and jerked my arm free at the same time. The next thing I knew I was rolling over and over down the shoulder of the road. Then I passed out. When I opened my eyes, there were people standing over me. I started crying and screaming, "Don't let him touch me! Please don't let him touch me!"

Louise told me that the men had left, and tried to calm me down. My arms and legs were scraped, bruised, and bleeding. She took me back to the car and drove me home. I went straight to the bathroom and began treating my injuries. The gauze bandages. The iodine. The sting. I had seen the Man only a few hours and here I was back digging through the medicine cabinet cleaning up the blood.

Nightmares tormented me for a week. I was eleven years old again. The rapes. The beatings. The hopelessness. Each night, reliving it over and over, waking up screaming. I dreaded going to sleep. I began to focus my thoughts on Elvis, flooding my mind with the images of our times together. But even these healing thoughts became increasingly negative. The memories weren't enough anymore. I needed a flesh-and-blood savior. I needed Elvis. He had chased the darkness away before. Only he could do it again. But would he want to? Two years had gone by. Elvis was maturing. The army boasts it molds boys into men. I knew the boy loved me, but I wasn't sure about the man.

Months passed. The morning paper began bringing bittersweet news. America's most famous soldier was getting ready to come home. Even the most conservative newspapers couldn't ignore the growing anticipation. I was excited but equally perplexed about what to do. I had run from him. I promised I wouldn't, and I did. I let him believe I was dead. Could he ever forgive me?

There was something else feeding my doubts. The papers

started dropping hints. The fan magazines fleshed out the story, but those publications could never be trusted. It was the brief accounts in the morning paper that bothered me. The reporting was free of exaggeration. It differed little in tone from the coverage of President Eisenhower's latest speech or the stock market report. The stories hinted that there was a young girl Elvis had found in Germany. I glanced at the latest edition of the paper. I wanted to read about Elvis. I didn't want to read about her.

I directed my attention to a more positive prospect, a phone number he had given me before he left. It was his number at Graceland. I searched through my address book and found the code I used to disguise Elvis's numbers. The instant I saw the scribbled digits my mind flashed back to the moment I wrote it. It was our last time together in Memphis. It was fall, late fall. So many of our meetings had been in the fall. The trees were nearly bare. The ground was a sea of leaves. We rolled around in them. Elvis burst out of a huge pile and began tossing leaves at me by the handful. I laughed at first, but some were dirty and sprayed my eyes with sand. I motioned him to stop and he rushed over, apologizing profusely. He treated me like fragile crystal the rest of the day, acting as though he had to win my forgiveness for the awful thing he had done.

The memory gave me courage. I grabbed the book and went to the phone. I just wanted to make sure the channel was still open, that I still had a way to reach him. A woman answered. I paused an instant, then fell into my businesswoman voice and asked when Mr. Presley would be home.

"We expect him in a month," the lady said. "Who is calling?"

"Just a friend. Desirée. Thank you very much."

The short, meaningless conversation thrilled me. The avenue remained open. It would be as simple as that. The next time, maybe Elvis would answer. That sent me bounding into the living room to pick up the newspaper. I instinctively turned to the same page and corner of the paper where the Elvis updates always appeared. There was a picture this time, and the story was longer than the usual paragraph or two.

ELVIS HAS SWEETHEART, the small headline said.

The story was written in a more whimsical style, beginning with a tease about bad news for all the young ladies in America. It quoted Elvis christening a teenager as the girl of his dreams. He was going to bring her back with him or send for her later.

It got worse. For the first time, the girl had a name.

Priscilla.

So it was true. He did have another.

I dropped the paper. I had to get outside. It was raining and unseasonably chilly, but I was oblivious. The girl's name kept repeating in my mind. Priscilla. Priscilla. Priscilla.

I tried to convince myself it wasn't true, it was another of his manager's ploys. Elvis had explained before that the romances were publicity stunts dreamed up by the Colonel. I believed him then, but this was different. The Colonel wasn't in Germany. I sensed that this girl wasn't going to disappear with yesterday's news. My despair quickly turned to resolve. I had made a decision two years before to protect him by running away. I would continue to stay hidden, and I could never tell him about his daughter. He was moving on with his life, finding new romances and gearing up to re-establish his career. Desirée and I couldn't interfere. I had to accept that.

I went back into the house and walked directly to the night table in my bedroom. I opened the drawer and reached for my Bible. I picked it up, flipped open the back cover, and took out a small, rectangular piece of paper—Desirée's birth certificate. I had used his last name for the document because I wanted Desirée to have the right one day to choose to use the name of her real father. Deep down, I thought we would eventually be a family. The certificate had now become a taunting reminder of a life that could never be. I silently tore it apart, folding up the pieces and shredding them beyond recognition. I was tearing Elvis out of my heart once and for all. It was killing me, but it was the best thing for him.

The next day, back at the boutique, Jack called me into his office. That worried me. Business had declined. The small specialty store couldn't compete with the discount department stores in the area. Maybe he was thinking of closing up? Trouble always comes in bunches.

I sat in a chair in front of his cluttered desk and tried to read his face. I couldn't. Jack was a reserved and emotionless man. He was in character this morning.

His topic of discussion was bizarre.

In the same tone he used to order dresses, Jack proposed to me. He termed it a "partnership." He said it was the proper time in his life to marry and have children. He figured that I needed help with the heavy burden of supporting four children.

"I don't really believe in love," he explained. "I feel if people can work together, a marriage will succeed. I've evaluated your situation and it's obvious you need someone."

If there were a *Guinness Book of World Records* entry for the world's worst marriage proposal, that would be it. I tried to stay calm. It was difficult. I was steaming inside. In a few short sentences, he had turned me back into an object. I was a business deal again, a chunk of property to be bought and traded. How dare he! We had never even dated. It was crazy. I didn't need anyone. I never needed anyone except Elvis.

I quickly suppressed my anger and acted surprised. I still had my job to think about. With my dream of reuniting with Elvis shattered, that became crucial. Besides, I couldn't accept his proposal even if I wanted to. I was still legally married to the Man. Nobody in Alexandria knew, and I had no intention of dredging it up.

"This is all rather sudden, Jack. You can't actually expect me to say yes."

He responded that I should give it some thought. With that, he dismissed me. The meeting had ended and I was back in the display area checking the latest fashions for unsightly wrinkles. My mind raced. I had severed myself from Elvis, at least symbolically, just a few hours before, and now this dilemma.

I survived the rest of February by avoiding both Jack and the section of the paper that updated Alexandria on the latest Elvis news. In early March the paper played dirty. The story had moved from its safe corner to the front page. Elvis was home. His arrival created a frenzy. Forcing myself to read the description, I began to weaken. I still loved him.

I saw him on TV later that evening. He looked good. His hair was short. He cut a fine figure as a soldier. The television pictured him seated at a press conference. He was shy and uneasy. His answers were brief. The military experience had enhanced his natural meekness and quieted some of his wildness. A reporter asked him if there was someone he wanted to especially see now that he was home. Suddenly he brought his hand to his ear. Was he sending me a message, or was it just a twitch of tension? I chose to believe the positive. I rushed to the phone and tried to reach him, knowing the interview was taped. I had to take advantage of my highest moment of optimism. If I delayed, the paralyzing doubts would return. It sounded like the same lady on the phone. She said Elvis wasn't home. I tried a few more times over the next week, but the phone was busy. My rush of anticipation was dashed by the irritating sound of the busy signal. Slowly my determination dissolved.

The newspaper and television kept me informed of Elvis's whereabouts. His career was on the rise again. The Colonel shoved him back in headfirst. There was a new album, a welcome-home television special with Frank Sinatra, and a new movie. I wanted to cut in and shout, "Elvis, I'm here in Alexandria! I want to see you!"

I couldn't interfere. He was back on top, as big as ever. The world was still watching his every move.

The stretched-out arm signals that Elvis had previously promised to send Lucy when he performed, a switch from the earlier ear signals, are harder to discern because they are a dramatic staple of many performers and became frequent in Elvis's later performances. However, the strange and sudden arm movement at the end of the song "Stuck on You" during Elvis's appearance on the Frank Sinatra special in 1960 appears to be a signal, and a moving confession that he still loved her.

Lucy had to work late that evening and missed the show.

E ACH NEW ACCOUNT OF HIS CON-tinued success made him grow more distant. I stopped reading the stories. I turned the channel when he appeared on TV. I tried to ignore his existence and almost convinced myself it was possible. I could forget him. God would help. God wanted me to forget.

In early summer I made the final payment on the loan from Dave Silverstein. Though I felt good about meeting my obligation, I was still ashamed that I had to ask for it in the first place. Now I could work on saving for the divorce. It was absurd. I had been separated from the Man for nearly seven years but was unable to raise the three hundred and fifty dollars it took to get a legal divorce. I couldn't get ahead. Everything was a struggle. The future looked worse. My job was far from secure. The store continued to lose money. Jack couldn't go on pumping capital into the place.

But it wasn't all bleak. The daylight began easing into that soft yellow quality of fall. It reminded me of the good times with Elvis. Fall was my time to heal. I was born in October. My mother called me *fille d'automne,* meaning "daughter of autumn." Fall offered hope.

Jack was also full of hope that autumn. He sensed a calming in me and began acting less dour. I agreed to have him over for dinner. Desirée rushed to the door when he entered, froze in her tracks, and stared wide-eyed at him. She had such serious eyes. I saw Elvis in so many of her expressions. Forgetting him appeared impossible.

Jack was bent on changing that. His low-keyed pursuit lacked overbearing aggression. That made it tolerable. His cards were on the table, and he was content to give me all the time I needed to evaluate his offer. After dinner Jack upped the ante. He had purchased a spacious ranch house in Alexandria's most prestigious suburb. He told me that he bought it for me. I was welcome to move in whenever I wanted. For the first time, I felt a twinge of temptation. I was tired of my old, creaky rented house. A ranch house set on a nice lot would certainly please the children. And Jack wasn't such a bad man. He had been an executive with a large oil company and had his own business, even if it was struggling. He was nice-looking, well groomed, had good manners, and didn't appear to be violent. Many women around town considered him a good catch.

I came back to reality. There was a giant flaw in that version of the American dream.

"But you don't love me, Jack. You said it. You've admitted it. Don't you love anyone?"

For the first time, I saw emotion in Jack's face and eyes. There had been someone.

"I did love once. She ran off and married somebody else. Love gets you hurt. You must be strong."

What a sad outlook. But weren't those my own sentiments? Did I appear as emotionally barren to Jack as he appeared to me? I realized it was true. We had both been scarred by love and neither of us expected to love again.

His confession made me open up a little. I told him about my previous marriage. I warned him that my estranged husband was still capable of anything, including violence. I explained that I had never had enough money to pay for a divorce. Jack offered to rectify that on the spot. I thanked him and declined. Just as things were beginning to warm, a scream came from Desirée's bedroom. I ran in and found her rigid. Blood was trickling from her mouth. I grabbed Desirée and Jack rushed us to the hospital, narrowly avoiding an accident on the way. For an instant I thought Desirée was going to die. The emergency team was quick to react. Desirée had gone into convulsions and was burning with fever. They packed her in ice to cool her down. When things stabilized, I was surprised to see Dr. Easterling coming out to talk to me.

"Your baby is going to be okay, Mrs. Presley," he said. The joyful relief braced the shock of hearing the name. I had forgotten about that. He explained that Desirée had a throat infection and had bitten her tongue. He advised me to go home but didn't protest when I insisted on staying. In the quiet of the darkened hospital, my anguished thoughts turned to Elvis. Did he care that his daughter had almost died? Couldn't he sense it? Wherever he was, wouldn't some inner feeling alert him that his child was in trouble? I was being unfair. Even I was beginning to expect Elvis to be superhuman, and I had known him as a young country boy before he was a star. If he knew, he'd be here beside me. He'd hug me and cuddle Desirée and assure us that everything would be all right. That was the type of man Elvis was. He couldn't have changed.

That was the reason I could never tell him about his daughter.

If I called him, Elvis would come. He'd dutifully take his place beside me, beside a twenty-four-year-old married woman with a dark past and four children, one of whom was his. The shining new image of the obedient soldier that the Colonel had cultivated would be gone, the comeback washed away in scandal. I couldn't ask that of him. Not for myself. Not for my daughter. Maybe one day the sacrifice wouldn't be so great. Elvis would grow weary of being the King and pass the crown to a new singing sensation. The crowds would dwindle and the spotlights would dim, and nobody would care if Elvis Presley slipped away and married a divorcée with four children. The fame had to let up. It was so intense, it couldn't last forever. I would be patient.

Desirée recovered quickly and was released from the hospital a few days later. I was able, over the next few months, to stash away the money for the divorce. I traveled back to Monroe to go through the final procedure. I didn't look forward to it. I spotted the Man as I entered the courtroom. He looked older, smaller, and not as threatening. I thought again of all the things he did to me, all the times he beat me and forced himself upon me. I still hated him. He was to blame for my losing Elvis. Without him, I really would have been Mrs. Presley. He had destroyed both my past and my future.

Don't even try to talk to me, I thought. I don't want you near me.

When the routine hearing ended, I tried to leave without a confrontation. I saw him approaching.

"You were wise never to see that punk again," he snarled. "I told you I was right. See the kind of person he really is?"

The statement stung. It was the last thing I expected him to say. I turned and rushed out of the courtroom.

Outside, my anger quickly subsided. My slavery had lawfully ended. I could shut that door forever.

It was time to walk forward.

Lucy's instinctive belief that their relationship would damage Elvis's career was on the mark. Similar scandals grounded both Jerry Lee Lewis and Chuck Berry, and destroyed Eddie Fisher. In 1958, at the height of Jerry Lee Lewis's fame, he married his fourteen-year-old second cousin, Myra Brown. The public was appalled. Lewis's concert tours were canceled, his records blacklisted, and his career nearly vanished for a decade. Chuck Berry was convicted in 1961 of taking a fourteen-year-old girl across a state line, a violation of the Mann Act. He was sentenced to three years in prison. (He served less than two.) In a closer parallel, Fisher left his all-American bride, Debbie Reynolds, and their two young children to marry Elizabeth Taylor in 1959. His fans were shocked and sent his career into a nosedive from which he never recovered.

Chapter 13

MONROE HELD SUCH MIXED EMO-
tions. The horror of the Man and the beauty of Elvis were mixed
together in that same small town. After leaving the Monroe courthouse, I spent my first day as a free woman going back to all the
places that rekindled the good memories. The levee at Forsythe
Park, the St. Matthew's choir loft, the Paramount Theater, and
our spot on the river across from the country club. Sitting in the
grass unleashed a fresh sequence of memories along with the usual
stream of tears.

I returned to Alexandria, the store, and aimlessness. John
Wayne called and cheered me up. It had been two years since we
met and yet he called now and then to see how I was doing. It
was nice to have someone in whom to confide. He asked me to
come to Los Angeles for a visit. I told him that time didn't allow
it, too ashamed to admit that my meager finances were the cause.
I mentioned my plans to move, and he agreed. "Don't delay
decisions. Sometimes you just gotta pick up and go." We talked
a little about Elvis. His comments were a bit confusing, first
supportive and then more realistic.

"Elvis is out here doing a little work and a lot of playing," he
said. "He's young. He'll grow out of his conquests. Just don't hurt
yourself by holding on to the past. You need to go on with your
life. Come here and start over. You've got a lot of life yet. You're
just a baby. Make up your mind and call me."

He must have been reading the same stories I had about Elvis
having a new girlfriend each week. Or maybe he knew about it
firsthand? It twisted the knife in my heart another turn. If he
hadn't settled on one woman, that meant he was still searching.

Maybe there was still a chance. I fought the urge to try to contact him. Why couldn't I stick to my plan to stay away?

It was market time in Dallas for the spring and summer fashions. That helped take my mind off my problems. I brought Desirée with me and left the older girls—Deborah, twelve, and Melody, nine—to help my mother watch six-year-old Denise. During a break between shows I nonchalantly picked up a magazine that was lying around and noticed there was a big story about Elvis and his latest love. Only it wasn't his latest love, it was that girl in Germany. The story dubbed her his "bride-to-be" and detailed elaborate plans to bring the teenager to Graceland. She would finish school and then they would marry.

This story was unlike the accounts of his Hollywood girlfriends. It mentioned marriage plans and details. Was it true? How could I contact him if he was going to say, "Sorry, baby, I've found someone else"? It would destroy me to see the detached look in his eyes. My fear of rejection was so overpowering. I'd rather hide and hope.

There is a saying, "Once you love and the love dies, it goes back into the heart and returns in the form of tears to wash away the hurt." How true. My mother's words also came to mind: "God never gives us burdens we can't carry." That had always been my motto. But when would the burdens end? I carried enough for ten lifetimes. John Wayne's advice came to mind: "Start over. Don't wait. Forget the past. You've got a lot of life yet." A lot of life, and a lot more sorrow.

Jack had accompanied me to Dallas on this trip to learn something about the business he was in. That made it worse. At the Apparel Mart, I walked the long halls that were filled with clothes, trying to keep my mind on work but thinking only of Elvis and his teenage import. Jack asked me to lunch and said he had something to talk about. We sat down at a nearby cafe and ordered. With his business expression still intact, he asked me if I had thought any more about getting married.

"Oh sure, if you wish, why not?" I said sarcastically. He missed the sarcasm and heard only my words.

"How about right now?"

"You mean with no plans or anything?"

"Sure."

I had hit rock bottom. Unwanted. Rejected. My dreams shattered, my life over. Elvis didn't want me anymore. If he had, a man with his resources would have found me. How could he want me? He had his little girl and all the other women in the world. Even if Elvis wanted to, the Colonel would never let him marry me. If I got married, at least my children would have a home and would be taken care of. Maybe by getting married I could solve my problems. My children's future would be assured. Elvis would be behind me, forever. I could end the agonizing emotional tug-of-war going on in my heart. If he did find me, a marriage would prevent us from starting up again and facing the same problems that destroyed our relationship before. I didn't think I could go through that again. Elvis was better off without me. Hadn't I always believed that? In the grief that swept over me after reading the story about Priscilla, marriage appeared to be a solution.

Jack called for a judge and somehow rounded up one on the spur of the moment. We left for the Dallas courthouse, and when we got there, the license bureau clerk wanted proof that I was old enough! Where was he thirteen years ago? I had to call someone at the market to confirm that I was older than eighteen and didn't need my parents' consent. I went through the process in a daze. Judge Pierce McBride said, "You're supposed to say 'I do,'" snapping me out of my fog. I hesitated. I forced myself to think dark thoughts. Elvis had referred to Priscilla in the story as "the only woman I've ever loved." It was over. I had to let go. I had to let him go.

"I do."

We left immediately after the ceremony and drove back to Alexandria. Shortly after our marriage, Jack told me that he was losing money at the store, and now that I was his wife, I had forfeited my hundred-dollar-a-week salary.

Wonderful.

When Lucy married, Elvis's relationship with Priscilla was not as threatening as she believed. According to Priscilla's account in her book *Elvis and Me,* he called her only sporadically and often talked about other women. Priscilla had no assurance she would see him again. The media, however, were full of stories about them, as they were about all of Elvis's girlfriends. He had made some comments about her, hinting that she was special, and that was all it took for the sensationalistic magazines to announce the marriage. Priscilla didn't visit Elvis until the summer of 1962, almost two years later. She didn't move into Graceland until 1963.

At the same time Lucy was getting married, Elvis's song "Are You Lonesome Tonight?" was working its way to the top of the charts. An old Al Jolson weeper, the song contains a sorrowful spoken bridge addressed to a woman who ran away. The singer says he is willing to forgive her if she will only come back to him.

Lucy said she never heard the song. With four young daughters playing radios night and day, including Deborah, an Elvis fan, that seems improbable. "Are You Lonesome Tonight?" was a monster hit that appeared on the Hot 100 chart for months and was the number-one song in the country for six weeks. During this troubled time in her life, Lucy was so determined to forget Elvis she apparently blocked him out.

WE ARRIVED IN ALEXANDRIA LATE the next evening. There were no lights on at my house, and no one answered the door. Something was wrong. Mother would never leave unless there was an emergency. I ran to the backyard and was stricken with fear. The large oak door was open and swinging in the wind. Leaves were blowing into the parlor. "Mother! Debbie! Melody!" I screamed. There was no answer. I ran to the phone and called Delphia. She said my children were with my sister Louise and then told me the awful news. My mother had suffered her second heart attack. She wasn't expected to make it this time. I went immediately to the hospital. Mother, once again, had rallied and was fighting for her life. It amazed me how she kept coming back.

Since we had no honeymoon, I was able to visit her every day in between moving to the large house Jack provided. It was a one-story, four-bedroom ranch house set on an acre and a half of land. The children loved it and were happy. They felt better about themselves now that we were a complete family. But my troubles would never let up.

A week after we moved in I found an opened letter sitting on the dresser. Jack had been frowning as he read it earlier, and that made me curious. It was from one of his relatives. "You should never consider marrying someone with such a background," the letter said. "If she's Roman Catholic and French, you know what they say. And she's been married before! She can only be a hindrance to you. And she's a singer and dancer? Those people are all alike." His parents, whom I never was to meet, must have felt the same way. I confronted him with it. He brushed it off, saying he didn't know what it meant.

"Why did you want to get married?"

"It was the only way I could have you," he said.

That was it. A dream marriage. There would not be any trifles like giving or receiving love. But there would be more children. That's something that never failed. A couple of months after the marriage I was pregnant.

"I knew you could give me a son," Jack said, welcoming the news.

My exalted status as wife consisted of working night and day at the store for free. Late one evening the Man called and said that he had two weeks to live. He had cancer. I felt nothing, neither happiness nor sadness, but my mind flashed back to the time he smashed my picture of Jesus and taunted God. He wanted to know if I would take care of his children. Imagine that. What did he think I'd been doing for the last thirteen years? "Don't worry about it," I said. He started crying and said he didn't want to die.

"I'm sorry that you're ill. I'll pray for you." I did pray for him. His blasphemy was an infinitely greater sin than anything he had done to me.

The familiar pains of labor struck in late August. My husband's relatives picked that moment to visit and assess the situation, so I escaped to my mother's. She was home again, having survived a third heart attack. A tremendous thunderstorm struck in late afternoon. We waited together while the thunder and lightning rocked the house. Since the storm wasn't letting up, I drove home through the wind and rain. As I was preparing to go to the hospital, Desirée looked up at me and said, "Mommy, if you go away, I won't get a birthday cake." Her birthday was coming up. She looked so sad. I dropped my things and went into the kitchen and made her a cake. The contractions hurt and were coming closer together, but I didn't want Desirée to be without a cake in case something happened to me. When I finished icing it, Jack drove me to the hospital. The storm had eased, but the damage was heavy. Trees were uprooted and wires were down and everything was a mess. We made it just in time. My son was born within an hour of our arrival at Baptist Hospital. There was little joy in having a child under the circumstances of my marriage. As with all my children, I learned to love little Jacques fiercely later on, but the night of his birth brought only despair. All I could think about was that his mother was a woman destined to live without love.

Things got worse after that. Jack sold the store at a loss of nearly $200,000. The psychological implications of the store's failure were severe. He had gotten into a business he knew little about as a means of obtaining me. Now he would forever associate me with the failure of the business and the great loss of money. He hung around the house for a time, then said he was going to Arkansas to start over. A week later he was gone. A few days after Jack left I received a call from my sister informing me that the Man had died. The children begged me not to send them to the funeral.

A story in the newspaper said that Elvis had earned $80 million in royalties since returning from the army. I was broke, alone, and he had everything in the world. Asking for his help now would be begging for pity. I had nothing left but my dignity. I would make my own way.

Jack called a week later and said he was in Dallas, not Arkansas. He said he'd leased a house and wanted me and the children to come. Dallas was as good a place as any, and at least we would have a roof over our heads. In a blur of activity, I moved, settled my children in school, hired a baby-sitter for Jacques and Desirée, and got a job in the credit office of Sterling Jewelry. I worked six days a week from 11 A.M. to 9:30 P.M. for sixty-five dollars. Jack decided he would go to law school and took a job selling cars. The year passed uneventfully.

In late 1962 I decided to try again to start a singing career. Despite having five children, I was only twenty-six. I went through the standard routine, making a demo tape, trying to get an agent. Most of the agents were leering bores, and the casting couch was very much alive. It was a humiliating experience. I finally settled upon a bug-eyed, roundish man named Tony Papa. He was your typical open-shirted, gold-chained, "stick with me, baby" agent. He felt I had a chance to make it big. Jack thought only "trash" made their living singing, and he gave me no support.

My mother became ill again. This time, she didn't recover. It wasn't her heart, it was cancer. She had returned to Alexandria, so I grabbed my youngest children, Desirée and Jacques, and drove to see her. She had been in a coma for a couple of days but came out of it shortly after we arrived. She was alert and clear-headed. "I want to see Desirée and Jacques," she said in French. She kissed them. "Let them go play in the sunshine." A nurse took the children. "Come here and sit down," she said to me, then clutched my hand.

"Ma petite Bee, please tell Desirée's father. Don't wait. Will you tell him for me?" I promised. She smiled, closed her eyes, and passed away. Her loss hit me hard. She'd had a difficult life. Elvis and I had sought success in order to help our mothers. Now they were both dead. Elvis's mother at least tasted success. Mine never did. I failed her.

In the summer of 1962 Priscilla visited Elvis in America for the first time. At that precise time he released a song entitled "She's Not You." The words spoke of a pretty blue-eyed girl who had it all, except for one major flaw, "she's not you." Elvis ended by singing, "It's just breaking my heart 'cause she's not you."

WHEN I RETURNED TO DALLAS, someone mentioned that a public relations job was available at the Cabana Hotel, which was owned by actress Doris Day and her husband Marty Melcher. The pay was better, $106 a week. I applied and to my surprise, they hired me. It was an interesting job that included advertising, customer relations, media relations, and best of all, auditioning talent for the hotel clubs.

President John Kennedy came to town in the fall of 1963 and everyone was excited. He was such a handsome man and well loved. I especially admired him because he inspired hope for the future. I took a day off from work because the city planned a parade in his honor and the streets would be jammed with traffic. Jacques needed a haircut and we went to the barber. Everyone was somber when we arrived. "What's going on?"

"Don't you know?" the barber said. "President Kennedy has been shot." I grabbed Jacques and left. The music on the car radio was interrupted with a bulletin. The president had died. I broke down and cried. How terrible his wife must feel. So much sorrow in the world. Dallas was in turmoil. Something new happened every day. A suspect was caught. Then he was shot. There were rumors of conspiracies and multiple assassins. It appeared as if the whole country was coming apart. It took months for things to settle down.

Elvis began appearing more frequently in the news. It was as if the country had been in mourning and now everybody needed a break from reality. The president was dead, but the King was still alive.

It became harder to avoid him. One of his songs struck a chord, "They Remind Me Too Much of You." Hearing it brought back all the memories.

"They Remind Me Too Much of You" was the flip side of "One Broken Heart for Sale," released in January 1963. Prior to this, Elvis recorded "Return to Sender." All were ballads about lost love.

I STILL LOVED HIM. I PUT UP A GOOD front for a while, but nothing had changed. My foolish pride diminished enough for me to realize I never gave him a chance to decide for himself what to do about us. I was busy making noble sacrifices without considering his feelings. All the newspaper stories about his girlfriends—didn't he tell me never to believe them, to at least give him a chance to explain? And how could I be jealous? He may have really believed I was dead. Now it was I who had explaining to do. That is, if I could summon up the courage to call him.

In 1964 I changed jobs again, taking a position as marketing director for Allen Case, Ltd. It paid a hundred dollars a week plus commission. Mr. Case was a stage and television actor who was opening a boutique as a sideline. He was trying to promote fur coats for men. He played on the television series *The Deputy* with Henry Fonda and later in *The Magician* with Bill Bixby and a Broadway play called *Hallelujah, Baby!*

I also began taking courses in Christian theology from the Paulist and Jesuit theologians at the Jesuit Preparatory School. That led to certification in 1965 to teach theology to junior and senior high school students in Confraternity of Christian Doctrine classes. I continued to study voice, including opera, for my enjoyment.

Desirée was growing into an extraordinary child. I began teaching her the piano at age four, and she picked it up quickly. Her personality was becoming more like Elvis's with each year. Gentle, respectful, positive, she was him in body and soul. Her eyes, lips, face—everything resembled his. Even the shape of her hands was identical to his. I loved her so much. The one thing that bothered me was she almost never smiled. Her little face was so serious. She reminded me of a lonely little girl who used to sit alone in an attic many years before.

Despite my great love for her, I couldn't bear to call her Desirée. Just before she entered the first grade I took her aside and said, "Honey, do you mind if I call you by your middle name, Romaine?" She said, "No, Mommy, that's okay." After that everyone used Romaine or just Rome.

All my daughters were beginning to display unusual and diverse talents. Debbie excelled at music and language. Melody was an artist and poet. Denise was an outdoors type and became a camp counselor. Often we would gather around the piano and sing songs. I enjoyed that so much. Everyone joined in except Jack. He was busy with his own life and grew distant. He complained about expenses, so I made sure he never had to spend a dime on my children. I paid for their food, education, lessons in music, dance, and art, everything. He didn't put up a fight to pay his share. Though the relationship lacked affection and fulfillment, the children had a happy home, so I endured it.

The Catholic Church remained a large part of my life, especially singing in the choir and doing occasional solos at St. Paul the Apostle. Desirée took her first communion at age six and looked like a little angel in her lacy dress and veil that I had sewn. On the way back from church I heard Elvis on the radio singing "Don't Leave Me Now." Tears started rolling down my cheeks. Desirée looked at me and said, "Mommy, don't be sad. It's a pretty song." I pulled the car over and silently hugged her.

In early 1965 I fainted at the end of a long day. A doctor confirmed my suspicions—I was pregnant. Jack apologized and said it would never happen again. He kept his word. He often reminded me how fortunate I was that he had rescued me "from the gutter." I confronted him a number of times and asked for a divorce, but he always had the same answer.

"You'll never disgrace me with a divorce."

My sixth and last child, Jacqueline, was born that September. She was daughter number five and of all my girls she would grow to look the most like me.

Cleaning, coddling, and diapering another baby and working to keep all the children fed took up most of the next two years. There wasn't much in the news about Elvis anymore and his songs weren't getting played on the radio. It was no secret why. Elvis had let himself get behind the times. His career appeared to be fading fast. I had stopped going to his movies years before, not because of the memories but because they were so bad. All those silly party pictures, each no different than the previous. What happened to the boy I knew who wanted to be a serious actor like Marlon Brando or James Dean? I never saw either of those two make a single movie of the type Elvis kept making. His so-called "brilliant" manager appeared to be managing his career right into the ground.

Priscilla had moved into Graceland, just as the stories said she would. It seemed as if she had been there forever. Every once in a while a story would pop up saying that they were married, but the reports were always denied the next day. I still cared deeply for him, but Priscilla's residency and our eight-year separation combined to take the edge off the pain. That meant I was crying only once or twice a month over him instead of every day.

I continued to stay busy and tried to improve my life. In the spring of 1967 I enrolled in paralegal courses at Southern Methodist University and volunteered as an entertainment coordinator for the International Visitors Program. The work consisted mainly of setting up schedules for foreign attorneys visiting Dallas and SMU.

After so many false alarms, Elvis finally married Priscilla on May 1, 1967. All the papers ran the story with pictures and fanfare. It was the most attention he had received in years. I had expected it and shaped a life without him, but it still hurt. I couldn't forget the memory of the boy on the hilltop who vowed to love me, and only me, forever. I went to church and knelt for over an hour, asking God to give me strength and to take the pain away. I prayed that Elvis would be happy, and pleaded with God to ease my guilt concerning Desirée. She could never know her father now.

Life went on. I changed jobs yet again, hiring on as public relations director for Blakeley Enterprises, a multifaceted company formed by attorney J. Alex Blakeley to handle his many interests, including oil, gas, and real estate. The salary was $162 a week, inching me up the ladder of success. One of the firm's former directors, a man named Lucien Camenish, was running a hotel in Acapulco. He called when one of his singers had to pull out of a scheduled engagement and wanted to know if I would fill in. That was a break. When I informed Jack, we had a bitter argument. He looked down on entertainers and related any upswing in my career to a downswing in my morals. The opportunity was thus squandered. My last chance to pursue the dream I wanted since childhood vanished for the same reason all the others had: Someone else controlled my life. I wanted to run away but thought of my children. I had vowed to always put their interests before my own. They were happy in Dallas, had many friends, and were finally settling in somewhere.

On a hot July day in 1967 I was home with Jacqueline when

the doorbell rang. A florist presented me with a bouquet of four-teen peach-colored talisman roses. The card read, "True love never dies." It wasn't signed. I called the florist and begged them to tell me who sent them. They stood firm, saying that they were like doctors, lawyers, and priests and weren't at liberty to reveal the sender. They wouldn't even tell me why there were fourteen roses instead of the normal twelve. It suddenly occurred to me. Fourteen years, 1953 to 1967. Could the flowers really be from him?

At work my mind wandered so much it was pointless to try to get anything done. I told Mr. Blakeley I wasn't feeling well and went home. Sitting around idly made it worse. We had a reception and promotion for a French champagne coming up, so I steered my attention to the preparations. Mr. Blakeley called and we discussed the guest list and other details. The phone rang again. I expected it to be Mr. Blakeley with a forgotten question. My "hello" was greeted by a long silence. The connection sounded scratchy, like it was long distance.

"Is this Lucy?" The voice made me tremble.

"Yes," I said, the lump in my throat nearly stifling my words. "Who is this?"

There was another long silence, then a click. I held on, hoping the voice would come back. The dial tone came instead.

The caller was Elvis.

Chapter 14

I COULDN'T SLEEP THAT NIGHT. WHY did he call after all these years? How did he find me? Would he call back? Why did he hang up? Nothing but questions, tormenting questions. The next day at work was impossible. My mind was far, far away. Ten years in the past by a river in the fall.

That night, my stomach was churning so much I couldn't eat. At eight-thirty the phone rang.

"Hello."

"Lucy, is this you?"

"Yes."

"This is John Jones." He paused. I paused. What could I say?

"Is this Lucy?"

"Yes."

"Do you remember me?"

I couldn't speak.

"Are you there?"

"Yes."

"Are you Lucy?"

"Yes."

"Do you know who this is?"

"Yes."

"I just found out where you are. Is it all right to talk to you?" He sounded so unsure of himself. The confidence was missing.

"It's okay. Where are you?"

"In L.A. I gotta see you, Lucy. We gotta talk. Please. Please." He was pleading. Something was wrong.

"How?"

"Please come out here. I have to talk to you. How are you?"

"Fine," I said. The tears were rolling down my cheeks. "How are you?"

"Wonderful now. I've found you! I must see you."

"I don't think I can."

"Do you want me to come there?"

Jack walked into the room and was staring at me.

"No, please. I can't discuss it now."

"Can I call you tomorrow?"

"Yes, yes, that'll be much better," I said in a businesslike voice.

"Please be there. I'll call at ten in the mornin' your time. Lucy, you'll be there, won't you?"

"Yes, I promise."

"You sound so good. You have no idea how this makes me feel."

"Thank you. Tomorrow will be fine, Mr. Jones."

"I feel alive again, Lucy. Just hearin' your voice. Tomorrow at ten. We must talk. Good-bye, Desirée."

"Who was that?" Jack demanded. I told him it was someone from the *Los Angeles Times* calling about one of the promotions. I immediately went to bed in my separate room. Another sleepless night. Why was Elvis so upset? What did he want with me? I wasn't the glamorous dancer he once knew, just a homemaker with six children. The next morning I realized that if he called at ten Texas time, he would have to get up at eight his time. That was almost unheard of unless he was working on a movie, or he had changed drastically. Maybe he was confused about the time. He wasn't. The call came precisely at ten. I was alone except for baby Jacqueline.

"Lucy?"

"Yes."

"Are you alone now?"

"I'm alone, Elvis."

"Oh God, you sound so good." He was so emotional it sounded like he was crying.

"How are you? And how did you know where I was? There's so much happening to you."

"I have to see you. I must know some answers. I still feel the same about you. I love you."

"My dear El, I love you. But you're married. Your wife is going to have a child. What is there?"

"You don't understand. I have to see you."

"I'd love to see you. There are many things to explain. Things you didn't know."

"Come now. Today. I'll arrange it."

"I can't. I have a concert Sunday, and I teach a Sunday school class. After that, I'll come."

"I'll get you a ticket and get a room. Don't worry. I'll call next week. Don't change your mind."

"No. I want to see you, too. But you don't have to make the arrangements. I'll take care of it."

"Same old Lucy," he said, laughing for the first time. "That's good, baby. Can you make it Wednesday?"

"Okay."

"I wish it were now. Today. You don't know what I've been through. They told me you died in a snowstorm. That nearly killed me. Then my momma died—" He was choking up again. "I lost everything. I didn't care about nothing no more. I had nothing. But you've come back. I have something again."

There was a long pause.

"Baby, why didn't you call me? Why'd you let me hurt?"

"There were so many stories. The other women. I thought you had changed."

"I'll never change. I wish nothing would ever change. Wednesday, baby. Okay?"

"Okay."

"Hey, before you hang up. Tell me something. What happened to your accent? I almost didn't recognize you," he said.

"It's gone. I studied hard to lose it."

"Why?"

"You won't understand. It made me self-conscious."

"Why? I loved it."

"I know you did. But sometimes a woman needs to be respected more than she needs to sound cute."

"What?"

"Never mind. We'll talk about it later."

"Wednesday?"

"Okay. Wednesday. Maybe I'll get it back by then."

"Can you do that? That would be great."

"I'm just kidding, silly. But don't worry. I still speak French quite well."

"Great. Okay. Wednesday."

For the first time in ten years my heart was soaring. Just hearing his voice made me feel alive. I was so happy I forgot to ask him how he found me. That wasn't important. It was enough that he had.

Mary Jo Webb worked at Silverstein's for twenty-two years. She said she ran into Lucy at the fashion market in Dallas in the mid-1960s and discovered that Lucy was alive and well. "After that, all the girls at Silverstein's knew Lucy was in Dallas. Whenever anyone called and asked for her, we told them where she was."

E LVIS DIDN'T SOUND LIKE HE HAD changed at all. He was so nostalgic. He wanted everything and everybody to remain as they were. In his mind change meant going from good to bad. He was determined to act the same, live in the same city, and surround himself with family and other familiar faces from his youth. That's why he was disappointed about my accent, but his had changed, too. He was less Memphis and more Los Angeles than ever. I wonder how he'd react if I asked him to start speaking Mississippi again? That made me laugh, the happy, gleeful laugh of a schoolgirl in love.

These thoughts diverted my mind temporarily from the real problems that soon made my head spin. What were we doing? Did I want to get involved again? Should I back out? We were both married. What was the point? Then I remembered a young man a long time ago who gently placed a ring of purple flowers in my hair. "Let's be together like this forever," he had said. "I'll love you and only you. No matter what happens. I'll love you forever."

The concert that Sunday was a small affair at the Melrose Hotel in Dallas. The recital was a part of the opera lessons I was taking, a chance to let the students perform in public. They had the concerts about every four months or so in one of the ballrooms, and about two hundred people attended. The instructors asked me to emcee the affair, probably because everyone else was so nervous they couldn't speak. I enjoyed it and introduced a number of novices with real talent. This Sunday I sang some songs, "And This Is My Beloved," "Make Believe," and "Adele's Laughing Song." For the first time in many years the words meant something to me. The next evening the family was gathered around the dinner table. That was a routine in my house we held sacred. We would all gather for dinner and discuss the day. I explained to everyone that I had to go on a business trip and would be gone for a few days.

"I need to depend on all of you. Can I?"

They assured me they were dependable. Deborah was eighteen and Melody sixteen, so they were put in charge.

"Won't Dad be angry if you go off to sing?" Melody asked. I explained that it wasn't that kind of business and said everything would be okay.

"Mommy, can I go with you?" Desirée asked. "I'll be good." She was nine and so beautiful. It would be so wonderful to take her. Maybe one day.

The next day I went to church and prayed for guidance. My mind was confused about what to do. Maybe it was wrong to go. Elvis called that night and told me to come on Thursday instead of Wednesday. We compromised on the arrangements. I paid for the flight while he got the room. He said there was a hotel in Beverly Hills that had private entrances. That sounded good to me.

Wednesday night was a disaster. I needed to sleep in order not to look old and craggy when we met, but my mind was spinning out of control. So many fears and worries. I was thirty years old. Elvis's image of me was frozen at sixteen. Would he be disappointed?

The next morning, I went to the linen closet, reached behind the towels, and pulled out a small paper bag. In it was a bottle of Drene shampoo. I had stockpiled a few bottles in case it went off the market, which it did. I washed my shoulder-length hair, then brushed it a thousand strokes to make it shine. My hands were shaking so I could barely get my makeup on straight. I smoothed my body with Royal Secret, a lightly perfumed French lotion.

Then came the hard part. What to wear? I decided on a simple olive green trench dress with a cinched waist. The green accented my eyes. Elvis liked me in peach, green, brown, and gray. The dress looked good on my 105-pound frame, but not too obvious. Another anguished debate followed. What shoes? Flats? Low heels? Or knock-'im-dead three-inchers? Forgetting subtlety or comfort, I went for the black three-inchers.

The flight was smooth. My stomach was turbulent. The anticipation was killing me. I tried to read a magazine, but my mind couldn't get beyond a sentence or two. When the seat-belt light flashed on signaling we would soon land, I nearly fainted. What if I got sick and looked miserable? I rushed to the bathroom to check my face one last time, which was silly because I knew Elvis wouldn't be waiting at the airport. Or would he? There was no telling what he would do.

On the ground I was approached by a chauffeur while waiting for my luggage. He was tall, rod straight, gentlemanly, and spoke with perfect diction.

"Are you Lucy? I have a car to take you to your destination." Despite his dignified appearance and manner, I was frightened. Elvis may have changed plans. Who knows where this guy was supposed to bring me? Maybe to a house full of people?

"Thank you, sir, but I've already made arrangements." He was surprised and insisted I go with him. The more he did, the more determined I was to resist. Finally he threw up his hands and gave in. I waited until he drove away in his long limo before waving down a cab. When I told the driver "the Beverly Hills Hotel, please," he arched his eyebrows and went into a long history of the famous place. Seems many famous people stayed there, including Elvis Presley, and they always stayed in the same bungalows. Great. Same old Elvis. Mr. Discreet. The reporters would probably bang on the door a few minutes after I arrived.

The taxi driver wasn't exaggerating. The bungalow was impressive. Lush carpeting. Beautiful draperies. A silky apricot bedspread. A breathtaking bathroom with bronze faucets and even a telephone. The window overlooked a lovely cluster of vines that were in full bloom. The setting was certainly seductive. I had to stay calm. He was married and having a child. It would be wrong to infringe upon that. My happiness couldn't be built upon another's sorrow. Turning from the window, I noticed a single red rose lying across the table. My mind flashed back fourteen years. "This rose contains all my love." How many nights had I lain in bed dreaming of being in his arms, kissing him, holding him, making love to him again? Now he would be here and I had to hold back.

The woman staring back at me from the mirror was more mature than the teenager in Monroe. The eyes were still bright green, but they held more wisdom than before. Her hair was full, black, and shiny. He would be pleased with that. The makeup was light in the French tradition of accenting beauty, not creating it. The perfume and body lotion were faint and fresh. The woman in the mirror looked good, but good enough? How did she compare to the other women Elvis had known? He would surely make a comparison. A light knocking at the door put an instant end to my mirror-gazing and almost caused my heart to stop. On the other side of the door stood the only man I had ever loved.

I slowly opened it. For an instant, I was awestruck. Before me was the best-looking man I've ever seen in my life. He nearly took my breath away. His hair was long and tousled, not what I had expected. He had looked so peculiar in his wedding photo with his hair piled up in an old-fashioned pompadour style, as if he had been in a time capsule. The man at the door was totally different. He was definitely with it. His pants were black and tight. Finally! No more of those baggy pants he used to love. His bright blue shirt was open at the neck and had laces hanging down in rows on each side. His face was tanned and his jaw set and ready for anything. I just stood there staring. He was magnificent.

Finally coming to my senses, I noticed he was staring just as intently at me. He made the first move, coming in and closing the door behind him without taking his eyes from mine. He grabbed me to him. We held each other so tight, as if we were afraid if one of us let go the other would disappear. I could feel his body trembling—or was it mine? He slowly released me without letting me out of his reach. His eyes were tearing. He lifted up his hands and ran them both through my hair, then came close again. I could hear him inhaling deeply, taking in the fragrance of the shampoo. As he did, he squeezed me tighter, his thank-you for my having remembered. His hands settled over both of my ears.

"It's good to see you, El, mon amour," I said, breaking the ice. "I missed you so much."

"My Desirée," he whispered.

He walked me over to the bed and sat down on the edge. He clutched both my hands as he spoke.

"I thought I'd never see you again. I used to lie awake and wonder exactly how you died. I called a few times, all the old places—the TV station and store—making up a story about who I was. Some people said you ran away with a singer. I knew that wasn't true 'cause I must have been the singer. Some others said you died in a snowstorm. But nobody knew for sure. I kept callin', even after I came back from Germany. Then one day someone at the store told me they heard you'd married a Texas oilman. That really hurt, baby. Knowing you got married. I tried to hate you.

"Before, when I was in Germany, a friend brought this little girl over one day. When I saw her I couldn't believe my eyes. She looked so much like you, Lucy. She was all I had."

I put my hand to his mouth. "Shhhh, you don't have to tell me. I know you brought her to Graceland to be your wife. That hurt me very much, knowing you had gone back on our vows. The pain hasn't gone away. My marriage is a 'mariage de convenance,' as we call it. It was security for my children. You had your life set by then. Nothing mattered."

"Lucy, you must listen to me. This girl was so much like you, and I was so lonely over there. I was attracted to her and she liked me as a person, not a star. The way you did."

Elvis was anguished. There had to be something else wrong, but I didn't want to put him through it.

"You don't have to explain."

"Yes I do. You deserve that. I knew if you still were alive you still cared. Our love was different. I don't know. You were gone. Momma died. I used to moan like a sick animal at night and cry myself to sleep. I needed somebody. All those girls in Hollywood the guys wanted me to be with—they just used me. They had no feelin'. I needed something else. I couldn't find you, so all I had was the girl in Germany. When she came, I couldn't get myself to marry her. I kept thinking of you. I got trapped. The Colonel suddenly arranged the marriage. He said it was best. Her parents were gettin' pretty mad. I do care for her, Lucy. I thought I'd never see you again."

Neither of us knew what to say. We were silent a long time.

"El," I said, touching his face with my hand. "It's your turn to listen to my story. It's been so long. There were many things you never knew about. I used to be beaten, sometimes very badly. When he found out about you, he almost killed me. Then he said you would die within a week if I ever saw you again. I had to go because I couldn't risk that. Not just for me, but for everyone. It was apparent even then that you were destined to be someone very special. I loved you more than life itself. Without you I'd have no life. But I was just one person. I had to do what was best, not for me, but for everybody. Now things have changed again. You have to stand by your wife. Just pretend I died a long time ago. You must. It's the best thing."

"No it's not," he said firmly, shooting up off the bed and waving his hands for expression. "I can't let you go now. I still love you. That'll never change. I feel like I'm alive again."

"Elvis, have you ever broken our vow never to tell anyone about me?"

"No. I could never share you with anyone. The story is so complicated anyway, who'd believe it? I don't talk to people much, I mean I talk, but not like with you and Momma. It's different. The only person I talk about you with is God. I prayed that He would let me find you. He's answered."

He sat back down. He was so close to my face, looking into my eyes. He kissed me. It was a kiss of love, not lust. It couldn't be allowed to go any further. We couldn't betray our marriages.

"I'm sorry," he said. "I know you must think I'm unfaithful, but I do love you. How's your marriage?"

"Not good. We're different people. I was divorced and had children. I'm French and Catholic. It was too much. Too different. But that doesn't matter. You and I can't hurt others because of our mistakes. You have to remember that."

"What do you mean?" His eyes were dark and angry. Something was definitely wrong.

"You're married and going to have a baby. She must never be

hurt. Especially not now. And there's so many involved in my life. I've been running and suffering for ten years. I thought you didn't want me anymore. You had everything."

"Stop that! Lucy, didn't you listen to my songs? I told you if we ever separated, I'd send you messages in my songs. Didn't you listen?"

"I tried. But it was hard. It hurt. And there were all those stories about other women."

"You're the only woman I ever wanted. There might have been some others, but only a few. It's all a farce. Just publicity and image building. Tell me you believe that."

"I wanted to hear you explain it so often. Each time I read about another girlfriend. I finally gave up. Nothing mattered." This was getting gloomy. I smiled and changed the subject. "Look at us arguing. We never argued before." He laughed and changed the subject.

"You remember when you told me to be careful about all those leeches who attach themselves to me? Boy, were you right about that. These people aren't my friends. There's only a couple who are. Charlie. He's good. I met him in the army. And there's Larry. He's real religious. He's got these gentle eyes. You told me 'eyes are the mirrors of the soul.' Man, the Colonel doesn't like Larry. The Colonel doesn't believe in anything but money. That's his religion. The rest of the guys, they're the same. Hardhearted. But Larry, his eyes remind me of yours. He understands things. And he loves God. He's been helping me. And you know, they're trying to keep him away from me. Just like they'd keep you away if they knew."

"I'm glad you have friends. That's important. What about your wife? Does she care for you?"

"Sometimes, but not always. She's kinda restless and uncertain. She hasn't adapted to my life-style. Or maybe it's something else. I don't know. Anyway, tell me about you."

"I teach religion to teenagers on Sunday, like Sunday school but we call it something fancier, 'Confraternity of Christian Doctrine.' When I lost you, I began studying at night and earned a certification. Teaching gives me satisfaction."

"You teach people about God? Man, I'd love to do that."

We talked some more about Elvis's thoughts on religion. Some of it was confusing, but he was intense about it. He asked why I was living in Dallas and remained married, and I explained again that it was for the children.

"Why don't you let me help? I've got money. You've got to let me help."

"Let's not talk about that. You know me. If something comes free, it's meaningless. You know that."

He got off the bed and began pacing the room. He was wound up about something.

"My life is so mixed up, and yours, too. How did it get like this?"

"It's just the way it worked out."

"So what happens now? Will you disappear again?"

I walked to the window and gazed out at the vines.

"No, no more running. I've learned to turn and face my enemies. I'm not a little child anymore. And I'm not going to run away from love. We have to accept our destiny, whatever it is, and be happy."

"I can't accept anything except our being together," he said.

"Our lives crossed. Our love is written. No one can erase it," I continued. "You helped me when I needed help. The memories of you kept me going. It has sustained me. But memories can't hold a person. They don't hug or keep you warm. They can't make love."

He came over and embraced me warmly.

"I've fought my urge to want you physically, and I'm still fighting," I said. "There are more important things that still can survive. Our love. Our laughter. Our trust."

"That's not enough. I want more," he whispered. "You've touched my life and stayed. Others have come and gone, but you've stayed. I'm selfish. I've tried living without you. I'm tired of it. But I'll pray about it. I'll do that for you. We'll let God decide. He knows what's best. Isn't that what you always said?"

"Yes. I can't argue with that. I've always believed God brought you to me." We returned to the bed and sat on the edge again. Elvis began talking about other things, rambling a bit but confirming my suspicions that he was troubled.

"All this other stuff happening to me. I give myself to my

public. And those around me, they try to gain control, power. They can never control my mind. No one gets into my mind. I shut it off from everyone. There are things there that none of them know, no matter how close they think they are to me. They don't know me. Only you. We'll triumph. You'll see."

"Maybe," I said. "Maybe one day. We're not on the final chapter yet."

"No, but I like to remember those early ones. You know, I'd give anything to start over. It was better then, when I was nobody and struggling. It's hard to explain. But it's better to fight. Once I reached the top, it wasn't any fun anymore. I can't figure it. You know, a lot of what I've done was influenced by you."

"Really?"

"Yeah, *really*," he said, teasing me about my frequent use of that word. "One day I thought about us riding at the zoo. Remember that? So I decided to buy this ranch. Nobody else was interested in it much. The guys wanted to live the fast life in Hollywood. It was a nice place, but once I realized why I bought it, it didn't mean anything. You weren't there.

"Why didn't you listen to my songs?" he continued. "I kept thinking you'd hear the words and realize I was talking to you. Once I was singing, 'I'll Remember You,' and, baby, your face was right there in the studio in front of me.

"Work is all that keeps me going. The Colonel loves it. More work. More money. He keeps me so busy I can't think. Now it's movies, movies, movies. I hate those movies. I wish I could perform again. The Colonel wants religion out of my mind. If he knew about you, he'd blow. That's why I can't tell anyone. They tell him everything."

"Does anybody know you're here now?"

"No. I can think for myself sometimes."

"Maybe you should go. They must be getting worried."

"Who? My employees?"

"It seems like they're more than that."

"They think so. So what do we do now? I don't want you to leave."

"I have to. My life is somewhere else. I'm only as far as the phone. Will you call?"

"When will I see you again?"

"Whenever it's right. Remember, God is deciding. He'll let us know. You have Priscilla and your baby to think about. And you'll always have my love. Elvis, our love has given me something very special. Someday, when we can have a few stolen hours, I'll explain it." He never suspected I was talking about a beautiful nine-year-old girl.

"Elvis, you must go now."

"Why?"

"We both know why. Things will be right. You'll see."

We embraced. Elvis dropped to his knees and held me against his face. I placed my hands on his ears. Then he stood and we kissed.

"This is a new era in our lives, El Lancelot."

"Are you going to be here tonight?"

"Yes, Princess Desirée will wait in her chambers, so not a single sweet memory will escape."

"I'll call you later. And in the mornin'. Did I tell you how good you look?"

"Well, I was waiting. Have I changed much?"

"You're as beautiful as ever. Your body is still great and your mind is even wiser than before. I'll show you how beautiful you are."

He swept down and kissed me passionately. It came close to knocking the sensibility and guilt out of me and making me give in to my desires.

"You must leave, sir," I said.

"Only for a short time, madam. This is a new era. You'll see."

I lay on the bed after he left and wrapped my arms around myself, drinking in my newfound happiness. He hadn't changed much at all. The warmth in his voice, the tenderness in his eyes —it was all still there. I relived the whole wonderful afternoon, then drifted off to sleep.

Charlie and Larry, the friends that Elvis referred to, are Charlie Hodge and Larry Geller. Hodge, a diminutive guitar player, met Elvis in the army and performed with him off and on in the 1960s before settling in permanently. He was one of the few so-called

Memphis Mafia members who survived the subsequent purges, and was with Elvis until the end. Hodge is the man who held the microphone for Elvis during the 1968 comeback television special when the spontaneous jam session got cooking. He was also introduced during the 1973 Hawaii concert. Geller was Elvis's hairstylist. He was summoned to the King in 1964 when he was working for Jay Sebring, the hair salon owner who later died at the hands of the Charles Manson killers at actress Sharon Tate's house. Geller, a thin man with a mass of black hair, looked every bit the spiritualistic swami he turned out to be. Far from practicing the traditional Christianity on which Elvis was raised, Geller was into the theosophist doctrine of Madame Blavatsky. Elvis became interested in theosophy from 1964 until about 1968 or 1969, and read numerous books on the subject. Geller was indeed a thorn in Colonel Parker's side. The Colonel decided that the books were a distraction and ordered Geller not to proselytize anymore, going as far as having him watched when he cut Elvis's hair. Elvis eventually gave in to the Colonel's wishes and helped burn the books.

Chapter 15

THE ROOM WAS DARK WHEN I AWOKE at eight that evening. I showered, changed into slacks and a casual blouse, then went outside to walk, think, and enjoy the night air. There was a park nearby with a trickling fountain. The calming effect of the water did little to quiet my mind. Why had Elvis re-entered my life? Where would it lead? The questions were overpowered by the opulent surroundings. The lights and luxury of Beverly Hills were disquieting. Young couples in expensive clothes walked arm in arm, showing off rather than enjoying each other. Every other car was either a Rolls-Royce or a Mercedes. Beverly Hills wasn't my kind of place—too much materialism and too little heart. The sanctity of the lonely hotel room suddenly became appealing. I ordered a club sandwich from room service and stayed in the rest of the evening. The prospect of facing the displays of wealth again the next morning was disturbing. I called the airline and booked an earlier flight home.

Elvis called late that evening. He said he had tried earlier. He admonished me for going out alone, then said he wanted to come back to the hotel. That would lead to more temptation and at that late hour I would be weaker. I made the excuse that I was tired. He said he would come by in the morning. When I told him my new flight reservations prevented that, he became upset and accused me of shutting him out again. Then he offered to give me money. We went through the old argument. I finally exclaimed, "There is no room for the exchange of money in our lives!" Something about that struck him as funny.

"I ain't asking for any from you, baby," he said, laughing.

He gave me his phone numbers in Memphis and Los Angeles

and said not to worry if they were disconnected. The fans often discovered his numbers and he frequently had to change them. If that happened, he told me to call his uncle, Vester Presley, and he gave me that number. I couldn't shake the feeling that Elvis wasn't happy. It bothered me the rest of the night and the whole way back to Dallas. Maybe it was his career. We didn't talk about that. It wasn't my place. He would tell me in his own time.

The next few months were routine. Work, CCD classes, another opera recital, and the family. My children surprised me on my thirty-first birthday that October by chipping in to treat me to dinner at a fancy restaurant. We had a great time, but I couldn't help thinking how nice it would be to spend at least one birthday with Elvis. When we returned home, Jack said that some creep had called. He said it was a Mr. Jones. Elvis called again a few hours later to wish me happy birthday. He mentioned sending a rose. Although he was struggling to sound upbeat, it was obvious he remained depressed. When I went to my room, there was a single red rose on my desk. The card read, "From an admirer."

Despite my busy schedule, I began to feel more and more restless. To combat it, I caught volunteer fever, signing up with the International Visitors Committee and the Council on World Affairs, both branches of the federal State Department. I also placed my name in the language bank to interpret for French-speaking dignitaries.

One day in mid-November I was home rehearsing some songs for church. Debbie was playing the piano. The phone interrupted us. It was Elvis. He sounded angry and frustrated. He said he missed me and wanted to see me again. I told him we had to be strong. We talked about singing for a while and that calmed him down. We discovered that we both had recently sung the same song, "You Don't Know Me." Elvis had included it on one of his movie soundtrack albums.

"I recorded another song that made me think of you, baby. 'Stand by Me.' Will you stand by me and do you really know me?"

"Yes to both."

I told him his voice was maturing and he sounded better now than ever before, hoping it would cheer him up. It didn't. He sunk lower and complained about working so hard. That was telling.

Before, the movies and recording sessions had been nothing but fun. Now he viewed them as tedious labor, as if he were working in a coal mine. Hunting for a topic that wasn't upsetting, I asked him if things were going well at home. That was a mistake.

"Are you happy?" he countered bitterly. "Tell me you're happy without me and I'll be happy."

I couldn't say anything.

"Doesn't sound like you're happy to me. Well, I'm going do something about it. I'm going to end my marriage real soon. It's not working. It's not what I wanted. I want you."

"You can't Elvis. She's pregnant. That would look horrible. No matter how you feel, please wait."

"But what about us?"

"If it's meant to be, our time will come. But it can't be now. Not under these circumstances."

"Everybody tellin' me what to do—what I can and can't do with my life. Who I have to marry. What to sing. What stupid movie to be in. When does it stop? When is anybody going to think of me and what I want?"

He was about to explode. I said nothing. There was a long pause.

"I'm not blaming you. You're right. You're always right. And I know how it hurts you to tell me this. You're really something special. That's why I need you."

"I'm sorry you can't find peace, darling. Please be patient. Things will change."

"Not soon enough. They can try and run my life, but they can't take my dreams. Tonight, I'll be back with you on our hill in Memphis. Wanna come?"

"Sure. I know the place well. I go there all the time myself."

"Things were so much better then . . . well, maybe not for you. I'm sorry. I shouldn't have said that."

"That's okay. Really. It's over. There are no scars."

"You don't mind if I remember?"

"No. I remember only the good times with you. You can talk about it all you want."

"We've got to meet again soon."

"Maybe. We'll see."

My heart was heavy after he hung up. He seemed so sad and lonely. What was going on with him? Was there something I didn't know?

Elvis was serious about ending his marriage at this time even though such a move could have mortally wounded his career. In her book, *Elvis and Me,* Priscilla wrote that at this same time Elvis summoned her to his office at Graceland and started talking about a trial separation. "It's not you," she quotes her husband as saying. "It's just that I'm going through some things." Priscilla said she was shattered and angry and threatened to leave. A few days passed and nothing more was said. Elvis never elaborated, leaving Priscilla to speculate that he was worried over whether his fans would accept him as a father.

DECEMBER WAS HECTIC—WORKING, juggling the finances, and buying Christmas presents for my six children. They were all deserving, and not all were "children" anymore. Debbie was a woman of nineteen. Melody was equally mature at seventeen. Denise was thirteen. Desirée was nine. Jacques six, and little Jacqueline was two. On Sundays we would all go biking or horseback riding and have a picnic in the country. Through my children there was happiness in my life. A few days before Christmas we were practicing Christmas carols and other songs for church. Jack was working. Despite his law degree, he enjoyed selling cars and kept the job. It surprised me, but when we discussed it he always got angry. The phone rang and interrupted our singing.

"I'll have a blue Christmas without you."

I was stunned. It sounded like Bing Crosby. Then something clicked in my head.

"Bing, I told you not to call me at home anymore." There was a strange silence on the other end of the phone. I couldn't hold it anymore and started laughing. Elvis finally joined in.

"You had me going for a minute there, baby."

"So how are you, El Lancelot? You're quite a mimic."

"Honey, I wish you were here with me."

"Are you all right?" I asked.

"What is it they say? 'Loneliness and pain help you grow.' I must be ten feet tall."

"I'm sorry. Is it anything you want to talk about?"

"Yeah. When can we talk? How about tomorrow?"

There was no way I could see him with Priscilla so close to having their child. She needed him. I knew the agony of having a child alone with no one around to love and comfort you. I wouldn't wish that on anyone.

"I'm listening now," I said.

He paused for a brief moment.

"I want to laugh again and talk and walk with you. I want to go back in time. Young again. Me and you. The way it used to be."

"You can go back. In your mind."

"That's not good enough."

"Come on. Promise me you'll have a beautiful Christmas. And know that I'll be with you in spirit."

"It'll be an effort."

"Your child will be born soon. That'll make you happy. You wait and see." Saying that made me think of our child. Someday, when the time was right, I would tell him.

"Honey, when part of your heart is missing, it's hard to be alive," he said. "You know, we've never spent a holiday together. Did you know that?"

"I know.

"Oh, by the way, I have something to tell you," I said. "I've prepared some beautiful songs to sing at midnight Mass. I'm dedicating them to the memory of my mother and your mother. You'd like them. I'm singing 'O Holy Night,' 'Joy to the World,' and Malotte's 'Lord's Prayer.' "

"That's beautiful, baby. Momma will like that. You never met her, and I never got to meet yours."

"They're happy, Elvis. I can feel it. Maybe they are together."

"Unlike us."

"Try and be happy, okay? Life is too short."

"I will. Just for you. I love you. Merry Christmas."

He was worse than ever. What was happening? What could I do? Go to him? No. Not now. We had to wait. He called again shortly before New Year's. He was rushed, and there were voices in the background. We spoke briefly. He didn't call again until February. He told me they had a baby girl and named her Lisa Marie. Now I was depressed. In my heart I was hoping he'd have a son. My mind went back nine years to a hospital in Alexandria where our daughter was born. How much longer could I live with the secret? The older Desirée grew, the stronger my guilt. He had missed nine years of her life. She had missed being with him. I wondered if I was doing the proper thing. He had a right to know about Desirée. Desirée should know her father. But there were so many complications, especially now that he was married and had a child. As always, it wasn't our place to intrude.

Time passed. Like Elvis, I began to grow more unhappy. He called in the late spring and said he was preparing to do a television special. He was excited. He hadn't performed in anything but those movies in nearly a decade.

"I'm scared, man," he said. "I need you to pray for me."

"I certainly will. And don't worry. There isn't an entertainer in the world who isn't scared before they go onstage. You'll be fine. You wanted to go back to the old days. Now you can."

"You always make me feel so good. Why? I know why. You know me as myself, without all this other stuff. I need that. Someone has to be around who knows me."

"The people know you. Not those around you, but the fans. They remember. They love you because you give love in return. Remember that. They're your friends. I have a feeling you're going to be performing in a spectacular way very soon. I don't know why, but I'm certain of it. So you've got nothing to worry about!"

"You really believe it."

"I know it. You'll see. By the way, how's Lisa?"

"She's fine. I'm trying with this marriage."

He stayed on the phone as if he didn't want to hang up. He really was scared about performing again. Why had his manager done this to him? Live performances made him famous. Now he was trembling at the thought. It didn't seem logical.

So much happened after that. I found a three-bedroom, brick ranch house and, over Jack's objections, I bought it with money I had managed to save. It was a lovely place that sat on a hill overlooking a creek. We were packing and preparing to move in early June when the phone rang. It was a friend. She was crying and told me Robert Kennedy had been killed. We had worked together on his presidential campaign in Dallas, and I was a precinct captain. That made it personal. So much violence in the world.

We settled in our home and the summer passed. I had asked Elvis a number of times when his special would be on, but he never knew. I didn't pay attention that closely and ended up missing it when it aired in early December. Maybe I didn't want to see it. Elvis had continued to pressure me to renew our relationship. All my instincts, not to mention my religion, told me it would be wrong. My resolve was strong, but the flesh was weak. How do you say no to the only man you've ever loved? Missing the special was probably best.

Elvis didn't call for a long time after that. There were no Christmas or New Year's calls. I missed him, but what troubled me even more was he had been so unhappy when he called and had never explained what was bothering him.

Desirée began getting more proficient at the piano. She surprised me with the difficult compositions she played flawlessly, pieces like Durand's 'Waltz,' selections from Chopin and Czerny, along with pop tunes she picked up by ear. She was eleven and began teaching Jacqueline, who was four. One night, after they finished practicing, there was a commotion coming from their bedroom. Desirée came running out and said, "Mommy, my nose doesn't look like a man's, does it?" I told her of course not, then explained that little girls can take the features of their father, adding that I looked like my father.

"But this isn't my dad!"

I had no idea what she was talking about but suspected that a trip to the bedroom would shed some light on the situation. I entered the room and almost fainted. The girls had plastered the walls with posters of Elvis. He was everywhere. The kids all grew silent and stared at me. They must have noticed something because no one said a word until Desirée finally spoke up.

"What's wrong, Mommy? Don't you like him? This guy at school gave out tons of these to everyone. He's neat. He's a singer named Elvis Presley. Have you ever heard of him?"

Lucy de Barbin
at age eight.

At age eleven in 1947,
shortly before her grand-
mother arranged the mar-
riage. Lucy had never even
had a boyfriend.

The dreams of Lucy's
ambitious young lover
begin to take shape. Elvis is
seen here with Memphis
disc jockey Charlie Walker,
one of the first to play his
recordings.

A young, smartly
dressed Elvis in an early
performance.

The Louisiana Hayride in Shreveport. Elvis got his big break at the country music showcase in late 1954.

Elvis and the Colonel. Elvis was initially excited about his new, high-powered manager, who thought big and promised to make him a movie star.

With his beloved parents,
Vernon and Gladys.

Celebrating Denise's sec-
ond birthday in July 1956
with daughters Melody (looking
up), five, and Deborah,
seven. Lucy was nine-
teen. "We were children
together."

The Steven Allen Show in 1956. Elvis was embarrassed by the silly skits, especially having to sing his hit "Hound Dog" to a hound dog. But as always, he did as he was told.

In his second movie, *Loving You*, released in early 1957. He dedicated the title song to Lucy.

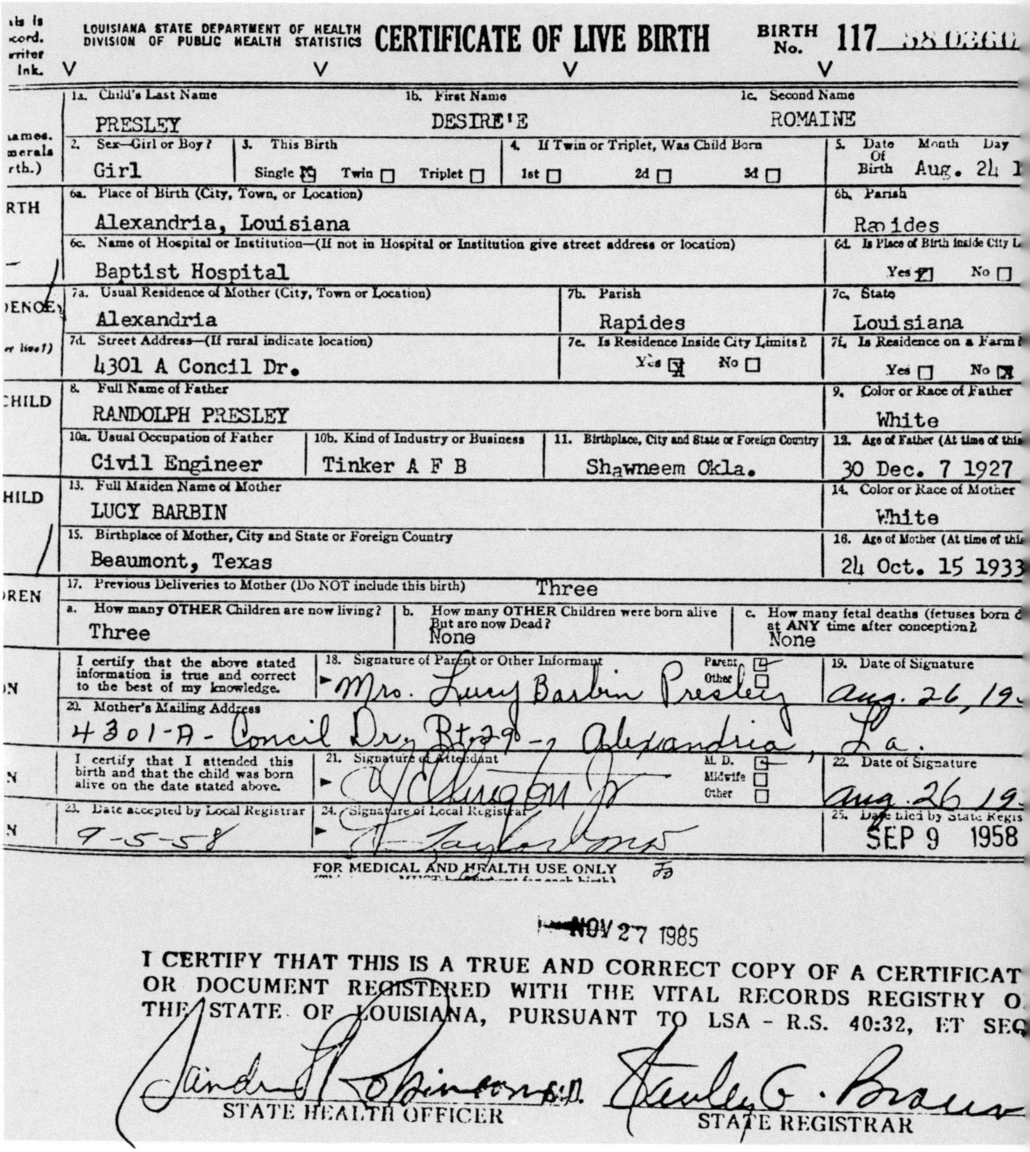

LOUISIANA STATE DEPARTMENT OF HEALTH
DIVISION OF PUBLIC HEALTH STATISTICS

CERTIFICATE OF LIVE BIRTH

BIRTH No. 117 [illegible]

1a. Child's Last Name: PRESLEY	1b. First Name: DESIRE'E	1c. Second Name: ROMAINE
2. Sex—Girl or Boy? Girl	3. This Birth: Single ☒ Twin ☐ Triplet ☐	4. If Twin or Triplet, Was Child Born 1st ☐ 2d ☐ 3d ☐
5. Date of Birth: Month Aug. Day 24		
6a. Place of Birth (City, Town, or Location): Alexandria, Louisiana	6b. Parish: Rapides	
6c. Name of Hospital or Institution—(If not in Hospital or Institution give street address or location): Baptist Hospital	6d. Is Place of Birth inside City L… Yes ☒ No ☐	
7a. Usual Residence of Mother (City, Town or Location): Alexandria	7b. Parish: Rapides	7c. State: Louisiana
7d. Street Address—(If rural indicate location): 4301 A Concil Dr.	7e. Is Residence Inside City Limits? Yes ☒ No ☐	7f. Is Residence on a Farm? Yes ☐ No ☒
8. Full Name of Father: RANDOLPH PRESLEY	9. Color or Race of Father: White	
10a. Usual Occupation of Father: Civil Engineer	10b. Kind of Industry or Business: Tinker A F B	11. Birthplace, City and State or Foreign Country: Shawneem Okla.
12. Age of Father (At time of this…): 30 Dec. 7 1927		
13. Full Maiden Name of Mother: LUCY BARBIN	14. Color or Race of Mother: White	
15. Birthplace of Mother, City and State or Foreign Country: Beaumont, Texas	16. Age of Mother (At time of this…): 24 Oct. 15 1933	
17. Previous Deliveries to Mother (Do NOT include this birth): Three		
a. How many OTHER Children are now living? Three	b. How many OTHER Children were born alive But are now Dead? None	c. How many fetal deaths (fetuses born d… at ANY time after conception? None
I certify that the above stated information is true and correct to the best of my knowledge.	18. Signature of Parent or Other Informant: Mrs. Lucy Barbin Presley — Parent ☒ Other ☐	19. Date of Signature: Aug. 26, 19…
20. Mother's Mailing Address: 4301-A- Concil Dr, Rt. 29-7 Alexandria, La.		
I certify that I attended this birth and that the child was born alive on the date stated above.	21. Signature of Attendant: [signature] — M. D. ☒ Midwife ☐ Other ☐	22. Date of Signature: Aug. 26 19…
23. Date accepted by Local Registrar: 9-5-58	24. Signature of Local Registrar: [signature]	25. Date filed by State Regis…: SEP 9 1958

FOR MEDICAL AND HEALTH USE ONLY

NOV 27 1985

I CERTIFY THAT THIS IS A TRUE AND CORRECT COPY OF A CERTIFICAT… OR DOCUMENT REGISTERED WITH THE VITAL RECORDS REGISTRY O… THE STATE OF LOUISIANA, PURSUANT TO LSA - R.S. 40:32, ET SEQ…

STATE HEALTH OFFICER

STATE REGISTRAR

The hidden b…
certificate. More t…
twenty years later, I…
would confess to…
bewildered daughter…
little on it is true excep…
time and place of b…
and the last nam…
Desirée's fa…

Lucy's family in 1959.
[M]elody, Desirée, Deborah
and Denise.

Desirée at age two
and a half.

A blurry shot of Lucy in 1967, the year she reunited with Elvis. She was thirty-one.

Elvis around the same time, as he appeared in his 1968 comeback television special.

Desirée in 1973 at age
fifteen—looking more and
more like her father.

Elvis and Desirée, the
daughter he never knew.

Elvis and Desirée.

Elvis played before half the world in his famous satellite concert from Hawaii in 1973. Despite the unprecedented audience, he moved sluggishly and gave an uninspired performance. Something was wrong.

Love Can Endure Anything...

Lucy's "credit card." A mischievous Elvis expressed his sentiments in this touching card he gave Lucy in 1973.

but I miss you

love

El Lancelot

A product of
THE SUNRISE CORPORATION
Atlanta, Ga.

Lucy in 1975, the year she and Elvis returned to their hilltop in Memphis. Lonely and unhappy, Elvis sought to recapture the joy of the past with the woman he never forgot.

Elvis in 1975, looking his best for the last time.

Desirée visiting Grace
in 1985.

Desirée with Vester Presley,
1985.

Lucy at Elvis's grave.

Desirée Pres

I recovered enough to say, "Of course. I haven't lived in a cave."

"Denise said I have the same nose he does. And he's a man!"

The blood was rushing to my head. I felt a little dizzy but tried to maintain composure. It was just a coincidence, but it was the kind of thing Desirée would remember when she learned the truth later on.

"Well, I wouldn't mind looking like him. He's so handsome. The joke's on them, Rome." Everyone laughed except Melody. She kept staring at me. That was trouble. Melody is an artist and is unusually perceptive. She is sensitive to emotions, vibrations, and facial expressions. Fooling the others was hard enough. Hiding my secret from her was becoming impossible. She stared at me strangely the rest of the evening. I tried to avoid her. The next day she couldn't contain her curiosity any longer. She cornered me.

"Mother, did you know Elvis Presley?"

"Honey, why do you ask?"

"The way you looked when you saw those posters. Was he your friend?"

It was a direct question. I couldn't lie to her.

"Yes, Melody. He was my friend and still is. We met a long time ago. We never get to enjoy our friendship much anymore. He's so busy. Darling, please don't mention it to anyone. You know how horrible Jack can be about my friends."

Melody looked at me, waiting. She wanted to know more. I explained that life is a constant evolution. Everything changes. You can have friends and still care deeply for them even though you can't be with them because of circumstances. She accepted that, or maybe she perceived that a clearer explanation would not be forthcoming.

Melody clearly remembers that day.

"We rarely had posters in our room," she recalled. "This was unusual. One of my sisters, I can't remember who, brought them home and we put them up. We were all crazy about Elvis. When Mother entered the room her reaction was so strange. You'd expect her to laugh or be indifferent. Instead, there was this look in her eyes, a deep sadness, and it was personal. I had been noticing things like that for years, and it always involved Elvis Presley. This time she had one of the strongest reactions I'd seen, probably because she was caught off guard. When my sister mentioned how his nose looked like Desirée's, the sadness in Mother's eyes changed to terror. It was like she didn't want the connection to be made. At that time, none of us had a clue about the truth, not a clue! Especially not Desirée. She was even more upset than Mother, but that was because she didn't want to have a man's nose. I thought about all this the rest of the evening. Mother had so many closed doors in her life. There was so much none of us knew. The next day, I asked her about it. For the first time, she opened one of those doors just a crack."

L IFE DRAGGED ON. IT WAS SO HARD to believe that with grown daughters, and all that had happened, I was still only thirty-two. Even so, there didn't appear to be much life ahead. Love for me seemed destined to be nothing more than a few vivid memories. Someone once said, "Love is the life of the soul." I added my own continuation: "It must flow through channels from one to another or it drifts into a dormant place to die." My love had been drifting but it hadn't died.

Elvis called in mid-January. He said he was in Memphis recording. He was stressed and extremely upset. The urgency in his voice was frightening. I thought something terrible had happened.

"I've got to see you. Come to Memphis. I'll arrange everything. I need to talk to you. There's so much going on you need to know."

"Are you all right?"

"No. That's why you have to come."

This was different than before. Something was definitely wrong. I couldn't deny him now.

"I'll come. Is anything wrong?"

"Oh God, baby. I tried to do what you said. Now I gotta see you."

He wanted me there tomorrow. A ticket would be at the airport and everything would be arranged. The desperation in his voice prompted me to agree to everything, even the short notice. I delegated authority to Deborah and Melody and told them there was urgent business in Nashville. I couldn't say Memphis because Melody was getting too smart.

That night sleep eluded me. My mind was overflowing with guesses about Elvis's problem. The next morning I didn't pay as much attention to how I looked as before. This was a mission of mercy. Elvis had called for my soul, not my body. He wanted a comforter, not a lover.

Chapter 16

Elvis had much to be troubled about in 1969. He had suffered through the worst two years of his life. His movie career was dead. The combination of bad scripts and Colonel Parker's iron-fisted belief that Elvis should do nothing deeper than beach-and-bikini movies had steadily diminished his value as an actor. The movies were actually little more than extended videos to promote the equally dismal RCA soundtrack albums. To that extent, they had been successful. The albums sold well and the movies made money. Everyone was happy but Elvis. The pictures destroyed his dream of becoming a serious actor like his idol Marlon Brando.

By 1969 no one wanted these travelogue movies anymore. Times had changed. The student-led protests against the Vietnam War were increasing and had gained the support of a wide range of Americans. When anti-war protesters turned to Elvis, they found that the rebel of the 1950s wanted no part of them. Instead, he decried their long hair and spoke disdainfully of "drugged-up hippies."

In the music world, too, Elvis was a has-been, a relic from another era. He hadn't had a number-one song in seven years, since "Good Luck Charm" in 1962. The Beatles were the new heroes, and John Lennon became the radical, anti-war voice the generation sought. Groups like the Who, the Doors, and the Rolling Stones were speaking to the American youth, while Elvis clung to his old-fashioned hairdo and movie songs. The Colonel, finally seeing what was happening, swung into action. Although he had steadfastly maintained that television was too small for his star, he did an about-face in 1968 and signed Elvis to do an NBC special. Critics jeered and said things like, "Next they'll bring back the Edsel." The show aired on December 3, 1968, and was a hit. The Colonel then set out to revive Elvis's musical career to keep the money rolling in. He was preparing to send Elvis back onstage before live audiences, something Elvis hadn't done in nearly a decade. He was terrified.

If consolation over a mismanaged career had been all that Elvis wanted in January 1969, he could have spoken to Lucy by phone. There was more to it than that.

I WAITED NERVOUSLY AT THE BAGGAGE area of the Memphis airport with my small suitcase at my feet. I had no idea what was troubling Elvis. All I could think of was how awful it would be if our relationship was exposed. Elvis had insisted on picking me up himself. He was so upset I didn't realize how dangerous that was. Elvis Presley could hardly swagger through the airport unnoticed. I imagined a mob descending upon me and Elvis springing from the center and giving me a kiss while dozens of Instamatic cameras clicked, capturing our secret and announcing it to the world. Shuddering at the thought, I didn't notice the stranger until he was nearly beside me. I jumped when he reached down to grab my bag.

"No, thank you," I said. "I'll take care of it."

The man looked up at me. He winked. It was Elvis! He was wearing a thick mustache, dark pants, a tweed coat, and a gray fedora turned down over one eye. I couldn't help laughing. I told him that he looked like Jerry Colonna, the bug-eyed comedian in the Bob Hope "Road" movies.

"Shhh," Elvis whispered. "Don't wanna attract any attention."

He leaned over and gave me a quick kiss. The mustache was stiff and prickly. He crooked his finger for me to follow. We left the airport unnoticed. No Instamatics in sight. I said a quick prayer of thanks and stepped into his black sports car. Elvis had a fleet of cars and took great pleasure in them, but I didn't know a Pontiac from a Porsche. The only ones I ever noticed were the small sports cars, and that was because they were so low and cramped and hard to get into. When I complained once, he laughed and told me how expensive it was. "Why do you spend so much money to be so uncomfortable?" I asked, and he roared with laughter, "That's success, baby!"

He'd been so playful at the airport, I was surprised when his mood began to change. He was getting more and more upset, obviously brooding. He took off his hat and mustache without a word. I stayed quiet. He soon pulled up to a hotel in that same cluster area near the airport where we had stayed before. "Go up to the room," he ordered. "It's reserved for Lucy Jones. I'll be there in a few minutes." His jaw was set and his eyes were angry. I was afraid he was mad at me.

I checked in and walked to my room in a daze, straining to think of what I'd done. I had barely finished washing my hands when I heard the familiar tapping on the door. I opened it, still drying my hands with the hotel towel. Elvis came in and practically collapsed in my arms. I was relieved that his anger wasn't directed at me. We kissed, but it was a cry for help instead of a preface of passion. "Is this the great Don Juan with all the damsels at his feet, hugging little old me?" I asked. It was an attempt at humor, but it also showed my insecurity. I was thirty-two. Elvis had an keen eye for both physical beauty and any threatening signs of aging. Could I hope to compete with the teenagers who threw themselves at him?

As we hugged, Elvis lightly pinched me. The pinch was a signal that he was okay. He tightened his grip for a few seconds, then relaxed it. "Honey, I want you to sit down and listen to me," he said. "Can you do that? I gotta talk to you."

I put my hands on his face, gently kissed him, then led him to a soft, upholstered chair and sat on the floor at his feet.

"Do you remember when I saw you in Beverly Hills and I told you about Priscilla?" he said. "You wanted me to tell you all those good things about her. You didn't want me to love you. I tried to do what I should, but I want you to know something. I put that wedding off so long because I was looking for you. I knew you weren't dead. I could sense it. I couldn't marry someone else. I couldn't go through with it.

"I even made Priscilla dye her hair so she would look more like you. I made her dress like you. Hell, I even had her take French lessons so she could speak to me in French the way you used to. But it didn't work. I was trying to re-create you, and she wasn't you. She's nothin' like you."

Elvis had mentioned before that he picked Priscilla because she looked like me, but he had never told me all this. At first I found it hard to believe. I didn't think Priscilla looked anything like me.

I saw the wedding photos. Her hair was piled so high it looked silly and out of style for 1967. Later, though, when I saw another picture of them, I was startled. I thought for a moment that someone had taken a picture of me and Elvis together. But I didn't want to think about it. Even if he had done what he said, she was his wife. I wasn't. That's all that mattered.

"The Colonel just planned the wedding and forced me into it," he continued. "He always has to get his way and acts like he owns me. He thinks he knows best about everything. I fought that marriage one last time, but things were already set in motion. After I was married, I discovered you were alive. You were the one I wanted, and you were still alive!"

I pleaded with him to stop. I didn't want to go over this again. It hurt, and I couldn't see any purpose for it.

"You stop!" he shouted, cupping his hand over my mouth. "You've got to listen this time. I always wanted it to be you havin' my baby. But it was done, I was married, I would have to live with that. I tried to make it work. I wanted to be a father. But all I could think of was you, and how you never wanted anything from me, nothing ever, not a dime. You just wanted me. You would have loved me if I was never anything but a hick in Memphis."

"Elvis, you mustn't—"

"Stop! Listen to me!"

He was furious. There was nothing I could do to stop him.

"You want to know about Priscilla? No more lies, Lucy. She's cold. So damn cold. There's no affection. I wanted her to love me for me. I thought I could build a home away from all the other stuff, the kind of life you and I wanted. It never worked."

The fury drained. Elvis became quiet. He sank back into the chair, lost and bewildered. He bowed his head and gazed at the floor.

"Lucy," he said, "she's seen someone else. She's seeing someone on the sly already."

I had never been certain how Elvis felt about Priscilla. I now knew he cared enough to be wounded by her infidelity. But I also knew how he felt about me. He was telling me this to make me feel less guilty about our relationship.

"The guys think I don't know it. They bring me girls to take my mind off her. Man, I'm not stupid. I get so mad about being used."

I winced at that "bring me girls" line and wanted an explanation, but I decided to let it pass. Instead, I asked Elvis if he was sure about Priscilla. It was possible that someone was spreading lies trying to break them up. I couldn't believe any woman who had Elvis could want another man.

"You would try to see some good in her," Elvis said, calming down, "even at your own expense."

I remained on the floor at the foot of the chair. I wanted to let Elvis get out all his anger.

"I know what's goin' on," he said. "I talked to Daddy about it. The guys, they don't care. They only want to play. They think I'm nuts if I try to be myself. If they knew about you, boy, you're all I have that's real. You're the only one who really knows me. You and Lisa are all I have."

When Elvis mentioned Lisa, I naturally thought of Desirée. She was ten and growing more beautiful, and more like her father, every day. I started the first sentences of my confession. "You have more than you know, Elvis. More than you know about."

I wanted to continue. If I could just say it: "You have someone else. A child born of love. Our love created something beautiful." Instead, the lump in my throat nearly choked me. I had a second thought: Elvis didn't need any more shocks right now. He was too upset and might do something rash. It wasn't the right time. The lump dissolved. "You'll always have me," I said.

"I know you love me, but there's always someone else. Someone keeping us apart. Why?"

Recalling our past would solve nothing. I changed the subject. "How much time do you have?" I asked.

"It's okay," he said. He dropped to his knees and lay his head on the bed, stretching his hands across the covers. He was worn and defeated. He turned and held out his arms. We climbed on the plush ivory spread and lay next to each other. We talked quietly as the sun set and the room darkened. Elvis asked me about my marriage. I told him it wasn't good.

"It's my fault. I just can't stop loving you."

"So why'd you marry him?" He knew. We had been over this before. But he wanted to hear it again.

"I ran from you because I loved you and I didn't want you hurt. I couldn't think only of myself. The world would have lost you, Elvis. The price was too high."

I laid my head on his chest. It wasn't the chest of the superstar everyone saw in the beach movies. It was the body of the simple country boy I loved. I told him how difficult it was getting to see him or even to call, that his staff seemed to be shutting him in.

"Baby, they'll never keep me from loving you," he said. "That's one thing I'll never allow.

"I'm staying here with you for a while," he said, rising up from the bed. "Let's order something to eat."

He went into the bathroom. I called room service and ordered a couple of hamburgers. It wasn't the time for anything fancy. He stayed in the bathroom for about five minutes and was less wound-up when he came out.

"I took something for my headache. It relaxes me. My head's been hurtin'."

It was obvious that Elvis was under strain because of Priscilla. I suggested that he confront her.

"She'll just say it's my fault. Everyone will blame me. They think I'm woman-crazy. I don't even mess with whoever the guys bring over. I guess I should tell them no, but it's hard sometimes. You know, attitudes. Guy stuff. They'll think I'm 'funny.' I have to take something to help me get through all this. I'm under pressure. They expect so much from me."

"You're letting them use you," I said. "The pills will make you weaker and make them stronger. Why don't you turn to God like you used to? Remember how you used to talk to God up on our hill? God listened then. He made you a star just like you wanted. If He could do that, He can surely get you through this.

"You can handle your marriage," I went on. "You'll find the answer. I know it. And whatever you decide, I won't change. You can depend on that."

"Honey, if I didn't take something to keep me goin', I'd go nuts. The Colonel is pushing and pushing and pushing. I've showed them what I can do. I'm recording everything I can. I just did that television special, and I have a show in Vegas coming up. Hey, why don't you come along?"

I didn't think that would be wise and said so.

"Maybe you're right. I don't want anything to hurt you. You're the only secret I've ever had. You're the only thing they can't ruin. I want to keep it that way. You've got to be outside all of that."

"Tell me about your new recordings," I asked, changing the subject again. "What songs are you singing?"

Elvis didn't answer. He was lost in thought. I got up off the bed and walked to the window. Earlier in the day there had been a lovely view of the Tennessee countryside—tall trees and rolling hills. Under the moon the same scene was even more beautiful. I sensed Elvis approaching. He stood beside me and looked out as he spoke.

"They told me I'd never make it. Maybe I'd have been better off."

"You don't mean that, Elvis."

"I'm not sure."

We stood together for a few moments, looking out the window. After a brief silence, Elvis started singing "Are You Lonesome Tonight?" He sang softly at first, then stronger as he went along. It was a new song, I thought, because I had never heard it. I was stunned by the beauty of the words and the powerful emotion in his voice.

"It's lovely, absolutely lovely," I said when he finished.

Singing the song cheered him up. "I've just recorded it. There's another one called 'Memories.' They all have to do with you," he said. "Baby, when I rehearsed those songs all I could think of was you. I wondered if you'd ever hear my music. Do you? I still talk to you in my songs."

"Of course I hear you sing. I hear you all the time. I pretend you're telling me all the beautiful things you're saying in the song. Do you really sing them to me?"

"Yeah. But I don't feel you ever hear me. You didn't hear 'Are You Lonesome Tonight?' when I wanted you to."

He grew forlorn again. I gently put my arms around him.

"I remember you singing once," he said. "A hundred years ago. We were together somewhere. I was your 'Beloved,' or somethin' like that, then I was supposed to be your 'Mr. Wonderful.' That made me feel great."

"You remember that? I can't believe it."

Elvis turned me around to face him. We stood staring at each other. He leaned down to kiss me. A loud rap at the door stopped him. We'd forgotten about room service.

I tried to eat, but the song and attempted kiss had aroused me. We hadn't made love in eleven years. I'd spent a thousand nights lying awake in bed, recalling every detail of our moments together. Now he was right there, close enough to touch. I thought about getting out of there before completely losing control. I knew I couldn't resist if Elvis attempted to make love to me. Although my marriage wasn't good, and Elvis's marriage appeared over, the prospect of double adultery was frightening to a woman raised in a Catholic convent.

As I watched him eat his hamburger, my thoughts turned. I knew things about him nobody looked deep enough or cared enough to realize. He was strong in his beliefs but weak in his need to please anybody and everybody. He wanted his business partners to be his friends. He wanted to be needed. He needed to be loved. Despite his huge success, his fear of losing it all remained overwhelming. Now he was taking pills to deal with the stress that was eating at him.

"Where you been, Lucy? You've drifted away."

"I'm just not hungry."

"You're worried about me, aren't you? You have that same look on your face Momma used to have. She was afraid the fame would take me away. Not from her, but from the things she'd taught me and my faith in God. She didn't want me to get caught up in show business and become cold and hard. She knew me pretty well. I did get caught up. And it wasn't any good. The anger makes you do things you wouldn't normally do."

"Elvis, you are letting it change you. I can see it. I'm so worried about what you're doing, pushing yourself with no direction. I know you love to sing, but you've got to change your course. The people around you are just there for the money. You must have satisfaction in what you're doing. Are you satisfied?"

"When I'm singing."

"Well, you'll always have that. You don't have to let them use you. And about your wife, I know what's going through your mind. You're like me, you don't want to hurt anyone. If she's using you, using your name for her own gain, you'll have to accept it and change it. You won't hurt Lisa, especially if you can do it now while she's young. But if these stories about Priscilla aren't true and you still have a chance to make a home with her, then try for Lisa's sake. Sweep her off her feet again. She won't be able to resist."

It hurt me to say that, but I felt that his wife deserved the benefit of the doubt, at least until he was certain she was unfaithful.

"As for your career, well, what is it you really want?"

"Lucy, I would like more than anything to teach others what it's like to love God. Like you do. So many people don't believe anymore."

It was a touching sentiment but sounded like someone trying to take on the problems of the world to avoid his own. But then again, it was precisely the kind of motivation that could give Elvis the direction he lacked.

"Well, you're a great singer," I said. "You're a communicator. Use that. Give them a message in your songs. Show them your love for God through your work. People love you and look up to you. If they see that you believe, they'll follow you. Give God the credit for making you what you are. Don't be afraid."

"You do understand me, Lucy," he said. "And you still love me when all I ever talk about are my problems. I want to give you everything, anything you want, but you won't let me."

"Elvis, don't you know that you do give me everything. I have your love and understanding. You're my friend. I have no regrets. Whatever I have, I have to earn it myself. I'm not trying to make things hard. I've just seen the other side of material possessions, the bad side. I was treated as a possession. Someone wanted to own me. I thought my life was over. Then I met you and fell in love. No one can take that from me. It hasn't been ideal, far from it, but it has been more than I ever dreamed love could be. I never want our relationship on any basis but love, pure love with no strings. I don't want to be just another woman in your book. I don't want any Cadillacs or houses to cheapen what we have. It must remain pure. Someday, when we can be together free and clear, I'll accept all the gifts you want to give me, whenever you want to give them, without the fear of having to hide them away so no one will find out. In the meantime, I'm proud of what I have accomplished. I'm proud of the least little thing. I want my children to be proud of me for what I have done. Can you understand that? I know you want to give so much, so just give me your love and your happiness. Your love is what I treasure more than anything."

There was something else. The words again formed in my mind. *You have given me something, Elvis, a child. That's better than any gift you could ever give.*

I couldn't say it.

Elvis fingered the tiny crucifix around my neck. It was one of the few gifts I accepted because it signified the vows of marriage we'd exchanged in 1953.

"Our love is crossed with God's love," he said softly, repeating the words he spoke when he gave the cross to me.

"I haven't made love to you in so long," he said. "We are fooling ourselves. My wife's cheating on me, and you don't love your husband. You don't have to stay there. Lucy, tell me what you want. I'll make everything right for you. We'll work it out. You love me. I love you. Why shouldn't we be together?"

"You have all the beautiful women in the world at your feet. Why do you want me?" I said, letting my insecurities surface.

"Don't you know how you shine?" he answered. "Don't you know how sparkling you are inside, and what you've meant to me?"

"But I'm not glamorous."

He ignored the remark and began kissing my neck. I was finally holding the body I ached for all those empty years. I ran my fingers down his smooth skin and traced his sensuous mouth. Elvis responded, first slowly, then eagerly. He was as thrilling in bed as he was onstage, energetic, powerful, and commanding. He explored all the nuances of my body, awakening desires I feared had long died.

"My Desirée," he whispered. "My Desirée."

He brought his face close to mine, kissed me, then kissed my neck, slowly descending to my bosom . . .

An hour later we dressed, pausing again and again for a few last tender embraces. Ending this meeting was especially difficult. I didn't know if I would see him again. I recalled a French proverb

I often quoted in times of sorrow: *"Si tu aime l'un que tu perds, tu ne perds jamais ton amour."* If you love the one you lose, you can never lose your love.

Elvis stopped me as I began buttoning my blouse. He placed his hand over mine and spread open the cotton folds. Gently he buried his face in my breasts one final time, kissing me.

"I never want to forget this day," he said. "You still belong to me. We should have been together from the beginning. Things would of been so different. We still can make a life together."

I didn't think we had much of a chance of that. There were more obstacles than ever before. We were both married. I had six children. He had a baby. Elvis was at a crossroads again, fighting to resurrect his career as a singer. The Colonel was still in charge and would view me with the same horror that he would have ten years before. Then or now, I was potentially fatal to Elvis's career. It was cruelly ironic that Elvis the man needed me the most when Elvis the superstar was most vulnerable to scandal.

Always oblivious of such concerns, Elvis began planning our future. The dreams soon gave way to anger.

"I have to figure out what to do about my marriage. I want my daughter happy. Damn this, they created this marriage."

I knew those feelings. Elvis, in his own way, had a marriage forced upon him just as I had.

"I don't want anyone to ever touch you," Elvis said. "I don't want them to ever know about you."

"They won't," I said. "We've kept the secret this long."

"Will you listen to the songs?" Elvis asked.

"Of course. 'Are You Lonesome Tonight?' and 'Memories.' Is it okay if I cry when I hear them?"

"Don't cry, baby. There's been too damn many tears already."

Two years after my taped interviews with Lucy, Priscilla Presley wrote in her book, *Elvis and Me,* that Elvis was forcing her to become someone she wasn't, suggesting that she dye her hair black and change its style and telling her what clothes to wear, how to walk, and how to act. Priscilla also wrote that to please

Elvis, she took dancing lessons "because he adored dancers' bodies," and learned French "because he liked the language." Elvis knew other dancers besides Lucy, but how did a man born in Tupelo, Mississippi, and raised in Memphis, Tennessee, become so enamored with French? I asked his friends, associates, and biographers, and no one had a clue. The only time he ever left the United States was during his army stint from 1958 to 1960, and he was stationed in Germany. Prior to Lucy's revelation, his infatuation with French was a mystery.

Despite the extensive physical and linguistic remodeling of Priscilla, Elvis apparently was not satisfied with the finished product. His bitter comments about being forced to marry her stand up under investigation. Many of the details have already been accurately documented in Albert Goldman's biography *Elvis.* My own investigation proved that this was one area where Goldman may have actually understated the truth. Currie Grant, the Air Force Special Services noncom who introduced Priscilla to Elvis in Germany, and often shuttled her back and forth from her home to Elvis's, explains what happened.

"In 1966 I learned through the Memphis Mafia grapevine that Priscilla might be on her way out. Prior to this I had already realized that Elvis was content to string her along forever without marrying her. He wanted her sequestered at Graceland while he lived his bachelor life in Los Angeles. The trouble was, Elvis had made a lot of promises to the Beaulieus [Priscilla's parents] in order to get Priscilla to stay at Graceland, including the promise that he would marry her. I went to bat for Elvis's integrity with Colonel Beaulieu. Priscilla's father respected me and I had put my honor on the line for Elvis. When I heard about what was going down at Graceland and that Elvis might end the relationship altogether, I felt an obligation to inform Priscilla's parents. I called Colonel Beaulieu and we had dinner at his house in San Francisco. I could tell he was upset about the situation. He called Elvis and firmly reminded him of his promises. I later heard he backed his reminders with some veiled threats. Elvis was vulnerable to serious charges of statutory rape and even child molestation because he started going with Priscilla in Germany when she was only fourteen, and moved her into Graceland when she was sixteen. Even so, Elvis initially refused to back down. He didn't want to get married. That's unquestioned. It was Colonel Parker who realized that Colonel Beaulieu wasn't bluffing. Parker took control of the situation and arranged the whole wedding."

Looking back, Grant feels he made a mistake.

"I had to do what I did because I had given my word. Had I known the anguish Priscilla would cause Elvis, I never would have made that call."

A large part of that anguish was Priscilla's infidelity. Elvis's admission to Lucy in 1969 that he was aware of it contradicts everything that has been reported up to now. We know from Priscilla's own account in her book that she had an affair with her dance instructor in 1968 after Lisa Marie was born. Later, she became involved with karate champion Mike Stone, which eventually prompted her to leave her husband. The question is whether Elvis knew. Biographer Goldman and his assistants interviewed more than one hundred of Elvis's associates for their book. They concluded that Elvis didn't know and then made an issue about it, saying Elvis's concern for Priscilla was so small that she was able to cheat on him for more than three years and lead a separate life with Stone.

The flaw in that investigation is they must have relied upon the least knowledgeable of Elvis's Memphis Mafia employees, that curious group of men who profess to know all there is to know about Elvis, but actually knew little about the man inside the image.

To the contrary, one of Elvis's closest friends, who asked not to be named because of an ongoing friendship with Priscilla, confirmed that Elvis knew about his wife's infidelity right from the start.

"I asked him if he wanted us to do anything about it—talk to her, take apart the guy, whatever—and he said no. He didn't appear to be concerned. He just said, 'There's a whole wide world out there and Priscilla has to learn about it. If she gets hurt, so be it.' I was pretty shocked at his indifference."

Elvis had become "indifferent" about a lot of things in the late 1960s. One statement during this meeting in which Lucy found little comfort was actually sincere. Elvis was speaking truthfully when he said, "I don't mess with whoever the guys bring over," a reference to the women his gang fetched for him. As self-serving as it sounds, previous biographies have reported and insiders confirm that Elvis often fell asleep without touching the women. As he had with so many other things, Elvis had become bored with meaningless sex.

As mentioned previously, Lucy had never heard "Are You Lonesome Tonight?" and regarded it as a new song when Elvis sang it to her. She quotes Elvis correctly about having recently recorded it. Elvis meant he "rerecorded" it. Some of the confusion is explained by the salesmanship of Colonel Parker and his cohorts at RCA Records. Colonel Parker was astute at wrapping the old in a new package and reselling it. Elvis had rerecorded "Are You Lonesome Tonight?" for a new live album based on his 1968 television special and recorded "Memories" at the same time.

Elvis's demand to see Lucy at this time establishes a new pattern to their relationship. Whenever he faced a crisis, whether professional or personal, he called her. If it was an especially trying one, he insisted on being with her in person. Almost all their meetings from this point on will show Elvis anguished over a major event in his life.

Chapter 17

DESPITE THE PHYSICAL REUNION in Memphis, Elvis's calls were as infrequent as ever. There was never a pattern or reason to them, or if there was, I couldn't detect it. It didn't upset me too much. In fact, I preferred it that way. He was such a mixed blessing. When we were together, he brought the only love, ecstasy, and passion I've ever known. But not without a price—a fear of being exposed, pressure to change my life, personal guilt about Desirée, and religious guilt about our adultery. When he didn't call, I missed him, but there was a sense of relief. When he did call, it shook up my life. Our relationship never had been routine, and it never would be.

He phoned in late July and said he was rehearsing for his live performance the following month. He was going to play the huge new International Hotel in Las Vegas. The choice surprised me because he had flopped in Las Vegas many years before and hated the place. I knew enough not to bring it up. He was still terrified at the thought of performing again, though less so than before. The fear was a fair trade-off to the positive effects. Rehearsals were going well. The comeback was diverting his attention from the things that had troubled him over the past two years. He was in much better spirits and appeared genuinely excited about life. He was working hard, but there was no more bitter talk about the Colonel working him to death. He was enjoying himself again.

He had called a month or so earlier wanting to know about what he should wear onstage. I had never been to Vegas, but I knew a little about the entertainment style there from my work selecting acts for the Cabana Hotel in Dallas. I explained to Elvis that Vegas had a style of its own. The people who went there wanted to be dazzled with glitter and sparkle. They were used to that kind of aesthetic excess from the minute they arrived in the gambling city and would demand even more in the shows. We talked about the kinds of acts that were successful in Vegas. The big-production "follies"-type shows with the women in the scanty clothes and giant headdresses were typical of what worked there. The performers who drew the Vegas crowds were people like Liberace, whose blinding outfits were perfect for his audience. I told Elvis that he should think along those lines, but more masculine and suited to his personal style.

Elvis said he had been watching an English singer who was packing the houses there, Tom Jones, and enjoyed his performances. Jones played before a full orchestra and Elvis decided to do the same despite the Colonel's objections.

"Are you gonna come? You'll like it. You know what you said about going with elaborate costumes. I have a surprise you'll like."

He offered to pay my way and set me up. As usual, my pride wouldn't let me accept, and I didn't want to be discovered. Our brief argument ended with me saying I'd try to make it.

"You're going to be magnificent. Don't worry about a thing," I said. "Remember my premonition?"

"Yeah. I've been thinkin' about that. Baby, you'll never know how that's eased my mind. If you come, call me when you get there. And please, try and come."

I wasn't planning on going, but as the time drew near something compelled me to make the trip. I just wanted to make sure he was okay, to see firsthand that his career was back on track so he could be happy again. It wasn't easy. The new house had taken my last cent. I had to get an advance on my salary from Mr. Blakeley to pay the two-hundred-dollar round-trip airfare. He was happy to give it to me because he thought I wasn't enjoying life enough. My plan was to fly to Vegas, see the show, then fly home that same evening.

I arrived in Las Vegas and was startled to discover that the city looked like a carnival called Elvisland. His name and image were everywhere. Some billboards pictured him twenty times larger than life. Others simply said "Elvis" in giant letters. I shared a limousine to the hotel because it was cheaper than a taxi. The people who rode with me asked if I was planning to see "the show," as if there were only one in town.

"Which one?"

"Elvis, of course," they squealed.

The hotel was Elvisland central. It was plastered with Elvis's image. Your couldn't look anywhere without seeing him. The posters led to a booth where the coveted tickets cost something like fifteen dollars each, a lot of money back then to see a performance. Elvis had always wanted to keep his ticket prices low because he knew his fans weren't the wealthiest people in America, so the steep price puzzled me. When I walked up, there was another shock. "Sorry, we're sold out," the ticket seller said. I flew all this way and now I wasn't going to get into the concert. A ratty-looking man in a cheap suit approached me. He took me aside and started babbling about the concert and how great it was going to be and how a pretty lady like me should have a chance to go. Then he pulled a pair of tickets out of his coat pocket and said he could "take care of my problem."

"How much?"

"For you, only twenty-five dollars."

"All I have is twenty." It was the truth. He furrowed his brow, then said okay.

"How many ya want?"

"Just one." He was surprised. Nobody went anyplace alone in Las Vegas.

I went to change in my private dressing room—the ladies' room —and put on a simple black dress with lace at the neck and hem, and added some pearls for contrast. Elvis watched me the whole time—at least his image did. The bathroom, like the hotel, was covered with Elvis stickers and posters. They didn't miss a spot. When I flipped up the commode lid, there was Elvis smiling at me. The Colonel must be enjoying this as much as his client.

I hunted for a coffee shop to kill the time. Next to pictures of Elvis, the most abundant item in the place were those gambling machines with rolls of fruit in a window. To me they symbolized everything evil and decadent about Las Vegas. I treated them as if they held some contagious disease. In the coffee shop I opened the menu only to see Elvis staring at me again. His image was clipped to it like he was the catch of the day. I lifted him up and scanned the menu looking for a crumpet. It wasn't listed so I asked the waitress. She didn't know what it was. The waitress was friendly and said she would try to come close. A short time later she brought apple pie with fresh whipped cream. After eating, I wandered around the lobby for a while, read some magazines, then decided to try to reach Elvis. I hadn't intended to, but changed my mind, thinking he would be upset if I didn't. I called the hotel operator and she rang his room, or somewhere, and a man curtly answered, "What is it?" I asked to speak to Mr. Presley. The man snickered and said, "Sorry, he won't be speaking to anyone until later."

"Will you wish him luck for me?"

"Who is this?"

"A friend. Desirée."

The conversation made me feel stupid. Of course he wouldn't come to the phone. How many others must have tried? At least he would know I'd been there.

I sat near the back during the show. This wasn't my choice. That's where they seated me. The fast-talking ticket man's "prime" ticket was hardly as advertised. Still, the performance was magnificent. Elvis looked great, dressed all in white in what looked like an embellished karate suit. The crowd went berserk from the moment he walked onstage. Elvis sang a mixture of his old songs—"All Shook Up," "Love Me Tender," "Don't Be Cruel," and "Heartbreak Hotel"—along with his newer ones, "In the Ghetto" and "Suspicious Minds." Then he sang one that pierced my heart: "Are You Lonesome Tonight?"

It was too much. The tears started spilling. We were as separated personally as we were physically in the huge auditorium—Elvis glorious onstage, me hidden in the back. Except for that first year in 1953, hadn't it always been like that? Elvis's fame and my problems standing in the way of our love. I couldn't take it anymore. I rushed out of the room, through the lobby, and out the front entrance, flagged down a cab, and told the driver to take me to the airport.

The trip to Vegas answered my prayers. Elvis was back on top. Instead of joy, though, it filled me with pain. Everything had become clear. He had found me because he was depressed and needed me again. These performances in Vegas would instill in him a new confidence and launch his career into an even higher orbit. He wouldn't need me anymore. My mixed feelings about him had been only a cover-up to rationalize his infrequent calls. I loved him. I needed him. I couldn't have him. Once again, I was alone with my tears.

He called two weeks later, happy and pumped up as I expected. The depression of the past two years was erased.

"You would have liked the show, baby. There were so many people and they still liked me. The place was packed every night. I could feel your presence with me and kept thinkin' about what you said about me coming back bigger than ever. But then, I always feel you with me."

"Didn't you get my message? I saw one of the shows. I tried to call, but someone told me you weren't talking to anyone. That's all right. I loved seeing you, even from afar."

"What? You were here and they didn't tell me? Who was it you spoke to?" he demanded. "I'll kill him."

"I don't know. One of those guys. It doesn't matter, really. I had to get back after the show anyway. I told the man to wish you luck from Desirée."

"Damn them. I'll find out who did this, honey. It won't happen again. I'm sorry. I knew I felt your presence. What did you think of the show?"

"You were sensational. You looked great and sang great. It really made me miss you."

"I miss you, too. But I don't want you around these creeps here. Damn! Did you come alone?"

"Yes, but I left right away. I don't like that place."

"Neither do I. But the Colonel wants me here. I'm gonna go to Europe soon, and I want you with me."

"Really? I can be your interpreter in France."

"That would be great. First, I've got to clear up things here.

Lisa's in the middle. I love her and don't want to lose her."

I reminded him that God would help him with those problems. He said he would call again soon.

Elvis did take care of the problem of not being notified of Lucy's calls. Former Los Angeles supercop John O'Grady, then working as a private detective, later handled the phone lists of people who would and would not be allowed to reach Elvis after the frequent phone number changes. The mysterious single name "Desirée" was on the list. "I always wondered who she was and when she'd turn up," O'Grady said.

THE BIRTHDAY SEASON CAME AND went. Denise's fifteenth in July 1969, Desirée's eleventh and Jacques's eighth in August, Jacqueline's fourth in September. My thirty-third and Deborah's twenty-first in October. Melody started it all in April with her eighteenth. We celebrated Deborah's and my birthdays with an outing at a local park. The children played ball while I sat by a rushing creek watching the water. That evening we gathered around the piano and sang songs. Father Bill Dougherty of St. Paul the Apostle Catholic Church dropped by and he played the piano. He was a Paulist priest who baptized Jacqueline and became a dear friend. We sang "Little Things Mean a Lot," "I Believe," and "Memories." The florist delivered the now-familiar talisman roses with the standard note: "All my love—your secret admirer." The children teased me about it.

"Mother was always getting roses," Deborah, thirty-seven, recalls. "It was so strange and mysterious. We kept wondering who was sending them. We knew it wasn't my stepfather. My sisters and I got together once, after another bunch came, and started asking each other, 'Is Mother involved with someone?' Nobody knew. We never came out and asked her either. If she had something going on, we didn't want to put her on the spot. She's such a private person. She never opened up to us. It was the same with the phone calls. She got phone calls all the time, day and night, sometimes very late at night. We had no idea who was calling her."

THE MORNING AFTER CHRISTMAS, I carried the trash to the metal can outside. Opening the lid, I saw twelve fresh talisman roses lying on the bottom. It was apparent that Jack had had enough of my secret admirer. My feelings for this distant admirer were also beginning to strain. He hadn't called in months. His career had rocketed back to the top with unprecedented speed. He performed in Vegas again in February 1970, and introduced his trademark glittering white jumpsuits. He followed up his doubly certified Vegas comeback by touring the country giving concerts. He created a sensation everywhere he went and even managed to fill the huge Houston Astrodome for a series of concerts. I felt lonely, left out, and unimportant.

Time passed. I threw myself into my work, CCD classes, and my lifetime campaign of instilling in my children a taste for the creative arts and music to go along with a strong faith in God. They were growing and progressing so fast. Debbie earned a scholarship to study language and music at the Sorbonne in France. Unfortunately, she contracted a heart infection known as pericarditis and had to turn it down. She recovered in time to accept a merit scholarship to the University of Dallas. Melody was becoming more proficient at art and poetry, and was the only one of my children who sang publicly with me. Denise was studying psychology. Desirée was growing tall and continued to excel at the arts. She and Jacqueline were studying ballet and music through a gifted-students program offered by Southern Methodist University.

Desirée, of course, continued to haunt me. She was developing into a woman, and had a full mane of beautiful black hair. Never once did I look at her face without thinking of her father. What would he say if he knew? Would he hate me for not telling him? Now that he had Lisa, would it matter?

Desirée was still a serious and solemn child. She became attached to Father Bud Powers, another priest at St. Paul the Apostle, where she attended school. He spent hours with her. He sensed an inexplicable loneliness in her, as if something was missing. I'd see them together, walking, talking, always close. He was the father she never had.

Elvis called in September. He said he tried to call me many times but never got through. He left messages from a "John Jones" that I never received. It wasn't hard to figure out why: flowers in the trash, no messages from him. My relationship with Elvis had reverted to the dismal triangle of the past. I felt guilty for having doubted him.

"I thought you had run away again," he said.

"I'm sorry. Things are just bad here."

"Come to Memphis. I need to see you."

I tried to beg off, telling him he didn't need me now that he was back on top. He countered by saying that he needed me more than ever. That was the right answer. I flew to Memphis the next day and took a cab to the Admiral Benbow Inn, a hotel near the city. I felt that wonderful nervousness again, brushing my hair, checking the mirror for telltale wrinkles, and waiting for the familiar knock. When it came, Elvis was dressed more casually than ever before, sporting a dark blue jogging suit, a floppy beige golf hat pulled low over his eyes, and another phony mustache. He wore that for sentimental reasons. I burst out laughing. That set the tone for the whole evening. Laughter and loving.

"I've recorded another song for you," he said. " 'Snowbird.' "

"I love it!"

"That's you. My little snowbird."

He was so different than before. The concerts had renewed his confidence and brightened his outlook. He presented me with a yellow porcelain rose. Finally, one that couldn't wilt!

"I want you to place it on your dresser to forever remind you of my love," he said, giving the mandatory speech.

We had a great time enjoying each other without any outside problems intruding on the moment. We even danced together for the first time. The song "Mona Lisa" came over the hotel radio, and we waltzed around the room. When I left later that evening, there was little sorrow in the parting. It was as if the dark cloud hanging over him had passed. His happiness made me happy. He spoke again of making our relationship permanent, and for the first time in more than a decade, I began thinking it was possible. Our haphazard affair continued to work its magic. Prior to this meeting, I had been slowly sinking into my own depression. His rejuvenation energized his body, and in turn, the energy poured through mine.

The next month, on my thirty-fourth birthday, he sent a dozen roses with a new inscription on the card: "You're My Snowbird."

In late November I became deathly ill and began hemorrhaging. I knew instantly what was wrong. I was pregnant and was in danger of having a miscarriage. The pain was so intense that Denise had to drive me to the hospital. Aside from the pain, the implications of the pregnancy were churning through my mind. It was Elvis's child. My husband and I hadn't been intimate in a very long time. If the baby was saved, I would be forced to change my life, a change that would throw my family into turmoil.

As I rode to the hospital, I decided it was in God's hands. If I remained pregnant, this time I would tell Elvis, not only about the baby but about Desirée as well. I couldn't help feeling that Elvis may have wanted me to get pregnant. He was always so careful about taking precautions, but the last time in Memphis, just as in 1957, we let it slip. Maybe he wanted to force me to go to him, and this was his way. As Denise pulled up to the emergency room, my maternal instincts took over. Despite the problems it would present, I began hoping that the baby would survive. It would be wonderful to give Elvis a son.

At the hospital the pain increased and made it impossible to think about anything. I fought the best I could but I lost the baby. I was so sick afterward there was no immediate depression. It didn't hit me until a few days later. I had left it to God, and a decision had been made. There would be no pregnancy to force me out of my marriage and to Elvis, or at least into suddenly presenting Elvis with what would have been a difficult decision for him to make. Instead, I would return to my unhappy life and my secrets. The sadness of losing the child was tempered by my belief that it just wasn't meant to be, and by a strange sort of confirmation that I had been right all along in my decision not to tell him about Desirée.

In 1970 twelve-year-old Desirée was maturing in more ways than in body. She was old enough to recognize that there was something out of kilter regarding her status in the family.

"When I was twelve, my mother and Jack had their anniversary. I remember hearing they had only been married for ten years. I knew Mother had been married before, but according to my sisters, that marriage ended long before I was born. The numbers didn't add up. I couldn't figure out how I was twelve and they had been married for only ten years. So I made my own assumption that I must be adopted.

"I began to really believe it. For one, I didn't look like any of my sisters, or Jack, for that matter. Then one day a friend of Mother's was over and told me that I looked just like my mother. I was so thrilled because I adored Mother. I remember wishing I could be as beautiful as she. After that, I began to doubt whether I really was adopted. And if I wasn't, then who was my father? I built up my courage and asked Mother, not if I was adopted, but why she had been married only ten years. She told me that Jack was not my real father and that she couldn't tell me who my real father was until I was older. But someday I would know. She said she had never loved anyone more than my father and that they were not married legally, but they were 'married in the eyes of God.' I guess I was just so happy that Mother was my real mother that nothing else mattered to me, so I didn't ask any more questions. I felt special because I was close to Mother. I knew she was unhappy about the circumstances of my father, so I didn't bring the subject up again for four or five years."

Melody adds, "Desirée asked me several times who her father was during this period. I didn't know. I told her to ask Mother, even though I knew that wouldn't help. We all knew that we were never to talk about Desirée's father. It was an unspoken law in the house and we abided by it. The main thing going through Desirée's mind was that she was adopted, and that mortified her. She idolized Mother in every way. She wanted to grow up and look like her, act like her, be her. When she found out that Mother was her real mother, that was the biggest relief of her life. That was her main concern."

I WAS HOME ALONE ABOUT A WEEK before Christmas, taking a few days off from work to recover from a cold, when the phone rang.

"How are you, baby?"

Bad, but he didn't need to know that. He said he was lonely and had to force himself not to call me because he knew I didn't want to talk to him. That didn't make any sense until he mentioned calling and leaving messages but never hearing from me. I explained that the messages weren't getting through. He was down again. His mood swings were becoming severe.

"Honey, I'm leaving here. I can't take it anymore. I want you to meet me in Washington. Please don't say no. I need to talk to you again."

Why was he going to Washington? I couldn't meet him there if he was going to be with his entourage. He said he was going alone. That was hard to believe. He didn't go anywhere alone. He kept insisting he was going on his own.

"I'm not a child," he said. "I'm sick of all these people around me. Listen, baby, I need to talk to you. Please come."

"I really can't afford it," I said, still doubting whether he would be alone.

"I'm so sick of this mess, Lucy. You can afford it. You are my love and I have money. What I have is yours and you don't want anythin'. What is this? Just go to the ticket counter and everything will be arranged. I'll be at the Washington Hotel registered under Colonel Burrows."

"When?"

"Now, baby. I'm goin' now and I want you there when I arrive. I need you. Please."

He was agitated and insistent. I had no choice but to go.

Colonel Burrows, the name Elvis used at the Hotel Washington, was a variation of the name Colonel Parker used when he didn't want to be recognized.

Released from the shackles of the lobotomizing movie soundtracks, Elvis began to record in earnest again. The breakthrough song was "In the Ghetto," written by Mac Davis. It reached number three on May 3, 1969, and brought Elvis's seductive voice to a whole new generation of record buyers. (His last Top Ten hit had been "Crying in the Chapel" in 1965.) That August, "Suspicious Minds," the showstopper of his renewed live performances, gave Elvis his first number-one song since "Good Luck Charm" in 1962. He followed that with "Don't Cry Daddy," "Rubber-neckin'," "Kentucky Rain," and "The Wonder of You," all big hits. In the midst of this chart comeback, Elvis continued to earn universal critical praise and outright fan hysteria with his Las Vegas revival. His decision to take the Vegas show on the road completed the climb. In one short year Elvis went from being a has-been to having one of the biggest years of his illustrious career.

Still, it merely acted as a temporary diversion to the increasing darkness in his life.

Chapter 18

I TOLD EVERYONE AT HOME THAT
there was a business emergency that needed my attention but
didn't mention it was out of town. I took only a briefcase and the
clothes on my back—a calf-length black skirt, a blue blouse, black
French boots with leather laces, and a black cape. When we
landed, I took a cab to the Hotel Washington. The hotel was a
dull stone building, not Elvis's style. He liked things bright, shiny,
and new. He chose it because of the name. He was in Washington;
it was the Hotel Washington. The simplicity of his thoughts was
so endearing.

Picking up the hotel phone, I asked for Mr. Burrows. He was
in. This was a switch. For once, I was on the outside tapping on
the door. He smiled and we hugged from opposite directions than
usual.

"Oh, baby," he said. "I'm alive again."

He was dressed wildly in a purple suit with a reversible purple
and black cape. That was set off by a belt with a huge gold buckle,
and a gold medallion dangling from his neck. He carried a cane
that appeared to be embedded with precious stones. He looked
like Napoleon. He noticed my stare and twirled around to give me
a full view.

"What do you think?"

"You look wonderful."

"Are you gonna take it all off me?"

"Are you going to take mine off?" I teased back.

The outfit actually disturbed me somewhat. It was as if Elvis
didn't know where his real life began and the show ended. Despite
the vibrant clothes, he looked tired. His hair was long and hanging
in his face. His eyes were tender but a bit glassy. There was a pistol

on the table, but that was one touch that didn't concern me. I was from Louisiana and Texas and had been around guns all my life, including the small one I sometimes carried in my purse. He liked guns and that was fine with me.

I touched his face to feel his skin on my palm, then ran my hand through his black hair. He caught my hand, brought it to his mouth and kissed it, then kissed me frantically, as though the moment might be taken from us.

"My Desirée, say somethin' to me."

"I love you so much," I said. "I never thought I'd see you again. What's wrong, mon amour?"

"I can't take this anymore. Even Daddy turned on me because I spent too much money on guns and stuff. I can't believe Daddy, sidin' with Priscilla and the Colonel. Man, they're all using me."

According to published reports (*Elvis: The Final Years* by Jerry Hopkins, and *Elvis,* by Albert Goldman, among others), the argument started when two bills rolled into Graceland. One, from a ritzy gun shop in Los Angeles, totaled either $19,792 (Goldman) or $38,000 (Hopkins). The second, from a Mercedes dealership, weighed in at $85,000. Vernon and Priscilla were said to have been alarmed by this spree and ganged up on Elvis. In her book, *Elvis and Me,* Priscilla says the argument was between Elvis and his father and was about Colonel Parker. She gives no indication whether she participated or not.

Lucy's version of the argument that preceded Elvis's trip to Washington coincides with that offered by many of Elvis's associates, including the chauffeur, Gerald Peters, who met Elvis in Los Angeles later that evening.

Priscilla wrote that her marriage was severely strained at this time and blamed Elvis for spending so much time away from home. "To me he became increasingly unreachable," she wrote.

H IS RAGE WAS BUILDING. I TRIED MY best to calm him.

"You're letting anger take over. You know your father loves you, no matter what. Maybe he's also angry about your wife."

"I don't care what she does, I just want her out. She'll try to take Lisa, I know."

"Elvis, you must never replace love with hate. Try not to hate her. What about your friends, Larry and Charlie? You said they could be trusted. Talk to them. They'll help. And you have me. I'm your friend."

"You're my only friend," he said bitterly. "You're the only one who would never turn on me because you're the only one who doesn't care about money. Money is the cause of all these problems. And there are so many burdens. The kids that belong to Daddy's wife, Dee, they're a handful. They're all over Momma's house. Daddy shouldn't have done that. Not to Momma. He shouldn't have brought that woman there. I held it in, Lucy, but man, you can't know how that hurt me. I've got to straighten it out. Daddy's got to decide which side he's on."

He turned and embraced me.

"That's why I've kept you out of reach. It's like putting something you love away from everything so its beauty won't be tarnished. I want to be with you more, and them less. I want my life to change. You told me once you had a dream of running and not knowing where you were going. That's me, only it's real. I work and work and never finish. I don't have any destination.

"Do you know what I want?" he said, looking deep into my eyes. "I want what we had once, each other. Love. Remember when we had so many plans? What happened to our dreams?"

The question stung. What happened was that my life was a mess and I ran away.

"El, our love is real. That won't change. But no one connected with you would ever have let it survive. Look at us, hiding, being lonely. If they knew you were here with me, they'd probably destroy me."

"We'll change it one day," he said. "I want to clean house and start a production company. I want you to be involved in it. You can help me gain control of my life. I also want to write my life story. I want to show everyone how big a part of it you are."

We lay down on the bed together, holding hands and enjoying being close. Instead of being warmed, I began feeling old and insecure.

"Mon chéri, why do you keep coming back to me when you have all the beautiful women in the world? Look at me. Tell me."

He touched my face and looked at me so lovingly.

"I love you because you're you. Every woman I've ever been attracted to was a version of you. Only they were all missing something. None of them could match you. Until you and I can come together, I'll wait. And now, let me show you what I mean."

Our capes dropped to the floor, along with everything else . . .

"Why are you getting dressed?" he asked later.

"I have to catch the late flight back to Dallas tonight. I'm sorry."

"Tonight! You have to go back tonight? You can't."

"I have to. I'm sorry."

"Can't you stay? I need you to stay."

"I can't. Really."

"You're always leavin'."

"Someday, El, I'll never have to leave."

"I'd like that. You'll never know how much I'd love that. Home will be with me.

"In the meantime," he continued, "there are some more songs I recorded for you. I want you to listen to them. They're 'The Wonder of You,' 'You Don't Have to Say You Love Me,' and 'I Just Can't Help Believin'.'"

I caressed his hand and promised to listen to the songs. As I did, I noticed that his hands were bluish and swollen.

"They've been like that a lot lately," he said. "I don't know what it is. I have some strange pains in my hands and stomach. I haven't been feeling well."

"Will you please go see a doctor when you get back? That should be taken care of. I'm so worried about you. Do you feel well now?"

"I'm okay. I have doctors around all the time. I'm going to leave here, too. I don't want to be here without you."

"Where are you going?"

"First, let me tell you why I'm here. You know all the work you do with the government? Well, I want to do that, too. I want to work with the narcotics bureau—become an undercover agent like my friend, John O'Grady in Los Angeles."

He caught me looking at him suspiciously. I was always wary of his so-called friends. Everyone wanted to use him.

"He's really my friend. A real friend. Not like the others. He really is."

If that was true, a friend would be welcome. Sometimes it seemed that he had no friends. But even so, what he wanted to do was crazy.

"Elvis, you're a singer, not a policeman. You have to be specially trained for that kind of work. Besides, it's very dangerous."

"I want to do something else with my life. I want to be useful. I need a purpose. I'm gonna fly to Los Angeles and straighten some things out first. I don't feel too well now. But then I'm coming back here to volunteer."

"Are you sure you'll be all right?"

"Yeah. But I want you to keep carin' about me, baby. I need it," he said, smiling that same impish grin. He came over and hugged me tenderly.

Just before I left, he handed me a manila envelope and told me not to open it until I got home. It was my Christmas present. Later that night, at home in Dallas, I opened it and found nearly $7,000 in cash. My pride reared up for a minute and I almost sent it back. Then I thought of Desirée and decided to use it for her. I bought her a beautiful handmade, navy blue Swiss coat from Neiman Marcus. It cost $167, and for once, I splurged. Elvis would have wanted that. I used the rest of the money for Desirée's schooling, ballet, and piano lessons.

A few days later there was a picture in the paper of Elvis with President Nixon. The story mentioned that Elvis was going to support the president's war on drugs. He must have gotten his cherished agent's badge.

Elvis's trip to Washington, Los Angeles, and back to Washington has baffled biographers for nearly two decades. The first trip, when he traveled alone, is the one that has given writers the most headaches because, unaware of Lucy, they found no explanation for it. That left them with nothing to do but speculate, attributing it to everything from Elvis's "James Bond–ish" nature, to drugs or illness rattling his brain. Actually, his motivation was the oldest and simplest in the world: He wanted to be with the woman he loved.

The biographers got back on track in explaining why he picked

Washington and why he returned a few days later. Elvis was a police buff who collected badges from police departments around the country. His return to Washington was motivated by his desire to get an "agent at large" credential from the Department of Justice's Bureau of Narcotics and Dangerous Drugs. He learned about it through John O'Grady, a Los Angeles supercop turned private detective who Elvis hired to investigate a paternity suit in 1970. O'Grady, known as the "Big O," was formerly the sergeant-in-charge of the Los Angeles police department's narcotics squad and was responsible for 2,500 busts. He is also an accomplished storyteller, as attested to by his book, *O'Grady*. Elvis was fascinated by O'Grady's riveting stories of the danger and intrigue of the undercover life, and the two men became friends.

When Elvis arrived in Los Angeles later that night he was dead broke, having given Lucy every cent he had. He rounded up a former Memphis Mafia member, Jerry Schilling, saw a doctor, then flew back to Washington a day or so later to continue his quest for a badge. On the flight back Elvis befriended a soldier and ended up cleaning out his wallet again, giving the man the five hundred dollars he had acquired in Los Angeles. Also during the flight, he wrote a letter to President Nixon offering his help in the fight against drugs. Elvis went to the Bureau of Narcotics and Dangerous Drugs and met with deputy director John Finlator. Finlator denied his request for the badge. Elvis had better luck with Nixon. The President agreed to meet the King that same day, and when Elvis mentioned the badge, Nixon made a call. With a presidential recommendation, Elvis was dubbed an undercover agent.

The final irony is that the one person most hated by the bulk of rock 'n' roll fans of the late 1960s and early 1970s was the creature Elvis Presley aspired to be—an undercover narc. And Elvis himself was a heavy drug user, although he obtained his "legal" drugs through subservient doctors.

Instead of lost love, Elvis's new songs spoke of a woman who was always there when he needed her. "The Wonder of You" was released as a single in May 1970 and appears on numerous albums. "You Don't Have to Say You Love Me" was released as a single in October 1970 and also appears on numerous live and studio albums, including *Elvis: That's the Way It Is.* "I Just Can't Help Believin'" is also on *Elvis: That's The Way It Is,* which was released in December 1970.

L IFE WAS FILLED WITH WORK AND responsibilities. That Christmas my youngest children surprised me with a beautiful set of Norman Rockwell collectors' plates that showed the four seasons of the year. The children had used the money they made selling brownies to buy them. It was a lovely gift and touched my heart. They were such wonderful children. They tried so hard to give me enough love to fill the emptiness in my heart.

The year passed quickly. Elvis called periodically, but he was busy touring and playing Las Vegas. I resigned myself to enjoying what moments we had and enduring the separation. On Christmas he sent a single talisman rose. The card was similar to the previous year's. It said, "You're My Snowbird. All My Love, Your Secret Admirer." After that I had a horrible feeling that Elvis was sick, a feeling so ominous I decided to call his father for the first time. Elvis had given me his number. Mr. Presley was friendly and receptive. I explained that I was a friend and that Elvis had said it would be okay to call. He talked openly and said Elvis was working too hard and that Lisa was living with Priscilla away from Graceland, which made him upset. We spoke briefly and he told me to call him whenever I wanted.

Elvis didn't call for a few months, until February 1972. He was agitated again and spoke of things happening that were out of his control and all the pressure on him. The problems with Priscilla were continuing, and now he was having problems with the guys. Then he said something that he used to tell me a long time ago.

"Don't believe anything you hear or read unless you hear it from me."

That's what he used to tell me when there were published reports about his girlfriends. That usually meant trouble.

"Are you well? What's the matter, El? What's upsetting you?"

"I'm all right. But Priscilla is accusing me of womanizing so she can feel better about her sins."

There seemed to be something else wrong, but I couldn't put my finger on it. The newspapers and magazines were soon full of sensational stories about Elvis and Priscilla splitting up. She ran off with a karate instructor. Not long after that, the magazines were writing about and showing pictures of Elvis and his new girlfriend, a tall, attractive beauty queen named Linda Thompson. I felt like someone had ripped my heart out and crushed it.

What a fool I had been to think he loved me. The minute Priscilla was gone, he wasted no time bringing in a replacement. My pain turned to anger, then back to pain. It was so deep I was physically sick. Shortly afterward, I had chest pains and collapsed. I called my friend, Marty Harnden, and she rushed me to the emergency room of Presbyterian Hospital. The doctor was Henry Mobley, a noted cardiologist. He ran every test he could but couldn't find anything wrong. I wondered if it was truly possible to die of a broken heart.

When I returned home a few days later, there were messages that Mr. Jones had called. I was in no mood to accept them or to call him back. What good would it do? The stories weren't fabrications. This beauty queen was his official girlfriend. What could he say? At Christmas I received a dozen roses. The card said, "Always On My Mind. Love, El Lancelot."

Sure.

There are varying reports as to when Priscilla began her relationship with Mike Stone. In Albert Goldman's *Elvis* the chapter on the affair is attributed to interviews with Stone. The book itself is based largely on the recollections of longtime Elvis sidekick Lamar Fike and other members of Elvis's Memphis Mafia. In this account, the affair is said to have started in 1968, and includes the observation: "Priscilla concealed her affair for three and a half years (before revealing it in 1972). The great length of this subterfuge tells a lot about the Presley marriage. Clearly, the marriage entailed so little intimacy or even cohabitation that Priscilla was at liberty to make what was in effect a second marriage . . ." (As noted previously, Elvis actually knew about it from the beginning, along with the prior affair with her dance instructor.)

My own interviews with friends and associates of both Elvis and Priscilla place the beginning of the Stone affair anywhere from 1968 to 1970. In her book Priscilla says she met Stone in 1972, shortly before she left Elvis.

Chapter 19

Elvis's love life continued to make news. There were stories about his upcoming divorce, and more stories about Linda Thompson. There were also reports of shows canceled due to his poor health. What was wrong? My anger became concern. He must be more anguished than ever. Had I contributed to it? I gave up on him because of some stories, never giving him a chance to explain. And who was I to object to his having a girlfriend? He asked me to be with him so many times, and I always put it off. He needed someone, especially now that he was alone. Was he lost, alone, and hurting?

"Don't believe anything you hear unless you talk to me first." The words came back like thunder. He needed me to believe in him, not shun him. Hadn't we shared the most intimate feelings? If anything, I could still be a friend. Friends seemed to be in short supply for him. Wasn't a big part of love based on understanding and trust?

I called Graceland but he wasn't home. I left a message for him to call "Desirée." He called two days later.

"Baby, I've been through some wars," he said, sounding tired and depressed. "I've been sick."

"What's wrong? I've heard so much."

"I guess you have heard a lot," he said. "I tried to call you and see you. You really don't care anymore, do you?" He sounded pained.

"I'll always care. The question is whether you care. I've heard you have a woman with you. What am I to think? You want glamour girls."

"Honey, there's so much wrong. I have someone with me, but

it's only to have a woman around. I wanted to show you, to hurt you because you didn't care."

"I care enough to want you to be happy. Do you love her?"

"You know where my heart is. Damn it. I can't take this. Everyone tries to pacify me. They don't know what I want. Do you miss me? Tell me you do, baby."

"It doesn't matter what you do, El, I'll always love you. You don't have to love me back. I don't blame you. Life is strange. People grow apart. Other people influence them. I've kept our relationship pure in my heart, so pure no one can take it from me. Right now I'm more concerned about your health. I'm so worried about you. Are you still taking medications for pain?"

He was silent. Then I heard what sounded like a sob. I wanted so much to be near him, to hold him.

"Oh God, I need you. Nothin's goin' right anymore. You don't realize how much I need you. I've done everything with you in mind. Every woman that wanted to be around, she had to pass the test. The test was how she compared to you. The ones that had similar qualities, I kept, but at arm's length. I don't know . . . I can't stand all the pressure. I can't sleep anymore. I don't feel too well. But I'll be all right when this is over. I feel better just hearin' your voice.

"I'm performing constantly," he said, sounding exhausted. "You know the Colonel. He causes so much of this. I'd like to see you again, soon."

"I don't want to interfere in your life."

"Stop it!" he shouted. "You know what this is. There's always someone around. I have to have someone here to keep them from bringing me women. They're always pushing women so they can play. I don't want this kind of life. I never did. You know what I wanted. It could have started off differently right from the start. When we first met."

"I understand your wanting someone else. I'm not as young and pretty as I used to be. But if those around you are really forcing you to do things you don't want, why do you tolerate it? They're not your friends. I know you want to help everyone. But don't let them hurt you."

"I know, honey. I know. God is guiding me now. Larry is back."

"I thought he was always there."

"No. There've been changes. I don't want you to change, Desirée."

Whenever he used that name, it was like a hot iron touching my skin. Desirée was fourteen and had grown into a tall, beautiful young lady with long legs and lovely black hair. Should I tell him? Would it help? Had I waited too long? He already had a daughter.

"How's Lisa?"

"She's fine but confused. I want to leave all this behind and make a life for her, and eventually us. If I thought you wouldn't be at the end of this journey, I couldn't hold up."

He sounded so lonely and sad. Why did he always come back to me? It was so hard to believe.

"El, the most important thing is your health and happiness. I'll always care. That will never go away. God gives us burdens to strengthen us. My burden is missing you. I miss you more than words can express."

We were both silent. There wasn't much to say. Our love amounted to a few telephone conversations, and that would never be satisfying. It couldn't survive that way. I changed the subject.

"Are you recording anything interesting?"

"God, I want you with me," he said, ignoring my question.

"I'm always with you in spirit, El. No one can take that away. Now tell me about your best new songs so I can buy them."

"I recorded some of the songs you sang for those diplomats. 'Until It's Time for You to Go,' 'The First Time Ever I Saw Your Face,' and 'The Impossible Dream.' "

"Are you serious? I love those songs."

"I can't believe you didn't run out and buy them already. You're supposed to like everything I sing," he said, lightening up.

"I do. I'm just more concerned about what's happening to you. There's so much I need to tell you. Something I have to tell you. It's so important. You will be happy about it, I'm sure. I can't talk on the phone about it."

"What is it? Tell me now," he demanded.

"This is too special. I have to tell you in person, not over the phone." Why did I blurt that out? If I was going to tell him about Desirée, it couldn't be this way. I struggled to change the subject again.

"I heard you gave that big concert in Hawaii you were telling me about. How did it go?"

"Okay, I guess. I felt kinda sick, though. I almost passed out right in the middle of it. It's gonna play on television here sometime soon. Will you watch it?"

"When?"

"I don't know. Soon. I'll call you in a few days when I find out. I'm gonna be home for a while."

"El, is this Linda with you?" I really had no right to ask. Here I was, still living in the same house with my husband, even though things had been tense between us for nearly a decade. Still, I had to know.

"Lucy, please. She's just around. She watches me. I promise I'll get this settled. I love you."

"What does that mean, 'just around,' and 'she watches you'?"

"You don't understand. She's like a nurse."

"She doesn't look like a nurse to me. If you need a nurse, hire a real one. I don't understand you sometimes. You can't expect me to."

"You must!" he said, suddenly becoming frantic. "You gotta, baby. You're the only one who ever did, you and Momma. Don't desert me now. Please."

"I'll try. But it's hard."

I wish I could have gone to Graceland and thrown them all out, the guys, the women, everyone. Something was happening to Elvis, and it didn't appear that anyone cared. I drove out to the country and went for a long walk. I prayed God would keep watch over him and never leave his side for a moment. Weeks passed. I worried. He called again in February. He was talking fast, in spurts, and was more upset than before.

"Where are you?" I asked.

"Vegas. I had a dream. An awful dream. I was in court, on trial. Everybody was against me. The Colonel. Priscilla. The guys. They were all testifyin' against me. Man, I've been so stupid. I didn't want to believe it. All this stuff. Priscilla's not only taken Lisa, she's turning her into a hippie with this guy she's been sleepin' with. Lisa's just a baby. You don't know how this hurts me. And the guys, I've lost my patience with them. They've lost all their self-confidence. They're afraid of me. They think I lose my temper. The Colonel doesn't care whether I live or die anymore."

He was so frantic he was lapsing deeper into his old Mississippi accent. I'd never heard him this manic before. It was like he was lost, completely lost.

"What do you mean? Are you sick?"

"My body's dyin', baby. I can't go on. I hafta take pills to keep goin', to keep performin'. The pain never leaves. My stomach hurts. My head hurts. I can't sleep. I wish we could go off together and leave all this behind."

"Have you seen a doctor?"

"They give me somethin' to feel better, but I still hurt. I can't stop. The Colonel made all these deals. There's no time for me. I'm fightin' and it's a war. There's so much happenin'. I can't slow down."

"Elvis, honey, calm down a minute. Let's think rationally. You can't let this slip by any longer. Your life is at stake. Please don't let them do this to you. I'll take care of you. We can go to the Mayo Clinic. I'll go with you. Or anywhere you want. Do me this one favor. You're all that's important."

"Baby, I know you care, but let me handle it," he said, calming down. "I'll see you very soon. I don't want anyone dragging you into this mess."

It was so unthinkable that Elvis could be addicted to drugs. He didn't drink or smoke as far as I knew. It was so out of character. Anyone who knew Elvis when he was coming up—the driven, energetic boy determined to make it—would never have guessed he would let anything beat him, especially drugs. He hated drugs. It was horrible even to consider the possibility. He had so much compassion and love. How did it start? I didn't know what to do. How could I help him without exposing our relationship? If I tried to interfere, would he hate me for betraying his trust? If he was forced to go to a rehabilitation clinic, word would leak out eventually and the scandal would devastate him. Other stars could have problems. The public would accept it. Elvis believed he had to be infallible. He was trapped by his fame. I worried about him constantly.

His "Aloha from Hawaii" concert appeared on television in April. Everyone remarked at how wonderful he looked and performed. Everyone but me. The white suit, the hair, the sideburns, the voice, all were dazzling. The image looked fine. The man didn't. He was sluggish throughout the performance and his eyes were glazed. When he talked, he mumbled halfheartedly. That wasn't Elvis, not the teasing, snarling, wide-eyed lightning rod on *The Ed Sullivan Show* sixteen years before. After seeing that, I really began to worry. Then came reports that he had to cancel his Lake Tahoe appearances after a few shows because he was sick. He called a few days later and sounded bad. I asked him about his schedule, where he would be next, and he seemed mystified.

"It's crazy, as usual. I don't know. Why?"

"I'm going to Los Angeles on business and I'd like to see you."

"That would be nice. Just tell me when."

I worried about all those men around him. Could he get away? "Can you be alone for a couple of hours?" I asked.

"Why just a couple of hours? You're becoming distant again."

He knew why I was distant. Linda.

"I'm sure you're quite busy."

"Stop it, Lucy. You know I want to see you. Why are you acting this way?"

"I'll be there in a week or so," I said, trying to sound aloof.

"Would you stop it? This isn't you. Why are you actin' this way?"

"I didn't choose another over you. My situation is a bit different. I'll get out of this marriage. But this woman? You didn't wait a week. Why?"

"Don't do this to me. It's not what you think. I'll explain."

He was right. My jealousy wasn't important at this point. If he was sick and in trouble, then I had to swallow my pride and go to him. Maybe it wasn't just a line. Maybe she was a nurse. He didn't appear to be in control of himself, much less those around him. Could they be using his weakened state to take over?

"El, is it possible to see you alone? I mean, no men waiting at the door or in the lobby. No one driving you there or even knowing where you went. Is that possible? I'm beginning to think it's not."

"Of course. I do what I want. I'll send you a ticket."

"No, I can come on my own." It wasn't my pride so much anymore as my worries that he was being monitored. I didn't want my name or address showing up on credit card bills. I didn't even want him phoning me from his homes anymore. It's hard to explain, but I had a strong feeling that his every move was being watched.

"You know, baby, this is supposed to be the life I dreamed about. Remember way back. I'd have killed for this. Now look what it's brought me. Everyone meddling in my life. Givin' the same performance over and over. Is this it? Is this what I fought so hard for?"

"No, you're just feeling a little down, mon amour. Don't worry. Desirée is coming back. She'll make things better."

"Baby, that's all I ever wanted. My Desirée with me."

It was hard to be angry at him, and hard not to. Then I remembered a poem I'd read somewhere, "The Meaning of Love," written by a priest in the 1600s.

> True love is when you remove yourself from the throne
> And another's needs become more important than your
> own.
> Love is giving with no expectation of receiving
> And trusting with no reason for believing.

Elvis's life at this time was a blur of contrasts. On January 14, 1973, he appeared live, via satellite hookup, before a billion people around the world in his "Aloha from Hawaii" concert. To this day, it's remembered as a glorious performance. Looking at the videotape, one finds that Elvis was actually just as Lucy remembers—sluggish, with deadened eyes. Video clips of his press conference in Hawaii prior to the concert show him struggling to remain coherent. The following month he nearly died of a Dilaudid overdose in Las Vegas. Three months later, in May, the powerful prescribed "medications" he had become dependent upon forced him to cancel the last four days of his two-week stint. His weight also fluctuated from his normal 175 pounds to well over 200.

After these close calls Vernon Presley contacted Elvis's attorney, Ed Hookstratten, and asked if anything could be done. Hookstratten hired John O'Grady and another private detective,

Jack Kelly, to find out what doctors were supplying the drugs.
The detectives positively identified three doctors and one dentist.
When the detectives confronted the men, instead of backing
down, the practitioners defended their treatments as medically
sound.

O'Grady and Kelly turned over the results of their investigation
to narcotics bureaus of both the state of California and the federal
government. No action was ever taken against the doctors.
O'Grady has no animosity toward either drug enforcement agency
because he says the report they filed did not mention Elvis. "We
tried to protect him. The feds never had his name. It's very
difficult to turn in a report like that and not tell the police
everything. I think they thought we were being devious and had
an ulterior motive. That had to hamper their investigation."

Even if they had been successful in cutting this supply line, it
probably wouldn't have made a difference. Some reports say that
Elvis had nearly a dozen doctors and dentists supplying him with
controlled drugs. His main doctor, George Nichopoulos of Memphis, was not even part of O'Grady's investigation because Vernon
Presley assured the doubting detectives that "Dr. Nick" was
okay. (Nichopoulos later became the subject of an intensive investigation into Elvis's drug habits by Geraldo Rivera of ABC Television's *20/20*. That led to an inquest by the Tennessee Medical
Board. Nichopoulos was cleared of most of the charges, but was
reprimanded and suspended from practicing for three months. In
May 1980 he was indicted by the Shelby County Grand Jury on
fourteen counts of illegally prescribing drugs. Dr. Nichopoulos
was tried by a jury and found not guilty on all counts.)

There are many theories to explain what drove Elvis to his
depression, paranoia, and dependence on drugs. One of the most
convincing comes from Dave Marsh, a former *Rolling Stone* reporter. In Marsh's 1982 book, *Elvis* (a more sympathetic por-
trayal than Albert Goldman's harsh treatment in his *Elvis*), Marsh
concludes:

> The fact is, Elvis was bored and lonely. The loneliness
> was unavoidable—he'd lived with it for twenty years—but
> the boredom was unbearable: He couldn't stand it for
> twenty minutes. Neither the Memphis Mafia nor legions of
> women, buckets of pills, realms of land and fleets of cars
> could relieve him of it. Once Elvis knew for certain how
> passionately he was loved, and by how many, he had no
> goals left. He had shown 'em, but in the process he'd
> trapped himself. Now he was sealed off from any other
> avenues of growth.

Sonny West, one of Elvis's longtime bodyguards, offered a similar opinion in a newspaper interview.

"He's a very lonely person. He's a very unhappy person. I've been around him since he was an unpopular high school kid with acne who couldn't make the football team. After all that he's become, that kid is still inside him. He's Elvis Presley, but he's a lonely little kid."

While Elvis's health deteriorated, his workload escalated. In 1972 he gave 162 performances in 32 cities. In 1973 he gave 168 performances in 20 cities.

Chapter 20

I TOOK A TAXI FROM THE LOS ANGELES airport to the Beverly Wilshire Hotel where my room was waiting. I was Lucy Jones again. Elvis wanted everything to be as it had in the past. I knew the reservation was part of this. Lucy Jones. The name welcomed me like an old friend.

As usual, I had hardly put down my bags when the phone rang. Elvis sounded better and insisted he was okay. I hurried to freshen up, knowing he would appear within minutes of his call. I agonized over my appearance. I didn't feel pretty anymore. A woman has to be told she's pretty to feel beautiful because beauty comes from the heart. But there was hope. The moment I saw him I'd bloom. *"Une femme d'en amour est une belle femme"*—A woman in love is a beautiful woman.

Less than fifteen minutes passed when I heard his familiar knock. I took a deep breath, then braced myself. Opening the door after a long separation was a thrill. It was the same rush the fans experienced in a dark hall when the spotlight revealed Elvis for the first time. Sometimes it was impossible to discern if the light was shining down on him or magically beaming up from him. For me it was that and more. He would be right there where I could touch him.

Only this time the anticipation turned to sympathy. Elvis stood listlessly with his arms hanging limply at his side. His eyes were dark and brooding. He was overweight. Instead of wearing a swaggering outfit, he was casually dressed in a black warm-up suit with yellow stripes down the sides. I recognized the symptoms immediately. Dejection. He was a picture of dejection. Yet despite the added weight and the lack of spark, he remained handsome. He would always be handsome to me.

"Hello, El."

He kissed me warmly, then walked to the bed and eased down. He was exhausted. What phantoms hung over him now? I sensed for an instant he was going to be taken away forever. I slid to the floor with my back against the bed. I didn't want to look into his eyes. It hurt to see the desolation there.

"How are you, El? Please tell me everything. I'll listen. I've always listened. Just tell me everything."

"I've been sick, really sick. I was in the hospital. I was bad off, baby. I thought I wasn't gonna make it. The only thing left is to take more medication. I can't go on without it."

That was his solution? That was the *cause*. How could he be so mixed up? He appeared to be walking willingly toward his death. I was horrified at how far he had fallen.

"No, no, I won't let this happen," I said, climbing on the bed beside him. "Why? Why don't you get help? Who is your doctor? Who is he?"

"Baby, I can't stand the pressure. I can't take it anymore. All I do is work. Now Priscilla wants more money. Do you know she filed for more money? That means more work. I can't take it. She wants everything."

Priscilla had filed a lawsuit demanding a new settlement in their divorce. The newspapers reported that she had charged him with fraud and was seeking a huge sum of money. Elvis took it hard.

"I can't perform unless I take something for the pain."

"This isn't the answer," I said. "You have to find the cause of the pain and stop it. You can't just cover it up. The drugs will destroy you. They won't help."

I was fighting for his life. He may have given up, but I wouldn't. I never would.

"What's wrong with you? Where's the pain?"

He ignored the question.

"The pressure will be gone soon. I'll make things right. Don't worry."

He sat up on the bed. I continued to avoid his eyes.

"Baby, look at me. I'm not so ugly, am I?"

I turned to face him, finally lifting my eyes to meet his.

"I need you," he said. "I feel love when I'm with you."

I was skeptical, especially since Elvis was still living with his beauty queen "nurse." I wondered aloud about Linda. Was she a comfort or feeding off him like the others? He ducked the question. Despite his condition, he was as nimble as ever in dealing with his inconsistencies. But I knew it wasn't as hypocritical as it seemed. He needed someone all the time, not someone he had to sneak away to see. A part of me understood, but another part refused to accept it. I knew the jealousy would surface if I let it. This wasn't the time. As I looked at him lying on the bed, I wondered if this dejection was what his mother had sensed before she died, the evil she warned about. Elvis misread my concern as anger over Linda.

"It's always been you, Desirée. Please believe me. I've had other women, but they never meant anything."

Elvis needed me to believe that. Our love could never weaken. He wanted it to remain forever at its highest point. I chanced looking into his eyes again. I saw a faint trace of the glint that had once been blinding. He must have seen something different in my eyes, a sadness, something he couldn't face. He fell back down on the bed.

"I never wanted this to harm you," he said.

He pulled me down and began stroking my hair. He held me against his chest. If only I could keep him this close and protect him from all the pain. Was it possible? After all these years, could I be allowed to at least try?

"I wish, more than anything, we could have been together," he said. "I still do. You ran away, but you never stopped lovin' me."

He stared off. The melancholy swept over him again.

"My darlin' Desirée," he whispered, almost too weak to talk. "I've made so many mistakes. Now I'm losing you. Nothing is right anymore. All I have is God. Will you pray with me?"

He rolled off the bed and dropped to his knees. I knelt beside him. I was relieved to see that he still had faith in God. His faith had been so strong.

"Forgive us our mistakes," Elvis prayed. "You know how many we've made. If this is my punishment for my sins, I accept it. But please, God, take care of my loved ones . . ."

I clasped my arms around him to give him support. His body

was quivering. I wanted to tell him, *Elvis, listen, let me tell you about our daughter. She's gorgeous! She has your face and eyes. You've got to see her. You've got to see what our love created.*

Instead, I continued his prayer.

"Dear God, please keep Elvis in your care. Don't let anything happen to him. Don't let him slip away. Help him with his problems. Lift the pressure off his shoulders and the burdens from his heart. Give him strength. Return his spirit. He means so much to so many. Don't take him from us now. Please let us have him a little while longer . . ."

I couldn't go on. Neither of us had the resolve to even pray anymore. We remained on our knees with our eyes closed, silently searching for something, anything, to lift the awful despair. Finally, we lay down together on the soft carpet. Our tears mixed as our lips met.

"Don't go, Desirée. You're all I have. I'm afraid. I'm so afraid."

His plea was chilling. He had once been so commanding. Now he was the shell of the man I once knew. How could this have happened?

"I don't have to leave so soon this time," I said. "It hurts me to see you like this, El. I wish I could do something. There's been so much left unspoken. We never seem to have the time to say it."

He never picked up on my hints about Desirée, but how could he? He didn't even suspect. If only I could get it out. But then I thought of what he had told me. Desirée couldn't enter the picture now. Elvis would wholeheartedly accept her as his daughter. He wouldn't think or care about the consequences. The bad publicity would hurt him in Priscilla's lawsuit. The magazines would have a field day. I had to hold on. But I wasn't secure in that decision. I wondered if the revelation might snap him out of his despair. Or had I waited too long? Desirée was fourteen. He had missed so much. Would he resent me for not telling him? Would it make things worse?

I examined his face, the wonderful face that was so familiar to millions. He was a caring man who had given so much of himself to others. Now he was distraught and it didn't seem fair.

"If only I could change things," he said. "I wish I didn't have to depend on medicine. The pain is so great. But honey, don't ever give up hope. Be my strength. Don't think bad of me. You're the only one who sees in my heart. You know what my problems are. That's all that matters. You can look into my soul. There's no need for words between us."

"I have confidence that you'll decide something soon," I said. "Whatever you decide will be right. But I want you to get help. And I'll stand by you. You know that. Promise me you'll get help."

"I need your prayers," he said.

He always had my prayers. I leaned over and pressed my forehead to his cheek. I guided my hands over his face like a blind woman trying to see the image through her fingers. He clutched my hand in both of his and kissed my palm. It was time to forget the agonies that clouded this meeting. This is how I can help him, I thought. I could just love him so much it would drown out the problems . . .

He was invigorated by our passion. His mood lifted.

"You know what?" he said. "You're the sunshine and laughter in my life. You're my inspiration. You're with me, and God is with me. I'm lucky."

"We'll both always be with you."

"So what's going on in your life? Have you been dancing any more?" he said.

"No, not in years."

"I met a girl once who danced just like you. She even looked like you." The glint in his eye meant he was up to something.

"Who?"

"You wouldn't know her. Just a girl."

"Who? Tell me."

"Nobody special."

"Who, Elvis?"

"Just a girl. I believe her name was Ann something. Yeah. Anna Maria, Ann Mary, no, Ann-Margret."

"You silly," I said, hitting him with a pillow. "She doesn't look anything like me. I heard you dated her. Did you?"

"No, not really. We were just friends."

I had one for him. I'd met a particular performer while working for the Cabana Hotel in 1963. He gave me tickets to his show and I took Debbie backstage to meet him.

"There was a guy I met once who had a voice a lot like yours and sang nice songs. He wasn't bad-looking either."

"Who?" Elvis said, getting serious as I knew he would.

"It's not important."

"Yes it is. Who?"

"You wouldn't know him. He's French, and very handsome."

"Who? Who?"

"Robert Goulet. He played Lancelot on Broadway."

Elvis snapped straight up from the bed. He got really angry and began grilling me about where I had met Mr. Goulet.

"I don't look like him!"

"You look better."

"I don't sound like him, do I?"

"No, but he does have a good voice." That's not what Elvis wanted to hear. His anger was building. I took the offensive.

"Did you know Ann-Margret real well?"

"Forget about that."

He began brooding. I became very loving, whispered some sweet nothings in French and assured him that he was my only Lancelot. He calmed down. I got up and went to my purse and got out a small box.

"Here, I have a present for you." The box contained a beautiful necklace of ivory-colored pookah shells. I had ordered it special from Hawaii. His eyes lit up when he saw them.

"How did you know I like these?"

"I just thought they'd look good on you. They match your teeth. Will you wear it?"

"Of course, baby. Put it on me."

I slid them around his neck.

"They feel real cool on my skin. I like that."

He kissed me, then frowned.

"Do you really think I look like Robert Goulet?"

"No, El, I was teasing. You look better." He was so upset. I couldn't understand it. Mr. Goulet was a handsome man. It was hardly an insult. What he said about me and Ann-Margret was a compliment.

"Baby, you shouldn't spend money on me," he said, rubbing his hand over the shells.

"They weren't expensive. Just nice."

"You really do love me, don't you?" he whispered in a soft, almost sad voice. Then he began smiling mischievously.

"I have a present for you. The credit card I promised."

He watched as my smile melted. Elvis had long wanted to give me a credit card to one of his accounts. He said it was just in case I ever needed something in an emergency, but I suspected part of the reason was that he wanted me to be able to hop on a plane at a moment's notice and go to him. I had always refused to accept the card. I felt it would cheapen our relationship and make me feel like a kept woman. We had argued about this briefly in Washington.

"We discussed this before," I reminded him. "I can't accept it."

He came close, took me by the shoulders, and said, "Honey, I had to get this card for you."

"No, Elvis. Please understand . . ."

He took it out of his pocket and pressed it into my hand.

"This is the credit card. I want you to fill it up."

As it touched my hand, I noticed the familiar feel of hard plastic but there were no raised numbers. I looked at it, then at him. He was grinning wildly. I blushed and felt ashamed of my previous anger.

He had set me up splendidly. Instead of a credit card, it was a similarly sized greeting card with a crying clown on the front holding a wilted flower. The inscription read, "Love Can Endure Anything . . ." then on the back it continued, ". . . but I miss you." It was signed, "love, El Lancelot."

"See, you can trust me," he laughed. "I've always honored your wishes. Haven't I?" Then his expression changed. "I've never wanted to, but I have. That's exactly the way I feel, Lucy. Love can endure anything, but I still miss you."

We talked for a long time after that. I struggled to keep his mood up by emphasizing the good things he had, his family, his daughter Lisa, his still fabulous career. Mentioning his fame reminded me of the risk we were taking being together. He always had those men around watching him, his friends or keepers, whatever they were. I asked him if somebody was waiting for him.

"I'm damn sick of this protection," he said, his mood darkening. "If I want to see you, I will. I make my own decisions. I kept you secret because that's what you wanted . . ."

I didn't want to stir up that subject again. I leaned over and kissed him as he talked. He loved it when I interrupted him that way.

"Don't be angry," I whispered. "I don't want anyone to hurt our families. You understand?"

"I have all these years, haven't I?"

All these years. The words echoed in my mind. I thought how strange it was that Elvis could be so dynamic and powerful onstage, so sure of himself, yet so weak at other times. Elvis hadn't just found success, he had become the most famous star the world had ever known. The enormity of his fame relentlessly pushed down upon him. There was no escape. He felt it, and for the first time, I did too. He soared too high and never came down. I was overwhelmed by it, as Elvis must have been for years. How could I provide the answers? How could I possibly have the knowledge it took to help him? I had been just a sad little girl who prayed for someone to rescue me. I wanted someone strong and kind to put his arms around me and tell me it would be okay. I didn't ask for a larger-than-life superstar. I longed for the old Elvis, the ambitious boy in the beat-up car who was determined to conquer the world. The handsome knight who gallantly slew the dragon in my life.

Suddenly it hit me. Everything became clear. Twenty years of heartbreak, for the first time, explained. There was a purpose for our extraordinary relationship. Elvis had been there when I needed him most, when I was chained in a black cellar of hopelessness. Now it was my turn. I would be a haven where Elvis could escape from the pressures of his exceptional life. We had kept our love pure. Nothing had touched it. The separation kept it alive. Elvis still had someone who loved him for himself, who hadn't been corrupted by his fame and wealth.

No matter what happened, I would be there. I owed it to him.

The discovery was energizing. I began massaging his back. I wanted the strength to run down my arms and into his soul.

"I wish I could stay," he said getting up to leave. "My place is here with you. It's always been."

"Good-bye, El Lancelot. My Everlasting Love. Good-bye for a short time. Mon coeur est pour toi, mon chéri. My heart is yours my darling, my dearest."

He kissed me one more time.

Then he was gone.

Earlier the same month, May 1973, Priscilla filed a lawsuit against Elvis charging him with extrinsic fraud and seeking a large settlement based on California's 50/50 law. She had signed a previous agreement in August 1972 and now was reneging and asking for substantially more. At the divorce proceedings in October 1973, she netted $2 million in cash, stock in Elvis's companies, and $5,200 a month in alimony and child support. The settlement was said to have devastated Elvis. Still, he could have made it all back in a couple of good weeks touring Europe. Japan alone would have covered it for a few performances, much more than he could make on his grueling American tours. It wasn't to be. Elvis never sang a note anywhere but in the United States. The Colonel was against Elvis performing outside America. Some reports say this was because the Colonel was an illegal alien and couldn't get a passport (Goldman's *Elvis*). Others say the Colonel was afraid of having Elvis leave America because of the large quantity of drugs Elvis and his men carried with them; passing through customs might pose a problem.

Touring Europe, at this time in Elvis's life, might have presented the challenge he needed to snap out of his drugs and depression.

Elvis disliked Robert Goulet. He would pull out one of his revolvers and blast the television set whenever the singer appeared. It's undetermined if the ill feeling resulted from his conversation with Lucy, or if Elvis reacted so strongly to what she said because of a previous dislike for the singer, who did somewhat resemble him. Some accounts say Elvis hated Goulet, Mel Tormé, and others he felt were all technique and had little soul.

Chapter 21

THE NEXT MORNING I WAS BACK IN Dallas with no answers and more worries. It was apparent no one was helping Elvis. Those around him either didn't care or had no way to control him. If I could only find a way to drag him somewhere to get help. The next few times he called he spoke of being sick and how personal problems with Priscilla and professional disagreements with the Colonel continued to torment him. His calls stopped for a few months and I went crazy with worry. I called Mr. Presley at Graceland and he was as friendly as ever, though he too was concerned. He said both he and Elvis had been ill. I wished him well and asked him to have Elvis call me.

He finally called in August, after Desirée's fifteenth birthday. It was sometime after midnight. He said he had called previously and was told not to call again. That explained the gap. He sounded the same, lonely and depressed. I asked him about his health, and he ignored me, choosing instead to rant about his heavy work schedule, the Colonel, and Priscilla's lawsuit.

"She's robbing me of my soul," he said.

I told him his hatred was making him ill and that he should just let it go. I mentioned my conversation with his father and my concern for his health.

"Daddy is also sick. He's upset about everything happening. My divorce will be final in a few months. I have to go on another damn tour. These Vegas appearances are killin' me. The expenses are tremendous. I'd rather play to audiences I care about, you know what I mean?"

"I didn't like Las Vegas much either."

"I'm gonna make some changes soon. When can we be together again?"

"I don't know. I'm afraid of those people around you. I wish I could be with you right now." For some reason, his anguish combined with my own and caused me to choke out those words.

"It's okay, Desirée. Don't cry, baby. I'll make things right. After this, we'll go somewhere together and walk. A long walk."

"I love you, El Lancelot."

There were more stories in the newspapers of Elvis's divorce. Priscilla made out well. For a day or two I began to feel that maybe Desirée could help fill the void in his life. I always wanted her to know her father and use her rightful last name instead of her stepfather's, but so many would be hurt. It was too complicated. Desirée would be considered illegitimate and the notoriety would be too hard to handle at fifteen, if ever. How could I tell her? The guilt was unbearable.

Around this time, Desirée was a breath away from unknowingly revealing the secret to her father herself.

"I was home one afternoon and the phone rang. A man asked for 'Lucy Ware,'" Desirée explains. "I thought that was real funny because I had never heard Mother referred to by that name. I asked who was calling and he said, 'Joe Jones,' or 'John Jones,' something like that. He asked me who I was and I said, 'Lucy's daughter.' He asked me my name and I said, 'Romaine.' That was the name my mother made me use, even though I hated it. Mother came home a few minutes later and I began teasing her about the caller.

"'Who knows you as Lucy Ware?' I said. 'Is this your secret admirer?' Mother went white as a sheet and asked me who called. I told her. If she was white before, now she was ready to faint. She got real angry and was almost shouting at me.

"'Who did you say you were?' she demanded.

"'Me,' I answered.

"'Who?'

"'Me, Mother. Me.'

"'What name did you use?' By now she was bordering on hysteria. I couldn't understand it.

"'Romaine.'

"When I said that, she immediately calmed down and said, 'Oh.' But a few seconds later she ordered me never to answer the phone again. I mean, what did that mean? For the rest of my life? Then she sent me to my room. What did I do?"

Had Desirée told Elvis during that conversation her first name, the lives of Elvis, Desirée, and Lucy may have gone through the turbulent shake-up that Lucy dreaded.

Consciously or unconsciously, Lucy had prepared for such a moment.

"This whole name business had been a sore spot between me and Mother for years," Desirée continues. "I hated Romaine. It sounded like cheese or a head of lettuce or something. They shortened it to 'Rome' and that sounded like apples. I loved Desirée. It was a beautiful name and it was my name, but she forbid me to use it. Every year it was the same thing. When she signed me up for school, she'd list me as 'Romaine.' I'd say 'But, Mommy, I hate that name. Why can't I be Desirée? That's my name.' She'd just say Romaine was easier to pronounce. We had this same argument for about twelve years. 'Can't I be Desirée this year, Mommy?' I'd beg to no avail. It was bizarre, but there was no denying her. I've spent half my life going by a name I hated, unable to use my real name, which I loved. My sisters still call me 'Rome.' To this day, I don't know why I was unable to use my name."

P RISCILLA MADE HER POST-DIVORCE debut by posing for a magazine photo layout in a scanty bathing suit. She was beautiful and it made me feel old and unattractive. Without Elvis, my life had been nothing but hardship, loneliness, and pain. Without Elvis, her life appeared on the rise. I tried not to hate her, but she had caused him so much pain. How could she reject a man who was capable of so much love? Elvis and I held our love in check because of her. I went out of my way not to interfere. We both wanted to be honorable.

After he gave her so much, she paid him back by hitting him with a lawsuit when he was at his weakest point, both emotionally and financially. He needed friends, not enemies. He was unhappy and overworked, and she put a huge monetary burden upon him. He would have to work harder because of her demands. It wasn't fair.

He called a few times that fall. We spoke briefly, touching base. He was leveling off, not getting better or worse. He mentioned something about buying a house in Florida where we could one day live together. He wanted it to be somewhere near Disney

World. That was just like him, always a kid at heart. It was a nice thought. If we ever did get together it couldn't be at Graceland. That was more a commune than a home, and memories of the others would linger forever. He also mentioned finding a house in Texas and even told me to start looking.

Elvis did attempt to purchase a home near Disney World at this time. He made overtures to buy a palatial seven-level coquina stone mansion on Sequoia Circle in the Pine Lakes Estates development of St. Cloud, Florida, a bedroom community about ten miles south of Disney World and twenty-five miles south of Orlando. The house was built by housing contractor Tommy Thompkins and was used as his personal residence until he decided to sell it. Thompkins said he was contacted in late 1973 by an associate of Elvis's who said the purchase was contingent upon acquiring a permit to build a private movie theater on the one-acre compound. Thompkins was unable to get proper zoning approval and that ended the deal. Although Thompkins says Elvis never stayed in the house, and probably never even saw it, that hasn't stopped the place from achieving near shrine status among the locals. Neighbors insist that Elvis spent at least one night there, and area newspapers have printed stories about "the house the King almost made his palace." The current owners, Ray and Barbara Brown, say people frequently drive by and take pictures. Mrs. Brown walked me through the sprawling interior. Upstairs, she pointed to an immaculate bed in the guest room and said, "That's the bed he slept in, or at least, that's what everyone says."

E LVIS CALLED ON CHRISTMAS EVE. I was busy baking cookies. The tradition in our home is to give something of your own labor. Elvis gave me his present—a much better mood! He wished me a Merry Christmas and we talked about how we were never together for the holidays.

"Baby, I'm alone and with you at the same time," he said. "You've been on my mind so much. I dreamed of you last night. It seemed so real. We were back in Memphis a long time ago . . . I've got a heavy schedule coming up. I'm touring practically the whole year. But maybe I can see you somewhere."

"How are you feeling?"

"Better. I'm not taking as much medication."

"Is that woman still with you?"

"Lucy, honey, you know why she's here. I don't love her. Until you and I can make it together, nothing will happen. This way the guys go their way and leave me alone. I hate their fighting and womanizing."

I wasn't naïve, just trusting. Something came to mind I'd heard long ago: "The cause of all sin in love is frustration and neglect." I didn't mind Linda being there if it helped Elvis, especially if he was ill. Loving someone is wanting the best for them. It also helped ease my own guilt of being unable to sever my marriage without hurting the children. If I couldn't be there with him, then I had no right to complain when he had someone else.

Things worsened at home. Denise, nineteen, was the most outspoken of my daughters. She and Jack had an argument. He told her to shut up, and she responded that she hated him and wished he had never come into our lives. Denise disappeared the next day. She didn't even leave word. My other daughters told me, "Mommy, Denise left and isn't coming back." She returned a few days later, but the atmosphere remained tense.

A letter from Elvis arrived a day before New Year's. On a piece of typing paper, he had scribbled a poem dedicated to me. That certainly was unusual. The poem was a touching statement of what our love meant to him. It was so beautiful! There was also a check for $2,000 which he told me to use to get a small gift, but that meant nothing compared to the poem.

Elvis wrote a simple and moving nine-line poem to his "Desirée," calling her his "greatest treasure." Although Lucy wanted to include the poem in this book, the Presley estate, which controls Elvis's letters and copyrights, refused to grant the necessary permission.

A question that intrigued me as I heard Lucy's story was how could so much have been going on—flowers, love letters, a secret admirer, frequent calls—without any of her daughters catching on. Meeting and interviewing the young women proved to be revealing. Deborah, Melody, and Desirée are demure, shy, soft-spoken, and obedient. As children or adults, they would neither challenge their mother nor force her into any painful conversations. Denise was made from a different mold. A lovely blonde who studied psychology in college, she is the antithesis of her sisters. Direct, no-nonsense, and frequently disobedient, she was the last daughter with whom I spoke. She was also the most difficult to interview, remaining loyal to her mother until assured by Lucy that it was all right to talk. Her comments, offered on a blistering hot Dallas night, were startling, but not surprising in light of her character.

"I knew Mother was having an affair, and I knew it was with Elvis. It started in the late 1960s. Or more accurately, started up again then, because it was a continuation of something that had gone on years before. She didn't tell me, not until much later, but I mean, it was obvious. He called her right at the house. There was no running off to a phone booth or anything. Mother received many calls, but I learned to detect which one was Elvis. She talked differently with him. Sweeter, more romantic. She was, you know, in love. She glowed when he called. You had to be blind not to see it. She called him by an endearing nickname, 'Lancelot.' That meant it was Elvis sending the flowers too because they were usually signed 'Lancelot.' Sometimes after he called she would be so elated she would talk to me about it. She would never come out and admit anything, but she would start talking about Elvis and how wonderful he was. She used the same voice and had the same look in her eyes as when he called, or the flowers came, or one of his songs came on the radio. And once I knew it was him, his voice on the phone was unmistakable.

"I also knew when she was going off to see him. Again, it didn't take any great insight. She'd suddenly pay intense attention to her looks and clothes. Her eyes would sparkle and she'd be so happy. I knew she wasn't going off to be alone.

"Of course, when I realized this, it was obvious that Elvis was Desirée's mysterious father. She looks just like him. And Mother loved only one person in her entire life—the man who called. The man who sent the flowers. Desirée's father. And Elvis Presley. They were one and the same.

"I wasn't going to say anything. Especially not to Desirée. That wasn't my place. Knowing put me in a difficult situation. I believed strongly that Desirée should know, but telling her would have killed Mother. I didn't know what to do. Plus, it was enough dealing with the fact that my mother was having an affair, although I never was angered about that. I was happy for her. I knew her marriage was a mistake. And I didn't think it was a big deal that it was Elvis Presley. That didn't faze me a bit. He was 'the King,' but he wasn't my king.

"I can't say why my sisters or brother didn't figure it out. They probably didn't want to accept the fact that Mother was seeing someone else. But I can tell you why I paid so much attention. I was thirteen or fourteen when Mother started going with him again. I had reached puberty and things like love, romance, and sex were flooding my mind. I'm thinking and wondering about that stuff, and I see Mother living it right in front of me. Naturally, I was curious. When the flowers came, I was enchanted. When he called, I hid in the hallway behind her door and listened. When she prepared to fly off to see him, I watched."

AT FIFTEEN DESIRÉE BEGAN TO take on even more of Elvis's looks. Her mouth was sullen and sensuous. Her eyes would look startlingly like his at times. Her expressions and mannerisms began to mirror his. She was so gentle. She seemed to have a bond with him. She was religious and carried her little Bible with her everyplace she went. Once, she spent the night with some friends and they made fun of her when she knelt to pray. She asked me about it and I told her to keep believing.

"Desirée never looked like she was part of our family," said Deborah, Lucy's oldest child. "My gosh, by the time she was sixteen she was almost six feet tall! The rest of us are tiny like Mother. She also has those super-high cheekbones. I often wondered who her father was, but Mother was so private. I just couldn't pry."

THE YEAR WAS HECTIC AND FLEW BY. Elvis called in March and said he was in Monroe.

"Honey, do you remember this place? It looks familiar," he said, laughing. He also called from North Carolina the next day. I couldn't help wondering why the Colonel was booking him in all these small cities and working him twice as hard. He was a guaranteed sellout anywhere he played. He didn't have to perform in those places. Why wasn't he playing huge concerts in Germany, France, and Japan? It didn't make sense. He called a few weeks later from another little town and I asked him.

"I've been wondering the same thing," he said. "You're the only one who's asked that. The Colonel is on the way out. He's tied up my name in his companies to make sure I can't do anything on my own. But I'll get this straight. Right now, I gotta keep working. I need the money."

"Are you enjoying the tour?"

"Lucy, I'm so tired," he said, sounding it. "It would be so easy if you were here. I miss you. I talk to God every night and ask Him to help me not hate this mess I'm in. Anyway, how have you been? Do you need anything?"

"No, I'm fine. Thanks for asking."

"Honey, there's something I want you to know. Linda is still around, but that will change soon. You were right. You can't believe all I see. I need someone to watch me when I take the medicine, but it's such a joke. They all play games. You're too innocent to know what's going on with those guys and what can happen. Don't worry. I'm smarter than they are."

Things certainly seemed to be coming to a head. If Linda, the guys, and the Colonel had turned on him, that meant Elvis had nobody. He continued to call from every small town in creation, talking about how tired and lonely he was. The months passed. Nothing changed. He worked and complained. Christmas and New Year's passed. I sent him a scapular for his fortieth birthday in January 1975. It was a Sacred Heart of Jesus I crocheted. I knew he would be traumatized by reaching that milestone and needed a lift. He wanted to hold back the years and make up for lost time. He called a few weeks later and told me how much he loved the gift. He asked me to come to Memphis, and I said okay, as soon as he could arrange his schedule to be alone. I vowed to myself to tell him everything the next time we met.

"So much has changed," he said. "I fired the Colonel and told him I knew about his deals. He made it so I can't do anything without his permission. Can you believe that? I can't make a movie or sing a song or start a production company or go to the bathroom without his approval. I trusted him and he did that to me. Man, I just lost my cool and made everyone listen. I was ready to kill them all. But I had to let the Colonel stay on a while to finalize all these bookings. I have to use him but I don't have to be around him. But don't worry, I'll clean house soon."

"How's your father?"

"Not too well, but he's takin' care."

I wondered if Linda was still around but had promised myself not to mention it unless he brought it up.

Weeks turned into months. I stayed busy at work and used what little money I had left to start a small jewelry designing business.

My older girls were off in college and were a source of pride. Desirée was named the Lions Club Queen. They wanted her to compete in a citywide pageant but she shied away. She was her mother's daughter, ducking in and out of the spotlight, hiding one minute, onstage the next. Music and ballet were her favorites. She also was intelligent and enrolled in a paralegal class at SMU while still in high school. Elvis would be so proud of her.

Jacqueline, nine, was a budding musical genius. Her school entered her in numerous competitions, including a prestigious contest sponsored by the National Fraternity of Student Musicians. Desirée had previously won city and state ribbons, and Jacqueline won those and went a step further, winning the international title as well. Jacqueline was more at home in the spotlight.

Desirée was often shy and nervous when she performed. Once, watching her onstage, I could see her legs literally shaking with fear. It reminded me of Elvis a long time ago. At home, she frequently played his songs on the piano. Each time she did it cut through my heart. I stood staring at her from the kitchen once while she played "Love Me Tender." I felt like telling her everything, but I couldn't.

She wanted to attend an exclusive Catholic prep school, the Ursuline Academy, but I couldn't afford it. Desirée then decided she wanted to be a professional ballet dancer and was selected to try out for the George Skibine International Metropolitan Ballet Company in Paris. She and a dozen others were put through the rigorous trials for an entire day in Dallas to see if they were up to the intense dedication required. When it was over, she took off her toe shoes and her feet were bleeding. I told her that was the sacrifice it took to become a professional dancer. We discussed it and she decided ballet wasn't the life she wanted.

On the way home, the radio was playing Elvis's version of "What Now My Love." The words tore into my soul. I fought to keep Desirée from seeing me cry. The song was about how the world was closing in on him. His voice on the phone meshed in my mind with his voice on the radio. He was saying the same thing. I wanted to be with him so badly. Desirée noticed my tears but said nothing.

"The tears were streaming down her face," Desirée remembers. "She was always trying to hide her feelings, but we knew. By then we all suspected that Mother had something special with Elvis. I just never suspected I was part of it. That afternoon, I didn't say anything about it. In fact, I tried to change the subject to snap her out of it."

E LVIS CALLED A FEW DAYS LATER. He was in a jovial mood.

"Is this my true love?"

"I don't know," I answered. "It depends on who this is. My true love is El Lancelot." It was nice to tease and have fun again. The previous calls had been so anxious and solemn.

"I assure you, madam, this is El Lancelot. And I ask you again, is this my true love?"

"Yes, yes, and very true she is. How are you, mon amour?"

"Answer me oh my love," he started singing in his Nat "King" Cole voice. "What sins have I been guilty of? How did I come to lose your love?"

"That's beautiful, El, why don't you record it?"

"I love you, honey. Are you coming here? I won't take no for an answer."

He waited. I said nothing.

"How about Thursday? Please come, Desirée. I need you close. Please."

"Okay. If you want me to."

"I can't believe it. You're actually gonna come! It means so much to me, baby. Have you really, really, really missed me?"

"Really. Really. Really."

"Are you real close to the phone, honey?" he whispered. "I want you to know I'll be kissing you very soon and holding you in my arms."

I envisioned his face close to the receiver and his lips pressing against the mouthpiece. It raised goose bumps on my body.

"Desirée. Desirée. I don't wanna wait till Thursday. I need you now. I miss your lips on mine and your hand touching my face. Your fingers running through my hair. Honey, we need a lifetime to talk and discover one another."

He was in a romantic mood and I was loving it.

"I don't think that's long enough."

"How about two lifetimes then," he said. "This one and the hereafter."

"Much better."

"Lucy, do you remember when I named you Desirée?"

Did I? How could I forget? I also remembered lying in a hospital bed seventeen years before, having his baby all alone. I had the dream of people trying to take her from me, a dream so frighteningly vivid I had hovered over her like she was a precious jewel ever since.

"Yes, I remember. You told me I would be your love forever no matter what paths our lives took. That you would always desire me. I remember each and every word you said."

"We'll weather the storms of the seas and grow together and no one will ever destroy our love. You still believe this, don't you, honey?"

"Yes, El Lancelot. I believe."

I fell asleep that night curled up on the sofa by the phone. I didn't want to move. For the first time in years I felt the warmth of love.

Chapter 22

THE RINGING PHONE JARRED ME awake. It was early, and it was Elvis, an unusual combination.

"Lucy, can you come tomorrow? I've made a reservation. Please."

"What's the matter? Is it urgent?"

"Yeah, but it's good. I've got a surprise for you. I can't wait."

"Okay, but I can stay only a day. I have work to do. Maybe we should wait a few weeks, when there will be more time."

He didn't make a sound.

"El, are you there?"

"Why do you do this?"

"What?"

"How long are you going to continue this? What I have is yours. Don't you understand what I want to do?" He was offended about my working. This was a touchy subject and we were both stubborn about it. It was hard for him to understand that I had to work and was committed to my life. I was also afraid of being with him now. His life had changed. There were so many people around him. I had always been a private person. There was no way I could fit into his crowded life-style.

"We'll talk when you get here," he said.

Worry replaced the normal anticipation on the flight to Memphis the next day. Would we be discovered? Where was Linda? Elvis wanted to pick me up at the airport, but I made him promise not to. Even a disguise would be too risky. I went to the hotel and waited. All the worry evaporated. I was a young girl on her first date.

As usual, he was there within a half hour. When the door

opened, the first thing that hit me was his weight. He was a bit heavy and seemed puffy and swollen. He had been overweight in Los Angeles, but the mind reverts to perfection during long separations. Not knowing the extent of his illness, I attributed it to his poor eating habits and life on the road. He was dressed casually in a blue velour warm-up suit. As before, the added weight soon didn't matter. A smile lit up his forever handsome face and nothing else mattered. He still looked better than most men could ever dream.

He poked me a few times in the ribs.

"I just want to make sure you're real," he said. We didn't talk much for the next hour. Our bodies did the talking. After the passion subsided, we lay in each other's arms for another hour, just holding on and letting the world go by. Then without warning, he jumped out of bed and said, "Let's go for a ride." He slipped out a side door, retrieved his car, and picked me up out front. We drove around Memphis, holding hands and enjoying the fresh air. We passed Graceland and he stopped for a moment. His voice grew low and serious with a tinge of sadness.

"Honey, this was supposed to be your home."

All I could do was squeeze his hand and force a smile. It was one thing to agonize from afar about the life that should have been. It hurt so much more to see it up close.

"Wherever we're together is our home," I said.

He pulled up to the gate, the one with the musical notes and outlines of him playing the guitar, and pointed to the gatehouse.

"That's my Uncle Vester. I want you to say hello. I want someone in the family to at least see you."

"Hello, Uncle Vester," I said. Elvis's uncle smiled brightly, returned my greeting, and asked my name.

"Are you comin' in?"

Elvis looked at me pleadingly. I glanced back at him terrified and shook my head.

"No, we're going for a drive," he said. Elvis floored the car and we sped away. My tension eased with each mile. As we drove I noticed a small, black, shaggy dog trying to cross the street. It was scared and in danger of getting killed. Elvis noticed my concern and asked if we should stop. I said no but kept looking back at the little dog. Elvis whipped the car around in the traffic, drove back, got out of the car, grabbed the dog, and brought it to me. Poor thing was trembling with fear. Elvis asked if I wanted to keep it. The dog had a collar, so it must have been someone's pet. I took it from him and told him to wait in the car so he wouldn't attract attention from passing cars. I brought the dog to the other side of the street, put it down, and watched it scamper on its way. Saving the dog set the tone for the rest of the day.

We drove for a time, then he pulled off the road. There were more bushes and trees, and the years had changed it quite a bit, but I recognized the place instantly. It was the hill where we said our marriage vows twenty-two years before. We walked up the incline with our arms around each other, too overwhelmed by the flood of memories to say anything. How many times had I dreamed of being here again with him. In its own way, the emotional ecstasy of the walk equaled the physical passion we had enjoyed in the hotel a short time before. He stopped, reached down, and picked a wildflower.

"For you, my queen. I'm nothing without you." His words weren't playful as before. He said it in a deep, sad voice.

"El Lancelot, my king. I love you. This is the kind of gift I'll always accept from you." I tried to be lighthearted, but my tears betrayed me. We embraced, trying to hug away the lost years.

"I need you, honey," he said.

"I need you, too, El, more than life itself. That's why you have to take care. Because I still need the knight that rescued me a long time ago."

I looked up and saw that he too was crying. It was as if we both knew, deep inside, that instead of wonderful moments like this, more pain lay ahead. We walked further until we came to the crest of the hill.

"Lucy, do you remember when we became as one on this very spot?"

"It seems like a hundred years ago."

"Are you sorry? Did it mess up your life?"

"I've never once felt sorry. You're the only good thing that's happened to me. Our marriage here was my only real marriage. You made me feel loved."

"Do you really believe that in my heart I belong to you and no one else? Tell me you do, Lucy. It's important to me that you know."

"I believe you. You made me a total woman. Without you, there would have been nothing."

A calmness swept over him. He started acting as if we had truly gone back in time and he was trying to win me all over again. This was the Elvis with whom I had fallen so deeply in love. Behind the image and problems and pressures, the young boy was still alive, overflowing with love, poetry, and romance. He smiled mischievously and pulled a small velvet bag from his pocket. He opened it and took out an object that glittered in the fading sunlight. He held it up to my face with both hands. It was a beautiful ring with a large diamond in the center surrounded by smaller diamond baguettes.

"I want you to have everything in the world. This is just a small gift. Honey, please accept it."

It was so hard for me to accept gifts. I never felt worthy. Then I remembered what happened years before with the bracelet and how he angrily threw it into the river. He would be hurt if I refused. I silently held out my hand. He slipped it on my finger. The size was too large so I held my hand closed to prevent it from sliding off. I hugged and kissed him.

"I've always dreamed of wearing a beautiful white lace wedding dress and walking down the aisle of a magnificent church like St. Patrick's Cathedral. The organist would be playing 'And This Is My Beloved' and I'd look through my veil and see you standing at the altar waiting for me. Elvis, I want that to happen, even if we have to wait forever, I want that moment. You know, I've never worn a wedding dress."

"You will, baby. The most beautiful dress in the world. It'll happen just like you dreamed. I promise. We'll make it exactly like that."

He searched every inch of my face, his stare so intense it made me blush. What was he thinking? Did I look old? I forced a smile and looked away, watching the sun trying to shine through the clouds.

"Baby, I never knew there could be anyone like you. I've

known so many women and seen how they act. You're my special angel. I want to put you up in a castle and never let anyone touch you. That's how much I care."

"El, have you known many women intimately?"

"I didn't mean sexually, just know them, you know," he said. "Hey, you're jealous."

"I can't help it. I want to belong only to you, and you to me."

"The other women were just a human need. You and I weren't together. It wasn't like you think. It was never like with us. It never came close. What we have is special, above all that."

He could be so sweet and disarming. I felt guilty about allowing my jealousy to interfere with our precious few moments.

"Will we ever be together? Or is loneliness our destiny?" I said.

"It's not all loneliness. With you I've known my greatest happiness and love."

We continued walking and enjoying the cool breeze. He talked about our families. Lisa was seven, and he adored her. I could see it in his eyes and expressions. He said he wanted me to meet her one day. I thought of a young woman I wanted him to meet. Maybe we could all be together. Desirée could know her sister as well as her father. Maybe one day.

It started to rain and we made a dash to the car. Halfway there, he stopped and called me to him.

"Darling, I kissed you for the first time in the moonlight. Then we became as one in the setting sun. Now I want to kiss you in the rain." He pulled me to him and we kissed as the raindrops bathed our bodies. The wetness made the ring he gave me slippery. I took it off and slipped it in his coat pocket as we hugged.

"I don't want us to be separated anymore," he whispered. "We've lost too many years already."

We slowly returned to the car, holding hands in the rain as we walked. We both entered the hotel through a side door, since we were drenched. We dried off and I changed into a robe. He wasn't as wet because he had worn a jacket he had in his car. He started talking about his career. We hadn't mentioned it the whole day.

"All those nights on the road. I endured it because I could black out everything but you. You carried me," he said, hugging me tightly.

"Do you really mean that? I'm not as young and pretty as all those women around you."

"Stop that," he said. "You're the most beautiful woman in the world. I love you. I've always loved you."

He traced the contours of my face with his fingers and touched my lips. I tasted his fingers and felt a desire to love him. Our love was uninhibited, yet we both felt the same about sex. We were not to exhibit or flaunt our bodies except in moments of true love. Then we were totally unrestrained, giving to each other freely. We also had to accept the changes in each of us. He was not the slender young man of long ago, nor was I the young woman.

"I don't think I can let you go this time," he said.

"When we part, it's only temporary. Our love is forever."

"Lucy, I've been worried about something. I'm afraid you'll be hurt by gossip about me, or you'll believe it. Don't ever believe anything bad about me. Promise me. There's so much trash out there." He was frightened about something and saddened. What upcoming revelation did he fear?

"Are you still taking medicine?"

He had a strange look in his eyes, a mixture of pain, fear, hopelessness, and defeat.

"I am because I need to right now. I need the money to meet all my obligations. Once everything has changed, we can make a life together. I dream of this. When I'm home I can shut myself off from them and just be alone or see my family. If I could only see you more often."

I explained again how much trouble that could cause. His family. Mine. The Colonel. The risk that trying to be together might cause us to lose what we had. I wasn't sure if he was strong enough to make a stand for me. His drug dependence was eroding his will. He had been so elated about firing the Colonel, but then had turned around and hired him back within weeks. Part of that was because he felt guilty. He hated to see anyone sad, especially if he was the cause. The Colonel had helped him in the early years, and Elvis felt he owed him. Another part was that he was insecure. He was lost without the Colonel. That firing and rehiring incident revealed how quickly Elvis could change his mind and give in to those around him. Would he do the same with me if things became difficult? Without the drugs, I wouldn't doubt him for a second. With them, I couldn't be sure.

"Right now, El, no one can touch what we have because they don't know. We're safe."

"But it's not enough. This is where we belong. Together," he said.

I started to sing to him in French. "Darling, je vous aime beaucoup . . ." barely whispering each word. He closed his eyes and listened.

"Baby, that's what I remember. Your voice and your mouth, your beautiful mouth." We held on, not wanting the moment to end. I felt in my heart that I wouldn't see him again for a long time. That made me worry about his keepers.

"They're not too smart. They think I'm sleeping. I escape them all the time. But they treat me like a prisoner. We're both prisoners. We've got to change that."

He started talking about the production company that he wanted to start. He told me to have all my work finished by then so I could work for him. He also said they took tests at the hospital and found he had problems with his liver. That was serious and it shocked me, but he didn't appear too concerned. He said his father had a bad heart and was also ill.

"I'm afraid he's gonna be taken from me," he said. "I don't know what I'd do if he was gone."

"Just place your trust in God."

"I will."

We said our good-byes. He kissed me warmly, then disappeared out the door. Alone in the empty room, I sat by the window and watched the evening darken, reliving the entire day. I returned to the bed and hugged his pillow. It still contained his very special scent. What would happen if we threw all caution to the wind? Others would be hurt, but what about our happiness? Would he ever be free? Those around him had their interests and would never let go. His debts were high. His health was failing. When he ran in the rain he was short of breath. The drugs were taking a toll on his body. He needed help, and he no longer had control. Why couldn't those around him see it?

He called later that evening to ask if I needed anything and to talk. I remembered the ring and told him about putting it in his pocket. He said not to worry. He asked me my size and said he'd have it fitted and give it to me the next time we were together.

"Don't worry about me," he said, reading the concern in my voice. "I can handle it. You're going to be part of my life soon. You'll see. Then you can care for me personally. I need that because you're the only one who ever really cared for me."

I wanted so much to believe it.

When I spoke with Vester Presley, seventy-three, the gate-keeper at Graceland, he couldn't recall exactly how and when he met Lucy, but said he knows her well and has known her since the early 1970s. When I reminded him of the introduction at the gate, he remembered and said that was probably the first time he met her. Lucy called him periodically after this meeting, has visited him, and remains in contact.

Chapter 23

I RETURNED TO DALLAS AND FOUND MY family in the midst of a whirlwind of activity. Desirée, seventeen, was preparing for her first tests of her senior year of high school. Jacqueline, ten, was in the finals of another piano competition; as usual, she won. Jacques, fourteen, was in a Jesuit school and had two jobs on the side, one working in the school library and another as a waiter for the Spring Valley Country Club. The other three had left home. Debbie was married and living in California. Melody was in London, Ontario, working as a commercial artist, and Denise was studying psychology at Arizona State. All my little birds were darting in and out of the nest, and it was getting impossible to keep up with them. As any mother of a big family knows, you get pulled in ten different directions. Instead of the children becoming independent as they grew up, they appeared to need me more.

At the same time, Elvis was pressuring me to visit him more often and spoke again about making it permanent by our getting married. So many things were tugging at me. I wanted to be with him but didn't have the strength to go through what it would entail. Shattering my family, dealing with the people around him, surviving the wrath of the Colonel—it appeared insurmountable. Elvis was angry about the goings-on at Graceland and Vegas and swore he was going to make a purge. Even though he said it with determination, I knew he was afraid. He didn't take change well and would do anything not to have to instigate it. He called frequently during this period, sometimes three or four days in a row. We talked about the old times and assured each other of our love.

The holiday season was hectic, as always. I was volunteered to head a fund-raising show for the church. I worried about Elvis's health and decided to call his father again to get a straight answer. It was a touchy thing to do because in order to prod Mr. Presley into telling me what he knew, I had to tell him what I knew. That would betray my trust with Elvis and might make him angry. It was a risk I had to take. Something had to be done or Elvis was going to get worse. Mr. Presley was warm and friendly and said he remembered me from previous calls. I told him how worried I was about his son and expressed my growing suspicion that his doctors were contributing to his problem by prescribing so much medicine. Mr. Presley was silent for a moment.

"Lucy, are you the person he said would stand by him no matter what? He never told me your name. He said it wasn't important, but he had someone he could depend on when everyone else turned on him."

I didn't know if that was me or not, but it didn't matter. Getting Elvis help was critical.

"You're very nice to be so concerned," he continued. "I'm also worried about him. We're tryin' to find out what's wrong. We will soon."

I wanted to shout, "Don't you know what's wrong? It's so obvious!" But it might be taken as an insult. Mr. Presley was my last hope. I just reiterated my concern.

"Honey, I promise we'll find out who's contributing to this," he said, sounding so much like his son. "Now tell me, how long have you known him?"

"I've known Elvis twenty-three years, Mr. Presley. Since we both were very young." I didn't elaborate and asked him about his own health to change the subject. He said he was doing better. I begged him not to tell Elvis about my call, and he agreed. Mr. Presley opened up and began telling me about the people around Elvis trying to destroy him financially and emotionally. That did little to make me feel better. In fact, the whole conversation scared me.

Mr. Presley was locked into his belief that his son had some kind of sickness that needed treatment. I sensed he was unable or unwilling to face the truth, that Elvis was addicted to drugs. Even though it was inspired by love, it was this kind of head-in-the-sand thinking that Elvis didn't need. He needed to stay away from doctors and their pills instead of soliciting new ones. If Elvis wanted something, good or bad, he got it. His power, wealth, and fame were such that he could turn respected doctors into gofers. Elvis appeared to be heading over the cliff, and not a person around him was going to raise a finger to stop it. I searched my mind to find a way to get through, but I felt so helpless.

Elvis was performing in Vegas through much of December, then gave a big New Year's concert at a stadium in Detroit. He called later that week, glum and exhausted. The same Vegas that renewed him six years before had become a dreaded albatross around his neck. He had long tired of the shows but was powerless to end his commitment. His only way out was to get sick.

"I've always neglected you," he said, barely whispering. "I'll make it up to you. When I hear your voice, I know there's something else besides this madness. You're like a dream I keep in a special place. A place I can return to when everything is bad. I have to protect you, honey."

When he spoke like that, about protecting me, that usually meant he'd had an argument with someone, or there was a shake-up in his inner circle. He was so weary I didn't ask him to elaborate. A few days later I read that he had celebrated his forty-first birthday in Vail, Colorado, with Linda and all his cronies. I couldn't believe it. He was telling me how he hated all these people and how they were using him, and then he takes them to a ski resort and throws a big party. Was he just stringing me along? That hurt as much as anything he had ever done. He was using me like a yo-yo, pulling in the string, vowing his love, calling frequently, then spinning away with someone else.

I healed as I've always healed, turning my attention to my work and my children. Desirée was preparing to graduate from high school. After my visit with Elvis in Memphis, I began to seriously consider telling him about her. Now, thanks to his snow bunny party, my doubts returned. If he wasn't strong enough to make his own decisions, if the people around him were in control, then there was no way we could ever be accepted in his life. Those around him would see Desirée and me as a threat. He would be forced to take sides, and he wasn't healthy enough to handle that pressure on top of everything else.

Tall and striking, Desirée was a natural model and was soon approached by one of my associates to work at a sales presentation for food products at the Dallas Convention Center. She begged me to let her do it. I was reluctant, but gave in. She looked beautiful when she left the house. Denise was home from college and we both watched her leave, the crowning moment of her transition from a teenager to a woman.

That night, Denise was sitting alone reading. It grew late and we both expressed concern about Desirée. Finally, there was a knock at the door. I went into my room to put on a robe. From the bedroom, I heard Denise scream, "Oh my God!" There were men's voices and Desirée was crying.

I dashed in and saw two police officers standing in the living room. Desirée ran and embraced me. She was shaking and crying violently. I was crying myself by now, trying to determine what had happened but at the same time deathly afraid of finding out. The policeman said Desirée had been attacked by a man who tried to rape her in the parking lot after the food product show. She escaped, but the attacker had ripped her clothes and cut her slightly with his knife.

The effect of the attack on Desirée was devastating. She hadn't participated in the normal teenage activities because of her strong interest in music, ballet, and Bible studies. After the attack she withdrew and lived in constant fear. I suffered with her through it all, feeling all the pain and sharing her fear. It was such a bad time for both of us.

Elvis was out of my life again. He called and left messages, but I never called back or went to the phone if I was home. I was angry at him and worried sick about Desirée. I was afraid to get into an argument with him because I was liable to blurt out that while he was playing in Colorado, his daughter was being attacked in Dallas.

I cooled down enough to answer one of his calls that April. I showed little enthusiasm, and he sensed it immediately. He asked if I was sick or angry. We argued briefly about Linda and his ski party, but my heart wasn't in it. He quickly came to his own defense, saying the same things as before. He hated the guys. They were jerks. Linda was just his nurse, and it wasn't like it appeared in the papers. The same old tune he'd sung before. Despite knowing this, I was weak and lonely and began swallowing it again.

"Do you really need me?" I said. "Do you really care? Tell me the truth."

"Desirée, I love you," he said in a deep, convincing voice. "You gotta believe me. You're my lifeline. Listen to me. We'll always be together. Honey, you have to be patient and remember what we vowed long ago."

He wore me down. That he still sounded sick also worked to gain my sympathy. He said he was having financial problems due to lawsuits filed against him because his men had roughed up some people, and that his father's condition was growing worse. He painted such a gloomy picture of his life that I ended up apologizing for starting the argument.

"I'm getting things done slowly but surely," he said. "I'm cleanin' house. Daddy and I had a long talk and we're going to get rid of these guys. Linda, too. She's taken enough from me."

He said he was so angry he found it difficult to record. "There's no inspiration." We talked about his new releases, "Danny Boy," "Solitaire," and "Moody Blue."

"I really like 'Moody Blue,' " he said. "It's faster. It was written by Mark James, the same guy who wrote 'Suspicious Minds.' He's a good songwriter and can come up with a sure thing."

He talked about his tour, how tiring it was. He reminded me that he was playing in Fort Worth soon and wanted us to get together. I told him that would be nice, but inside I knew it probably was impossible. I couldn't see him when he was traveling with his entourage. I asked him about my ring and he said it had vanished; either he misplaced it or someone took it. He said he was missing a few things and suspected one of the guys was the thief. He promised to get me another.

"Honey, I've been talking to God and reading the Bible again. You're right. He has all the answers. And one of the answers is that we'll be together. I have so much to tell you. We'll change everything. Just wait."

He had won me over again. What had started out as anger ended with renewed hope that our long and unfinished story might be heading for a happy ending. My elation was tempered by Desirée's continued depression over her attack. She decided to move into her own apartment. I fought it, but she said it was the only way she could lose her fear and regain control of her life. When she did visit, she was sullen and strange. She stared at me, often with no expression on her face and nothing in her eyes. It troubled me, but I thought it was a delayed reaction to the assault and would pass.

Two months after she was attacked, Desirée received a startling phone call that had an even deeper effect.

"The call was from a woman who, at the time, was a friend of Mother's," Desirée explains. "She said they had just had a long talk and Mother told her who my father was. Then she told me my father was Elvis Presley. 'Are you sick?' I said. She insisted that Mother told her. I was in a daze for weeks. It couldn't be. Why hadn't Mother told me? Then I thought of all the things that happened in the past. Mother's reaction to Elvis's songs and movies. The time in the car when she started crying and began hugging me so tightly after hearing his song on the radio. That happened more than once. Then there was the way she often looked at me. Her expression was love mixed with a deep sadness, like she was seeing me and someone else at the same time. By then we all suspected that Mother had once had something going with Elvis, but nobody ever speculated that he was the mystery man who was my father. It was still too hard to believe. This woman kept calling and telling me I had to confront Mother, and Mother should tell Elvis. I just couldn't do it. Mentioning anything about my father had always upset her.

"As if my life wasn't troubled enough, I now had this to contend with. Was I Elvis Presley's daughter? And if I was, what did that mean, and why had Mother kept it from me? That made me mad. But still, I couldn't confront her."

Lucy was not aware that Desirée had been told this until ten years later, during the writing of this book. She said she had never confided to her former friend about Elvis being Desirée's father, that the woman had just put it together because of Desirée's resemblance combined with Lucy's emotional reaction to Elvis's songs. The woman then took it upon herself to tell Desirée.

Denise, aware of what was happening with Desirée at the time, tried to get her mother to open up.

"We were driving to the Dallas Market Center where I worked. I told Mother that she should tell Desirée who her father was, that it wasn't fair not to tell her. She started crying and crying and telling me that I didn't understand. She was right. I didn't understand. Desirée was going through hell and needed to know. Mother never even asked me how I knew, but she did finally admit it was Elvis. Then she made me promise not to tell Desirée. Despite how I felt, I promised."

E LVIS CALLED PERIODICALLY WHILE on the road. He was doing a string of one-night stands and was growing more irritable with each. Once he said one of the guys had called him "El" and he feared it was because they were listening in on his conversations with me. He lashed out at the man and said no one was to call him that. "Only you, baby. I don't want to hear it in their filthy mouths." He had told me the same thing a few years before. During another call, he talked about the autobiography he was planning to write. He wanted it to be titled *Through My Eyes*. He asked me to help him write it. "You'll be a big part of my book. Won't everyone be surprised? I put somethin' over on them—the guys, the Colonel, everyone. You're my only secret." He took great pleasure in that. Elvis didn't have very many secrets left, if any.

"We'll disappear and just write," he said. "Maybe even find the time for a few hugs. Why can't I have a normal life? I'm sick of this touring. I can't stand these hotels. I just want a nice house, a few kids, and a wife who really loves me."

In May I had a horrible nightmare. Elvis was out on the road, performing in some nowheresville. Someone gave him some pills backstage. When he went out to perform, he started dying right onstage. The audience just sat in their seats and did nothing. It disturbed me so much that I called Graceland. They said he was performing out west somewhere. He called a few days later. It was a relief to hear his voice, but the relief didn't last. He sounded worse. I begged him to take care of himself and to go easy on the medicine. He promised he would. He asked to see me in Memphis or Los Angeles, and I said I would when he completed his schedule.

I came home early a week or so later and saw Desirée's car in the driveway. I was elated that she was home because we needed to talk. Only she wasn't there. I sensed something amiss and went to the car. There was a note on the windshield. It read: "Mother, I'm leaving for a while and going to L.A. I'll contact you later. I have to be alone. I love you—Love, Desirée." I went rigid with shock. How could Desirée run off to Los Angeles with nothing more than a vague note? Where was she staying? How would I reach her? We were always so close. How could she have left without talking to me? Had I failed her in some way? My agony was complicated by the fact that I didn't have a shoulder to lean on. I needed someone to share my worry. Her father. But what could I tell him? "You have a daughter, she's seventeen, and she's run away?" That was too much to drop on him out of the blue, especially considering how sick he was. I had to endure the pain alone.

A few days later a friend of Desirée's called and told me that Desirée was with her and not to worry. She said Desirée would call me later when she got some things straightened out. I was happy she was all right, but still upset over the way she left. What did she have to straighten out? She had always turned to me whenever she had any problems. She turned to me for everything. Now she was shutting me out. What had changed? Weeks passed. I concentrated on my two youngest children, Jacques and Jacqueline, but I couldn't get Desirée out of my mind. Whenever I called, they said she wasn't home. Finally, she called. She was sad and aloof. We discussed the assault trial coming up, then she dropped a bomb. She said she was using her rightful name, Presley. I was stunned. How did she find out? What did she know?

"Why?" It was all I could say.

"That's my name, Mother."

I was silent. I didn't know what she knew and was too afraid to find out. If we talked, I didn't want it to be over the telephone two thousand miles apart. Maybe she didn't know. A couple of years before, she had defiantly announced she was going to use her first name, Desirée, the name I couldn't bear to call her. But this was different. I would have to tell her soon—and Elvis, too, before she decided to do it herself.

"When I told Mother I was using the name Presley, I waited for some reaction, a confession, revelation, anything. Nothing happened," Desirée says. "But she didn't deny it either. That kind of confirmed it, but not really. I needed more answers and she wasn't talking. To be fair, I still didn't pressure her to tell me. I felt she should be the one to come to me. When she didn't, I began to build up a lot of resentment toward her. To complicate matters, Mother's friend, the one who told me Elvis was my father, wouldn't let up. She wanted me to go to Las Vegas where Elvis was performing, march backstage, and tell him. I couldn't do that. First of all, I probably wouldn't have been able to get near him. And besides, it was a preposterous idea to begin with. I had nothing to say. I didn't know anything."

A FEW DAYS LATER SOMETHING HAP-pened that changed my thinking about telling Elvis and Desirée. I received a call from a man with a deep southern accent. He refused to identify himself and told me never to contact Elvis again if I valued my life.

"If you know what's good for you, don't try and see him when he comes to Dallas," the voice threatened.

What was going on? I had hid my secret for twenty-three years and suddenly, in the same week, everything began to unravel. Who told Desirée? How did this man know about me? Did Elvis tell someone? He couldn't have. I had a good idea why the man called. Elvis was coming to Fort Worth to give a concert in a few days, in early June, then was returning for a second concert in July. They didn't want me around. It verified all my fears from the beginning. His associates would forever prevent our being together.

Those around Elvis knew he was seriously ill and they wanted to keep it a secret. Onstage he just looked fat to the fans in the front rows. Many entertainers have gained weight in their later years. The fans accepted it. Anyone beyond row twenty just saw the image, the dazzling white rhinestone-covered jumpsuit, the sideburns, and the thick black hair. He still looked great from this perspective. His voice, despite his poor health, remained rich and powerful. Yet if those who knew Elvis personally saw him up close, they would instantly know something was horribly wrong. These were the people Elvis's controllers must have feared. Someone like Lucy was certain to raise hell. Currie Grant, Elvis's friend from his army days, saw Elvis in concert in Long Beach, California, that April and was so shocked that he walked out at intermission.

"Man, I couldn't take it. I left the arena with tears streaming down my face. I didn't know who that was up there, but it wasn't the Elvis I knew. He used to be quick and lean, good-looking and full of life. Instead he was fat and sluggish, forgetting the words of his songs. A lot of people, close friends of his, tried to get to him, but they couldn't get through those jerks around him. They weren't letting anybody through."

John O'Grady offers a second reason why Elvis was so tightly guarded. "If anyone of Elvis's employee inner circle thought someone on the outside was a threat to their own position with Elvis, you couldn't get through to him for a million dollars."

The phone numbers of people Elvis regularly called could have been gleaned from the phone bills at Graceland or Los Angeles. All it would have taken was for someone to match area codes with Elvis's concert schedule, and his paranoid associates could then work to keep the old friends at a distance.

N EEDLESS TO SAY, I DIDN'T GO TO either concert. I probably wouldn't have gone anyway. It was too risky. The reviews were good. That was astounding. Couldn't anyone see what was happening? When I saw his picture in the paper I was heartsick. He looked bloated and ill. He had to get into a hospital soon. When I got home the phone rang, but Jack got to it first. He was rude, asked who it was, and started cursing. How many times before had I missed Elvis's calls? I had to talk to him and I couldn't. Jack accused me of having an affair, and we argued bitterly. My life was tearing apart at every level. I felt like my head was caught in a vise squeezing tighter and tighter.

The following week I was performing at a graduation celebration for the international lawyers at SMU. Putting on these shows was one of my volunteer projects. I was about to finish when a lawyer from Italy stood up and asked me to sing some Elvis Presley songs. When Elvis's name was mentioned, the whole audience applauded and kept it up until I relented. I sang "Memories" and "Are You Lonesome Tonight?" When it was over, they gave me a standing ovation. It wasn't for me, it was for Elvis. I started crying onstage and nearly broke down. I ran backstage and collapsed in the bathroom. Elvis was loved by so many people, not just in America but all over the world. With such unequaled love and adoration, wasn't there anybody anywhere who could help him?

John O'Grady tried again. In 1976 he set in motion a plan to have Elvis secretly admitted to a detox clinic.

"My wife and I went up to Lake Tahoe and saw him. He was pathetic. Sloppy. Unsteady walk. He couldn't control himself. It was terrible. I got hold of Ed Hookstratten and he made arrangements to stick him in the Scripps Clinic in La Jolla. The problem was how was I going to get him in? I thought he would listen to his ex-wife, so I met with Priscilla and her sister. Priscilla just said, 'There's nothing I can do about it.' So I called Charlie Hodge and said, 'This is what I want to do. It's in his best interest.' Three days later Presley calls me and says, 'Goddamn it, Rev [O'Grady], I want you to stay out of my goddamn business. When you saw me up in Tahoe it was the air. I wasn't getting enough oxygen.'

"Horseshit, I told him. You belong in a hospital and you know it. He wouldn't listen. After that, it was hopeless.

"His associates? You have to understand, these people didn't dare confront him," O'Grady continues. "They couldn't go to him and say 'Elvis, you're a drug addict.' I could, and I did. But that was because I didn't rely on him for my livelihood. The others, he was their entire life. If Presley said, 'You're fired,' they were finished. That's the hardest thing for the average person to understand. And nobody in that group around Elvis had the type of strong personality it would have taken to get him help."

Despite the huge sums of money Elvis made, years of extravagant spending, heavy overhead including Colonel Parker's reported 25 to 50 percent take, Elvis's divorce settlement with

Priscilla, his father's divorce settlement with Dee, heavy taxes (he paid straight tax without any shelters), huge medical bills (for both pills and doctors), and poor financial management left him nearly broke in the mid-1970s—thus the necessity for the grueling road tours.

Chapter 24

H E CALLED A FEW WEEKS LATER, on a July afternoon, and said he was in Palm Springs. He was in a better mood, almost cheerful.

"Baby, I want you to know some things. We fired some of the guys, and I had John O'Grady throw Linda out. She's gone. You see, honey, things will get right. I want to see you soon. Did you miss me?"

This was a shock. I never expected him to take such a drastic step. It was good, but I worried about him. It must have pained him deeply to do it. He hated hurting people.

"Who are the guys you fired?"

"The Wests and Hebler. I don't want to think of them. They've given me misery and treated me like a kid. I've been payin' them for making me miserable."

Red West had been with Elvis for more than twenty years. They went to high school together. The other guy must have been Red's brother, and I didn't know Hebler. To fire Red, that was incredible. Elvis's cheeriness was for me. I knew it was eating him up inside. The veil quickly dropped. He wasn't good at false emotion.

"I feel so bad I can hardly make it anymore. I hate this life so much. Never havin' a home. No one to hold, or hold me. No one to love. I need you."

"Would it help if I came to you?" I asked. "I don't care about anything else. I want to be with you."

"You know how much I want you here," he said. "But I can't let you come. I don't want them to hurt you. I don't trust anyone anymore. They'll hurt you, too. I don't know if I can stop it. I have to take injections now."

That was the final step. All along, I tried to pretend, like Elvis, that it was only medication. He was overdoing it and abusing his power to get it, but it was still just medicine prescribed by doctors. But injections? That was going too far.

"Elvis, what are you saying? Please don't." I was near hysterics. "Don't do this. I don't want to lose you."

"Lucy, I'll be okay. I'll make it. I have to go on tour again. I have to keep it up. Just this last time. Then everything will change. We can be together. Don't worry."

The summer passed and the phone was silent. Elvis was gone and so was Desirée. She remained in Los Angeles. If Elvis called, I wasn't told. A few days before my fortieth birthday, in October 1976, the florist delivered another dozen bright orange talisman roses. The message was similar to the others: "Never doubt my love, El Lancelot." I was warmed that Elvis remembered, but I couldn't help worrying about his health. I wanted to thank him but had no idea how. He was on another of the Colonel's dizzying concert tours. Why wasn't he playing in Rome, Paris, and Tokyo instead of places like Ames, Iowa, and Odessa, Texas? What was the Colonel doing? I decided to call Vernon Presley for an update on his condition. This time, Mr. Presley's mood was dour. It was obvious that he was agonizing over his son's problems.

"It's bad, Lucy. They've put someone else in his bed to watch him. I'm losin' control. I want to know who's givin' Elvis those shots. He's sick, very sick."

I was stunned. I had never heard Mr. Presley sound so powerless. I was also jarred by the bed reference. What did that mean? I asked him if there was anyone Elvis listened to anymore, anyone who could help.

"We got rid of some of the problems, but there are many more. The new girl for one. You can't imagine how trusting Elvis is. They're gonna kill him. But I'm workin' on it."

"Is it Linda again?"

"No, this is someone named Sheila."

I gave Mr. Presley my number and reiterated my willingness to help. We promised to keep in touch. Instead of easing my mind, the call turned my concern into anger. Another girl. The drugs.

It added up to one thing: Elvis had completely surrendered. Those around him were now pulling all the strings. I decided to endure my birthday on the fifteenth with as little fanfare as possible. That plan was disrupted by the telephone.

"Happy birthday, Desirée."

I asked him if I could call him back. It was risky making such a request. It was always difficult getting through to him, and he wasn't dependable about returning calls. I explained that my children were around and that prevented me from speaking freely. He said he was in Chicago and would call back in two hours. He sounded more alert. Was he feeling better? I prayed he would call again. This time, he kept his word. Two hours later the phone rang. I was alone. I tried to be upbeat, but I couldn't stop thinking about what his father had told me.

"I know you have another woman with you," I said. "How could you lie to me? I'm sure you have an explanation, as always. But you forget. I'm not as naïve as your little girls. I have a brain."

I was so angry I was shaking. Constantly having to compete with women half my age was a task I didn't feel up to anymore, especially on my fortieth birthday. I wanted to slam the receiver down before Elvis waltzed into his slick excuse. But I couldn't.

"Lucy, you know me better than that. You're the only woman I ever wanted. That's why I take those medications when I can't sleep. I can't bear it alone."

The syrup didn't work this time. I was angry, jealous, and embarrassed by my own stupidity. Even if Elvis wasn't in control of his life, he still had to be the King of his bed. His girlfriends made me feel old and unimportant. I knew Elvis, like many men, sought younger women to keep a grip on youth. It was an immature though typical male reaction. But with him, it went beyond that. A stronger Elvis wouldn't have needed the constant stroking of adoring fans turned girlfriends. There was something about these traveling bedmates that was perverse. I hated him for it. His frailty. His hellish descent.

"I'm sure you have what you want, and it isn't me," I told him. "You allow these drug addicts to congregate around you. I have to wonder . . ."

I had never said anything so damning to him. Once I started, it was hard to stop.

"Do you enjoy women young enough to be your daughter?"

I thought of firing the final blow: *Your own daughter is that age. Would you want her, too?*

It was an ugly image and brought me back to my senses. Desirée could never be used as a pawn in our relationship. I couldn't let anger and jealousy force me to blurt out such a startling confession. Calming down, I figured he would recoil from my anger and hang up. I was surprised when he started pleading his defense, not the old smooth version, but one that came from within.

"This stuff, the women, it isn't real. It's like my life. I don't know where the show ends anymore. All I know is I still love you. I always have."

Fogged by anger and dwindling self-esteem, I failed to realize that he was admitting his world had twisted too far out of focus. This new woman wasn't an affair of passion. This was, as Mr. Presley had said, "another woman in his bed to watch him." At the time this was beyond my comprehension. The distance made it impossible to perceive how fast he was sliding. I still clung to the dream that we would end up together. So it was the intruder, not the descent, that consumed my thoughts. It was anger, not compassion, that filled my heart.

"Give me a chance to explain," he said. "I'm not well. . ."

"All right. Tell me. Tell me why you have to have a woman with you every second. Because you're thinking of me? Because you love me? And now I'm the reason you have to take drugs? Look around you. Look what you're doing to the people who care. You're hurting me. You're hurting your father."

He didn't answer. I waited.

"It's all just a show," he said. "They expect it. It's part of the act, the performance. I never meant to hurt anyone."

His voice was softer now, almost childlike, but the words were beginning to sound familiar. When cornered, he always hid behind the Colonel or his fame. I had believed him before, but he was hiding too much now. The parade of women hadn't stopped. Maybe he was lonely, shut in from the world, and these young women were all he had left of life. No, that wasn't it. I was stretching again to give him the benefit of the doubt. The women were no different than the drugs. They teamed up with all the other pressures around him to form one dark, ominous force that he was allowing to destroy his life. I tried to blame simple jealousy for my distress, but I knew it was Elvis's personal degradation that was ripping out my heart. The anger that clouded my brain was lifting. I fought it. To see the truth was to realize it might be over, that the old Elvis was dead. I couldn't handle that. Not on my fortieth birthday. Not ever. I would continue to feed upon my surface jealousy to vent the frustration that festered inside.

"There's so much you don't know, Elvis. So much. I hate all of them for hurting you. They've changed you and you can't even see it."

"Lucy, I have to see you. Can you come to L.A.? When you see me, you'll understand."

"Why will I understand? Don't defend yourself."

"Please don't do this to me, honey."

By coincidence, I had a fashion show in Los Angeles the following month. I told him about it but stressed that it was a business trip and I might be too busy to see him. He couldn't imagine anyone being too busy to see him.

"You mean all that is more important than me? Those people out there will get to you. The men will ask you out. I don't want you there alone. Tell me where you're stayin'."

"You forget, Elvis, I don't have anyone furnishing me men. No one will get the wrong idea about me. I would like to talk to you, but this will be a hurried trip. I'm only going to be there for three days and I have a lot of work to do."

"I'll get you a hotel room."

I politely declined his assistance.

"I won't have this!" he shouted. "I'll call you tomorrow. Don't leave until you talk to me. I may fly in to pick you up. Don't leave without talkin' to me."

"You are not going to fly and get me, and neither will you take care of my flight. This is my business. I'd appreciate it if you keep out of it. If I have some free time, I'll see you. If not, you'll just have to cuddle up with your little girlfriend and make do."

"Lucy—"

"I've got to go. Good-bye."

I hung up. He deserved it. It made me feel good. So good, I didn't realize that a thin streak of mascara had betrayed my tears.

I went to Los Angeles in November. I had started a leather fashions business and was there to make connections and to introduce my line at a show for investors. Aside from the work, my intention was to track down Desirée. She had grown so distant. Between her and her father, I was coming unglued. When I called to arrange to see her, they told me she was off visiting friends in Santa Barbara.

The fashion display and cocktail party were held in a closed restaurant, the Daisy. It went well and a group of Japanese businessmen expressed interest in backing my line. I found the atmosphere difficult because everything was so phony in Los Angeles. The huggy, kissy "let's have lunch" world bored me. I even overheard some gossip about Elvis. Seems Linda Thompson had spent $20,000 on a new wardrobe right before he kicked her out. Was there no escape from him?

That night, alone and lonely, I became depressed. I felt so rejected. I thought of calling Elvis, but my pride, anger, and fear of further rejection kept me from picking up the phone. When I finally did, I found that his number had been changed. I couldn't even leave a message. My trip to Los Angeles had done nothing but cause more heartache.

Back home, Jack told me some creep kept calling, and that Desirée had also called. The "creep" called a few days later. He was angry, grilling me about my trip to Los Angeles. Asking me who I was with and what I did. He asked if it was me he saw getting into such and such a car at various places around town. He was just bluffing, trying to trick me into admitting something. It was strange how possessive he suddenly became.

"Who were you with when you claimed to have seen me?" I countered.

"I just went there to clear up some things about this trashy book the Wests are writing. Did I tell you? They're sellin' me out. Never mind that. Why'd you go there alone?"

"Who are they planning on putting in your bed now? What's

wrong with you? Do you really want this?" We were both ignoring each other's questions.

"Who were you with? Are you turning away from me?" His anger melted into his little-boy pout. "Don't you love me anymore?"

"I went there to work. That's it. You know me. But you were the one who turned away. You have a woman with you. You can't have me and her, too. I've had enough of that."

"You couldn't see me, could you?" he said, not giving me a chance to explain that I tried to call. "I guess that answers my questions. I guess you're right. Maybe we should let it end."

I couldn't believe it. After all we had lived through, all the obstacles we overcame, he was going to break it off because of this? I hadn't done anything to hurt him. I was just trying to stay away to keep from hurting. Why was he making me feel so guilty? This wasn't the sweet person I loved. This was a monster who wanted to hurt me. His dark side was now in control.

"Is this what you want?" I asked.

"Apparently this is what you want. Isn't it? That's why you went out there."

"If you're trying to hurt me, Elvis, you have."

"Why don't you leave Dallas, get a divorce, and get free? I can't do what I really want because you're still married."

His words were biting. I had to defend myself.

"The reason is I have six children. I have to think of them. And maybe I think you're stringing me along. You're asking me, as you always asked me, to take a big chance, to shake up my life and the lives of my family, and you never quite seem ready for it. You want me, but you don't want to give up anything. The other women can come along and enjoy the ride for a while. I can't. I'm responsible for the lives of my children. What would you do in my place? What if I was in some man's arms in bed? Would you believe me if I told you I loved you instead? Would you?"

"Baby, it hasn't been right, but things will change. The minute there's no woman around, the guys'll think I'm slipping. I'm sick of it."

Although that didn't make sense to me, he did sound serious. But it was still the same old cop-out. It wasn't his fault. Oh no.

They put a gun to his head and forced him to go to bed with beautiful women. The guys did everything else for him, they might as well take the blame for that torture.

"Am I hearing you right?" I said. "Well, my friend, you best stop talking so your bed won't get cold. You don't need anyone. Especially not me. Good-bye."

I felt so humiliated. Was this the end? Maybe he was just drugged and couldn't be held responsible. Or maybe that was just another excuse. The phone kept ringing. I refused to answer. I told my children to say I wasn't home.

The birthday season and the holidays passed quickly. There was little joy in any of it. I'd lived on dreams for twenty-four years, and now those dreams were gone. A few months into 1977, I read that Elvis was engaged to marry another former Memphis beauty queen. Did they hold those pageants just to provide him with fresh girls?

Elvis had to be the hardest man in the world to forget, because the newspapers and magazines were always ambushing me with stories and photos. He called at the end of March and said he was in Alexandria, Louisiana. How ironic. That's where his daughter was born. And where I had run from him the first time.

"Lucy, can I please talk to you? Just for a minute. Please." He was so desperate.

"How are you?"

"I have so much to say. I can't live this way—knowing you don't care, thinking I hurt you. I can't get you out of my head. I need you."

"I heard you're engaged to another beauty queen. I'm sure you need her more."

"I know I hurt you, but can I see you soon? I'll explain. I've got to see you."

"No, I don't think that's honorable, do you?"

"Can you believe me when I tell you it's not for real? I'll show you what I mean. Honey, sometimes I get confused. I'm so sick I find myself doing things I don't want to. I can't stop myself anymore. I never wanted to hurt you."

My head was spinning. I didn't know if I was glad he was back, or if I wanted his engagement to be true. I hated to see him so sick and alone, but I didn't have the courage to believe him anymore. What was unquestioned was my love. I loved him so deeply. That never abated. I didn't want to think about his sickness. The engagement, the arguments, the separation, I could deal with that. But his sickness, that was too devastating. I was relieved when I heard voices in the background and he said he had to go. "I'll call you later."

Ginger Alden, Elvis's new companion, had won a few local beauty contests and finished first runner-up in the Miss Tennessee Universe contest. However, it was her sister, Terry Alden, who was the reigning Miss Tennessee and was brought to Elvis as a possible replacement for Linda Thompson, who happened to be the former Miss Tennessee. Ginger, then twenty, was also invited. Elvis was said to have shocked everyone by picking Ginger instead of Terry.

Ginger Alden is a dead ringer for Lucy de Barbin.

"I saw a picture of Ginger once and almost fell over," Desirée recalls. "She looks exactly like Mother. Exactly. And she was wearing the same white-rimmed sunglasses Mother used to wear. It was eerie."

H E CALLED AGAIN THREE WEEKS later, in late April, a few days after Melody's twenty-sixth birthday. He was calmer, too calm. It took me a few seconds to recognize his slow, deep voice. He said he was tired and ill and had been in the hospital. Despite this, he was still touring.

"Please, El, just quit. Then when you feel better, you can regroup. Why are you letting them push you so hard?"

"Honey, I'll be all right. I promise. I just need to know you're there. That you still believe in me. There's no one but you. No one."

He paused, waiting for reassurance. That's what he needed. Soft, loving words. There had been so much anger between us in the past year, but this was not the time for it.

"Mon amour, don't worry. Nothing has changed in my heart. You're the only one I've ever loved. You still have that. All that's important now is your health. I'm scared because I don't want to lose you. You've got to slow down. Please don't go on the road anymore. Turn to your father. He'll help. Confide in him. Don't keep pushing. And maybe you should change doctors?"

"Honey, when this tour is over there will be some more changes. I'm prayin' everything will work out. Tell me, my Desirée, do you love me? Let me hear you say it." His voice was so hoarse and low. He was barely getting the words out. Was he that sick, or was it just emotion?

"I love you, El Lancelot. When all the others have left, I'll still be there. We'll grow old together. We still have time, mon chéri. The last years can be the best."

"I love you, Lucy. I'll call while I'm away."

It was nice to hear him so loving, but his voice was disquieting and he made it clear he was going through with his schedule. Why couldn't he stop? Why wouldn't they let him? Were those around him so blind?

May was a miserable month. The children were all busy with their own lives and suddenly every one of them seemed distant. Desirée had returned to Dallas and was a little happier, but we weren't close anymore and that hurt me terribly. She was working for a law firm and taking paralegal courses at SMU. Jacqueline was only eleven but she was ready to leave home, too. She had been accepted by the Royal Academy for the Arts in London, England, and was preparing to disappear to another country. I made a few calls and found out there was a similar academy in London, Ontario, where Melody lived, and steered her there. The older girls were building their own families, and Jacques, sixteen, was at the age where a mother was more of a hindrance than a help.

In the midst of this emptiness, tragedy struck again. One of Desirée's friends picked her up to take her to a movie. He pulled up to the house in a convertible sports car. They never made it to the theater. A car towing a second vehicle cut them off and caused their car to overturn. Desirée was dragged across the pavement and was trapped underneath. Some men turned the car over and got her out, and she was rushed to the hospital.

When I arrived at the emergency room, I nearly died myself.

Desirée was in critical condition. Her face was a bloody mask of cuts and bruises, and I could see the gravel still embedded in her cheeks. Her blouse was burned into her chest, and her arm was burned so badly she almost lost it. I wanted to scream, but I had to be strong for her. I stayed at the hospital all that night and for most of the next week. I thanked God for keeping her alive, and begged Him to let her heal.

The same day Desirée had the accident, May 29, I read that Elvis was sick onstage. What a horrible coincidence. I thought again of telling him because it was hard to share the burden of Desirée's suffering alone. But if he too was sick, it would only make things worse. Desirée was in excruciating pain for the next few weeks. She had to be suspended in a basket and lowered into a solution to treat her burns. She couldn't move one of her hands. I came every day to feed and comfort her. One day she was crying and asked if she would ever be able to use her hands again. I told her she would heal and be perfect, comforting myself as much as her.

A few weeks later I went to the supermarket to pick up a magazine for Desirée. At the checkout, there was a tabloid with Elvis's picture on the cover. It was shocking. He was bloated and extremely fat. The screaming headline mocked him. A smaller headline said he was planning to marry. I was so disturbed by his appearance I didn't care about that. I called Graceland, but they said he was out on tour and wouldn't be home for weeks. All I could do was keep praying, for both the father and the daughter.

Despite Elvis's failing health, he gave one hundred concerts in seventy-seven cities in 1976, and fifty-four concerts in fifty cities the first eight months of 1977. It was an exhausting schedule that would have knocked a healthy man to his knees, much less someone who was obviously sick. John O'Grady still becomes enraged when he thinks of it.

"What kills me is why the Colonel worked him so hard when he saw him that way for two years?" O'Grady asks, knowing the answer full well. "The Colonel's just money hungry. I hate him."

After they were fired, Red West, Sonny West (actually cousins), and Dave Hebler signed a contract with the *Star* tabloid to do a book revealing the dark side of Elvis's personality, including the fact that he had a drug problem. Elvis was mortified and solicited O'Grady's help in trying to prevent its publication. Elvis offered his former intimates $100,000 to quash the project. They refused. The book, *Elvis—What Happened?,* was published in July 1977. It caused Elvis great anguish.

Chapter 25

AUGUST 1977

On June 19, 1977, during a one-night-stand performance in Omaha, Nebraska, Elvis stood onstage and played out one of the most touching scenes in the entire Presley legend. He was grossly overweight, obviously ill, but still giving his best to his loyal fans.

"I'm going to do a song called 'Are You Lonesome Tonight?' " he announced to the audience, pausing to take a sip from a cup handed to him by an aide. He looked down, fiddled with his finger, and added, "I am, and I was." He quickly recovered from his aggrieved confession by bumping into the mike stand and attempting to laugh it off.

Elvis proceeded to sing the song in a beautiful voice that belied his appearance. When he got to the spoken part, about the woman who left him and shattered his heart, he was unable to say the lines, instead mumbling whatever came to mind. A tear appeared to well up under his right eye, then mixed with sweat and spilled down his cheek. Elvis again tried to laugh it off, but ended up exemplifying someone laughing on the outside while crying within.

The heartbreaking moment was recorded on film and can be seen near the end of some versions of the movie *This Is Elvis*.

THE SUPERMARKET NEWSPAPERS were now full of distorted pictures of Elvis and insulting headlines. I couldn't understand why he was allowing the world to see him in this condition. He had fought a weight problem for much of his life, but he never let the public see any sign of it. Now he was displaying himself like some kind of a carnival freak. This wasn't Elvis. He was proud of his lean, handsome image and understood its importance to his career. Discarding it proved something was seriously wrong.

At least Desirée was progressing. She was recovering quickly and making plans. Denise was moving back to Dallas from Tempe, and she and Desirée decided to share an apartment. I wasn't too happy about that. I wanted Desirée to recover at home where I could take care of her. Denise was expected to arrive from Arizona in the afternoon. Anticipating her arrival, I unlocked the front door. As I did, the phone rang. It rang only twice. When I picked it up, the line was dead. I sensed it was Elvis.

He'll call again, I thought, comforting myself. The phone rang dozens of times during the next two weeks. I felt nothing. Business calls, calls for the children, friends, everything routine. Then late one afternoon in the second week of August the phone rang again. My sensors switched on. I ran to grab the receiver, not wanting the lifeline to sever again.

It was a collect call from John Jones. That meant two things. It was Elvis, and he was probably at Graceland. I didn't want him to call me directly from Graceland. After receiving the threatening call, I was more determined than ever to keep my phone number from showing up on his bills.

There were too many people around to talk. I would be alone later. I gave him a signal. "She's not here," I said. "She'll be home in an hour." Elvis got the message. He called back exactly one hour later.

"Lucy, are you there? I'm so glad," he said, sounding relieved.

"Elvis! How are you? I've been so worried. I tried to call."

"Oh God," he sighed. "I really miss you. I've been through hell. So much is going on. I've been on the road. You've been gone. Where have you been?"

"Oh El, something horrible happened. My daughter was in an accident. She's all right now, but it was awful. I read some terrible news about you. You've been ill. Why didn't you call me? I was so worried."

"Whoa, go back some. How about your daughter? How serious is it? Do you want me to come there? How old is she? Tell me, how serious is it?"

"It was an auto accident. She'll be okay. Don't worry."

"Tell me about it. What happened? How bad was she hurt?"

I gave Elvis the details, again assuring him she was recovering.

I was touched by his concern. He was sick himself. He sounded terribly fatigued.

"Everything will be all right," Elvis said, taking on the role of the comforter. "Baby, I'm sorry you had to go through so much. I could feel that something was wrong when I couldn't reach you. What's your daughter's name?"

I'd had eighteen years to anticipate the question. When it finally came, I was caught off guard. There was a telling silence on the phone as I waited for my jumbled thoughts to clear. I had never spoken to him directly about Desirée. I mentioned my children collectively, or spoke of my family, but never anything specific, especially about Desirée. If I unexpectedly broke down, Elvis would demand to know what was wrong. It was not the way I wanted to tell him. But now he had asked. What could I say? I needed a diversion.

"First let's talk about you. Is it true you've been so ill?"

"Honey, I've been really sick. This touring is killing me. I'm also doing a documentary and some more concerts. I'm taking a rest right now. Do you know about the book? Those three guys are crazy. They're doing this to get even because I fired them. You can't believe all that trash they wrote. You won't believe it, will you, honey?"

"Why do you even ask? We're closer than that. No one could ever say anything bad about you to me. I would never believe it. I knew they weren't really your friends. Remember, 'good fortune makes friends, ill fortune reveals them.' You're better off now. Don't let it get to you. I know you miss them but they're enemies. They're money hungry. If they really cared, they wouldn't have done that.

"Are you at Graceland?"

"Yeah, Lisa is here with me until I leave the sixteenth."

"Leave for where?"

"Another tour."

"Oh, Elvis, another one?"

"It wasn't my idea. I don't want to think about it. I just want to spend some time with my daughter."

"I wish I knew her. I do love her. It's strange, but I feel a bond."

"I only wish I felt better and this was over. I've had some rough times. But the shows were okay. The fans are still with me, Lucy, even with my weight. I have to get it off. I've got to do it when this is over. When I can rest. It's been such a hard tour.

"What about you? How have you been?"

"I've been so upset since the accident. And I was worried about you. Are you really all right? Tell me exactly how you feel. I want to hear it from you."

"Lucy, it's that book. It's gettin' to me. I'm afraid it's gonna hurt the people I love, like Lisa and my family and you. Will you turn against me?"

"Elvis, that's so ridiculous. I'm on your side. I'm concerned about you and all the rumors. Are they true? I want the answers from you. And, by the way, are you going to marry this girl? Do you love her? If you are happy with her, then best wishes. That's all I want to tell you. The other things are trash, I know."

"Lucy, darlin'. Listen. Listen. There's been too much distance. I'm sick of all this. Are you ready to face it and blow their minds? I've taken some steps already. I want you. Ginger is a girl that George brought in. I even agreed to an engagement when I was trying to hurt you. I thought you were through with me. But we've got to understand one another and not let anybody come between us."

Elvis's voice turned soft and low.

"I'm sorry I hurt you, baby. Please believe me."

That was difficult to accept. Were others really dictating his every move, right down to who his girlfriend would be and when they would marry? Could the same marital nightmare that all but destroyed both our lives be happening again? It couldn't be.

"Elvis, she's pretty. I know she's been with you. Is she there now?"

"She's someplace around here with her whole damn family."

"Oh El, please."

"The only important thing is for you to know the truth. I told Daddy and Uncle Vester this marriage was never going to be. She wants to announce the wedding date. It won't ever be. There will be no such thing. Do you believe me?"

He was pleading. I had no alternative but to agree.

"Let me talk about us. Honey, do you need some cash?"

"No, no, Elvis. The insurance took care of my daughter's bills. I wish you would cancel this tour and go away for treatment. I'll go with you. I just want you to get well. What about your doctor? Doesn't he know or care about you? He should be concerned. Something's not right."

"Baby, you can't imagine the plans I have. All this will pass. I've already started. I fired the guys. When I finish this tour I'll rest. Then you're coming here to Graceland. We'll get married like we should have a long time ago. What do you think of that?"

"That would be wonderful."

"No more excuses from either of us." He became excited. "Why don't you come here? Yeah, come here. Do you know what? We'll start my book. We'll answer those guys. Will you help me?"

"I'd love to."

Despite the glowing picture he painted, I remained uneasy. He didn't sound well.

"El, I want to see you soon. And I want you to take it easy. Is your father going on the trip with you?"

"Yeah. He's been sick too, you know. It will do him good. I hope your little daughter gets well. What's her name? You never did tell me."

I went numb. I couldn't dodge it any longer.

"Elvis, she's not a little girl. She's eighteen and her name is . . . Desirée."

It was his turn to be caught off guard. Neither of us made a sound. It was a silence that screamed for an explanation.

"I didn't realize she was such a big girl," he finally said. "Honey, why'd you name her Desirée? Is there something you're not telling me?"

I steeled myself to answer, speaking in a low, unnatural monotone that gave me away with every word.

"It's because you like the name. Thank you for caring . . . There's so much I have to tell you."

"Honey, why are you acting so strange? Is there something wrong? Lucy, tell me, is there something wrong?"

I retreated deeper into my monotone. I couldn't let my emotions betray me. I had to tell him, but not over the phone.

"No, it's nothing. I was just thinking of everything and wondering if I would see you soon. There's something I have to discuss with you regardless. Regardless of what decision you make about your girlfriend."

"I told you my decision and it stands. I don't want any other woman. If I give her money she'll gladly go. Everything is a mistake. I thought you didn't care. Tell me who you love. Please. Tell me you love me. Please. I need to hear it."

"Maybe that girl loves you. Have you asked her?"

"Look, I know she's not interested. I'm not interested. Do you hear? I asked you a question. Do you love me?"

He wanted more than a mere yes. He needed me to sweet talk him as I had so many times before. He used to tell me my voice could snap him from the deepest depression.

"You crazy man. You know I love you, Elvis Presley. I've loved you since you were eighteen, a thousand years ago. I thought that my knight in shining armor had passed me by. Then you came into my life and chased the dragons away. You captured my heart and it's been yours ever since. I watched you grow and change and exceed all your wildest ambitions. I loved you through it all, El, and I love you still. With all my heart! And when you grow old, I'll be at your side if you want me. I'll always make you feel like a young man. But we don't need to talk about that now. You're still a young man. The same young man that turned me into a woman. I hold all our memories sealed forever in the most exalted place in my mind. When I'm alone and I need you, I bring out the key and unlock the door. They tumble out and dance upon my heart, filling my whole body with joy. But sometimes, El, even that isn't enough. Sometimes, I need you. This is one of those times. I need you. I've longed for you for two years."

"Baby, I want you here," he said, his voice choking with emotion. "I want what I want, and I want it now. No one has ever made me feel the way you do. Twenty-five years have gone by, and no one ever equaled you. Even over the phone. I could conquer the world knowing I'm loved by you. When I return, we'll be together, out in the open. I promise. I promise you, Lucy, this time is it. You know, Lucy, you loved me without any conditions. I've seen so much, I've done so much, and yet you remain special to me. You're the only one who never changed. Everybody else changed. Everybody. That's why I know you care. That's why I love you. And now I really need you. I need you . . ."

He was crying. It was a desperate cry, and it broke my heart. I fought to stay strong. He needed my strength now, not my tears.

"That was so beautiful, Elvis. I know you care. I've always known. I understand. Don't feel bad about the past. It's over. Let's look ahead. Promise me you will take care of yourself. Do it for me. If you want to show me you care, care for yourself. I love you. You should never, ever doubt that. You know how much I care. I'll love you and care for you forever."

I was crying, but tried not to let on.

"Honey, you can change your life," he said. "I don't want you in that unhappiness any longer. I want you with me. I want you to be my wife. Will you do that?"

"I will, Elvis. I've planned on leaving for a long time. I do want to be with you. And we will. I won't make any more excuses. We'll do whatever you want. We'll get your weight down and break your dependency. We'll get you healthy again. My darling, we'll plan it all when you return. I'm ready to leave everything and go to you. And there is something so wonderful I have to tell you. A wonderful surprise! But only when I see you, okay? You'll be so proud!"

Despite my tears, I was overjoyed. I knew I could finally tell him about Desirée. I would tell him the very next time we were together. No, better, I'd show him! I'd bring Desirée to Graceland with me.

"Is it a good surprise?" Elvis asked. "Why don't you just tell me now. I can't wait that long."

"You have to, mister," I teased. "It concerns both of us, and it's very special. You'll be so surprised. It's nothing you can think of, so don't try. Will I hear from you before you leave?"

"I'm leaving the sixteenth. I'll call you that afternoon. Will you be there?"

"Yes! Waiting by the phone. Just remember that I'm always with you. No matter where you go, I'm with you. And if you pray to God, anything is possible. God will guide us."

"You know what?" Elvis asked. "I can see life so clearly now.

I know what's important. God has given me great insight. I have so many things I want you to read. You know, you've helped me a lot over my life."

"You've helped me."

"I'll never know why there are so many people out there trying to hurt others," he said, his voice wavering. "But you, I know you love me. I know all the gossip is hurting you. I never wanted that. That's why I hate those magazines because they make up all those stories. I've never told you a lie, Lucy."

He was crying again. Being double-crossed by his friends and sliced open before the world was punishing him more than I imagined.

"Elvis, don't hurt yourself. Being betrayed is a horrible, horrible thing. I'm sorry. I hate everyone who hurts you."

"My Desirée. You—" He stopped abruptly. There was a quizzical silence on the line, then I heard him laughing.

"Aha! Well, I'll be darned."

"What is it?" I asked.

"Nothing," Elvis answered. His mood instantly brightened. "We'll talk about that when I see you. But I'm not letting you off the hook this time because I think I know. Damn, Lucy. I hope it's true."

I couldn't say anything. I was glad he was giving me more time.

"I miss you," he said.

We both hung on to the receivers, each unwilling to hang up even though the conversation was coming to an end. Holding on to the phone was like holding on to each other.

"Honey, will you pray with me?" he asked.

"I'm here."

His voice dropped another octave. It was raspy and slightly slurred. It hurt me so much to hear it.

"Oh God," Elvis began. "You know us better than anyone. Soften our hearts and help us release any feeling of bitterness toward our fellow man. Fill our hearts with love for one another. And heal us from within, dear Lord. Forgive those with anger in their hearts. Amen."

"God bless you, El. Please be well."

"I will, honey, but I'm really overweight. Do you love me anyway?"

"You silly man. I love you! Not because of any way you look. Simply because I love you. Whatever you feel, I feel. So remember that, mon chéri. And don't worry, you'll never have time to eat. I have plans. So think about what I said. Food for thought."

Elvis chuckled. It built into a robust laugh. He laughed so hard I thought he would drop the phone.

"What's so funny? Don't you believe me?"

"Yes, yes, honey. I do believe you," he said through the laughter.

"Do you know what?" he asked. "I've just discovered the secret of dieting."

"What? You don't know what I'm talking about."

He started laughing again.

"You always make me so happy. And we haven't been together very much. Just think how happy I'll be when we're together all the time. Someone who truly loves me and gives me honest affection. Honey, we're alive! Remember our signal? How I feel your hand when we touch? When we put our hands together? I love to rub my face against yours. These little things have meant so much to me. I need to hold you, my Desirée. I need you."

His voice was faltering again. He was yo-yoing from laughter to tears with disquieting speed. I fought to concentrate on the meaning of his words instead of being overwhelmed by his tones and severely bouncing emotions.

"At times, I need your touch. Just to feel your love," he continued, barely whispering now. "I need that so much."

I could sense his weariness through the phone.

"I'm so lonely for you, too, mon amour. I need you so much. So much. My arms are empty. I just wish you were here so I could hold you. I'm hollow without you."

"My Desirée," he said. "My Desirée. My two Desirées. In a few weeks we'll have a whole new beginning. Everything will change. You'll see. I'm coming to get you, and I'll never let you go. I should have done this twenty-five years ago. Oh, why did I wait? Why was I so stupid? All those around me, I don't care what they think anymore. They don't care about me. This will be a short tour. I'll be back in no time. Then we will be together. I promise."

"I'll be here waiting.

"Darling, do you feel well?" I asked. "You're not in pain, are you? It's so hard not being with you. I really don't know if you're telling me the truth."

"I'll be all right. I need to walk more, and I get stiff sometimes. But I'll get back in shape after this tour. You wait," he said, suddenly recharged. "I have something to shoot for now. You and me at Graceland. The way it was meant to be. And I'll get well. The old Elvis is coming back!"

"I know you will."

"It won't be long, honey," he said. "You waited twenty-five years. How long can two weeks be?"

"An eternity when I'm waiting for you. But I'll survive."

"I've got to go, baby. Thanks for giving me something to live for again. Thanks for giving me hope. I'll talk to you soon."

"Just remember to take care of yourself. Take it easy if you can."

"Trust me, please. Nothin's gonna happen. I'll call you before I leave. Never doubt me, Lucy. I love you. It's important that you know that now. Honey, when I see you I want to place your ring on your finger."

"Did you find it?"

"No, not that one. I don't know what happened to it. I'll have another one. Bigger and more beautiful than the other. The kind of ring I should have given you long ago."

"I love you, El. Take care. Waiting will be so much easier now. Remember, you and I have some very important things to discuss."

"Are you sure you don't have something to tell me now? This might be your last chance," he teased.

"El, you're a rascal. Right now I do want to tell you something. My heart is filled with so much love it's about to burst!"

"Baby, it's going to be great. We'll throw all the bums out! Clean house! I'll call you before I leave."

"Take care, Elvis."

I was elated. At the beginning of the conversation I thought Elvis was buried so deep he would never dig out. Then miraculously, he summoned up the old spirit. I honestly felt he had turned the corner. He would overcome his problems with drugs and depression. He would jump out of the darkness in typical fashion—decked in a spangled outfit, jet black hair cascading over his forehead and knifing through the high, proud collar, flashing that paralyzing smile, bounding with vigor and brimming with blinding charisma. He would make it back. All the way back. And maybe, just maybe, I would be part of it this time. I didn't want to live at Graceland, but I wouldn't raise a fuss for a while. Once there, I would present him with the most phenomenal gift he could ever receive—a beautiful daughter on the brink of womanhood. We would bond into a loving family. Elvis could use it as a springboard to complete the sensational comeback. I would finally have the life I should have had. Desirée would know her father.

The next few days raced by. I put my mind on automatic to set up another fashion promotion. I devoted the bulk of my attention to plotting my getaway. I would demand that Jack grant me a divorce. It shouldn't be hard. Ours was a marriage in name only. The children were older. They'd understand. And what if they didn't? It was about time I lived for myself. Everything was coming together. The timing was right. Elvis needed me now. He truly loved me. I was sure of it.

August was steamy hot in Dallas, as usual, but I refused to wilt. My joy was contagious. Even those around me could sense the dramatic change.

"You're really happy," Alex Blakeley said, passing by my desk at the office. "What's this all about?"

I leaped up and hugged him.

"I'm changing my life!"

"That's the best news I've heard in a long while. It's about time."

On Saturday, August 13, I sang the national anthem before a crowd of two thousand at the Foreign Visitors Committee Social at the World Trade Center in Dallas. Afterward, my friends were amazed by my spirit and rushed up to learn the secret. I begged off, smiling and allowing that things were going well.

On August 15, an associate called and said an unexpected emergency prevented her from presiding over the fashion and jewelry show I had arranged for American Airlines employees the following day. I called a half dozen people to replace her, but no one was able to free their schedules on such short notice. I was stuck with doing it myself. I decided to attend the morning session, make sure everything was going smoothly, then dash home in the afternoon to await Elvis's call. I got up at dawn to oversee the setup of the show. My youngest child, Jacqueline, eleven, tagged along and provided company. The show went without a hitch. I was confident I'd be able to escape as planned.

Around three P.M., I became dizzy and lost my balance. I sat down and waited for it to pass. When it did a few minutes later, I brushed it off as stress from rushing to put on the show. It was a good excuse to leave.

Driving home, I worried about missing the call. The phone was ringing when I got to the front door. I fumbled with the keys to unlock it, then ran to grab the receiver. It was Desirée.

"Mom. You're home early. How are you feeling?" Her voice was strange, much too soft and gentle. It chilled me. I knew something was wrong.

"I'm okay. Why?"

"Did you hear?"

I said nothing. My body stiffened.

"Elvis Presley died."

For an instant, the desire to keep my secret held back the grief. I couldn't scream out, not with Desirée on the phone. A lifetime of crushing the lid down on my emotions helped me through the next few seconds. A thought came: It's just a test. Desirée made it up. How could she be so cruel? That's it! Just a scheme to get me to confess.

A figure approached from the side.

"Did you hear?" Jack asked. "He's dead."

The combination nearly destroyed me. There was no reason to hide my rage from him. I slammed down the receiver, then faced him.

"Leave me alone!" I screamed, scorching my throat. "Leave me alone!" I shouted it over and over. He retreated to his side of the house.

"I was at the law firm where I worked as a paralegal," Desirée says. "A friend at the office came over very solemnly and said, 'Have you heard?' I had confided in her about my suspicions, and we had discussed it a number of times. My friend told me very gently that Elvis had died. I couldn't believe it. 'Are you sure?' She was. By that time it was on the news.

"It's hard to explain how I felt. I didn't know him. I didn't even know for sure if he was my father. The first thing I thought about was Mother. This would kill her. I had to call.

"When I told her, she said, 'Oh my God,' in the most horrible voice I've ever heard. Then she hung up. She just hung up. I started crying. I tried to call back but there was no answer. I didn't see Mother or hear from her for days. She just disappeared. I didn't know what to do or how to feel.

"When I heard my mother's voice, for that instant, I knew Elvis was my father. But then the doubts returned. I could never be sure until I heard it from my mother's lips."

I STOOD IN THE LIVING ROOM HOLDING my arms outstretched over my head, gripping my fists so tightly my nails dug into my palms. I made a few jerking starts and wandered around in circles. Through the blur of tears I caught a glimpse of my handbag on the couch. I grabbed it and ran out of the house. The summer heat was suffocating and made me nauseated. I leaned on the house to catch my breath. Recovering, I ran to the car, opened the door, and struggled to get the key into the ignition. I was crying so hard I could barely see. I backed out and headed toward the city.

Looking down, my eyes focused on the radio. I reached over to switch it on, then froze. "No! I don't want to hear it." I turned the car away from the city to where there was grass and trees. The greening of the scenery had a soothing effect. Scenes from my life with Elvis played from all corners of my mind. But even that turned harrowing. The scenes began fighting for my full attention, blocking out my view of the road. The good images were replaced by a surrealistic vision of Elvis's swollen, agonized face pressed up against the phone during our last conversation. I visualized him telling me all the things I'd only heard him say before. I saw him cry as he expressed his sorrow, then laugh at my unintentional play on words. This was it. I had finally snapped. With Elvis's help, I had survived a lifetime of pain, both physical and emotional. Now he was gone. I didn't think I could survive anymore. I didn't want to survive.

"No!" I screamed. "I won't give in." The spurt of emotion rocked me back to reality. I channeled my thoughts into the natural grief that had to be vented to keep me from losing my mind.

"Why, God, why am I being punished? We were so close to making it this time. So close. Why? My only sin was love, was loving him. Now You took him away. You've taken him from me. I'll never hear his voice again. Never feel him near me again. I was going to help him. I was going to help bring him back. He would have come back. He would have made it. Why didn't You give me a chance? Why? It wasn't his fault. He was kind and it made him weak. You gave him that kindness. It's not fair.

"He's gone," I screamed. "He's gone forever."

Blinded by anguish and pain, I nearly blacked out. I managed to pull over at the edge of a service station. I had no idea where I was. Everything around was unfamiliar. But that wasn't important. Directly in front of me stood a phone booth. A direct line into Graceland. I wanted to speak to Vernon Presley. I had to find out firsthand.

"It wasn't true. They made a mistake," I mumbled to myself, digging in my purse for change and my address book. "It couldn't be. I won't let it."

I misdialed the first two times. My hands were trembling so badly I considered abandoning the effort. I took a deep breath to calm myself and fight off the frustration, then dialed again. By some miracle, I got through.

"Mr. Presley is unable to come to the phone." The woman's voice was tense. My mind jumped on a thought.

Maybe they meant it was his father who had died. Maybe it wasn't Elvis!

"Is it true about Elvis?" I asked, forcing out the horrible words. The woman on the phone started crying.

"Yes. Yes, he's dead."

I dropped the phone. It slammed into the glass and dangled by its cord. The unwanted response set off another wave of hysteria.

Why did it happen? How? What happened? Oh my darling, how did you die?

I climbed back into the car and drove east until I got my

bearings. I then steered toward a quiet wooded area where I could be alone. I kicked off my shoes to feel the grass under my feet and make sure I was still whole. I walked for hours, reliving all the glorious moments I'd spent with him.

This would be a nice place to die, I thought. I don't want to live anymore. I have nothing to live for.

I turned to another guiding force in my life. One that I could no longer understand.

"This is Lucy, God. Sensible, conservative Lucy. The one who was unwilling to take a chance. The one who couldn't risk hurting anyone by doing what I wanted. The one who played by the rules. I'm back under control. No more screaming. You can talk to me now. Just answer me. He was going to get better. He had the courage. But You took him anyway. So take me, too, God. Take my life right now. I beg You."

I fell to my knees. Despite my semblance of control, the plea unleashed more tears.

"Take me, please. Take me now. I can't live without him. I can't go on. Please God, take me to wherever he's gone. I don't care where. Just take me to him . . ."

I pounded the ground with my fists, daring and goading God to still my life, to end a lifetime of pain once and for all. Then I collapsed on the cool grass.

The sun was softer when I awoke an hour later. The sleep had renewed me. My mind was working clearly again. There would be no more pleas for death.

"I'm sorry, dear Lord," I prayed. "Forgive me my weakness. Thank you for sparing my life. I don't know if I have the strength to go on, but I'll try."

I must go to him, I thought, pulling myself up. I must go to Graceland.

Filled with new purpose, I drove to the airport and bought a round-trip ticket to Memphis. I was on automatic, acting on each single impulse as it came to me.

After lift-off, I looked out through the window at the darkening sky. I saw Elvis's face outlined in the clouds. I could almost hear his voice.

"Do the chairs in your parlor seem empty and bare?
Do you gaze at your doorstep and picture me there?
Is your heart filled with pain?
Shall I come back again?
Darling dear, are you lonesome tonight?"

"I love you, my Desirée. You were the only one."

"The plane has landed, ma'am," the stewardess said, gently shaking me from my trance. "We're in Memphis. You're the only one left."

Chapter 26

Graceland was a scene from a nightmare. Through the darkness I could see what appeared to be tens of thousands of people. They were outside the gate, lining the streets, sitting on the curbs, lying in the grass; some were trying to climb the stone wall and get into the complex. The taxi's headlights revealed brief but unforgettable images of twisted, grieving faces. Men and women were crying openly without shame. At first the crowd comforted me. This outpouring of emotion showed, more than anything else, just how greatly he was loved. A giant wake for a man who touched a hundred million hearts. Then the surrealism of the scene became too much. I was no different than one of the gruesome faces in the crowd. Probably worse. I had been crying off and on for more than six hours. My face was a swollen, distorted mask. And what was I doing here? I was on the outside, shut off from the inner sanctum of Elvis's world. Graceland was as unfamiliar to me as it was to the most casual fan. I knew nothing of Graceland, the fans, his fame—I was never part of that world. As always, I didn't fit in. I would have to suffer alone.

I ordered the taxi driver to turn around and take me back to the airport. I sat there for who knows how long, waiting for a standby flight back to Dallas. The trip to Memphis was symbolic of my whole life with Elvis. It was daylight when the jet touched down in Dallas. When I got home I roused one of my daughters from bed, Jacqueline I think, and we went to Mass. After the service, when everybody had left, I went up and lit a candle for Elvis. I was crying so much Father Gale White came over and touched my shoulder.

"Please don't cry, Lucy. Nothing can be so bad. There is nothing that we can't handle. We need grief so our heart will know what happiness is. If you only have sunshine, you never know how wonderful it truly is."

He was being nice, but he couldn't know that I would never have sunshine in my life again.

Later that day there was a knock at the door. A young man handed me a single talisman rose. The enclosed card read, "All my love, till I return—El Lancelot." If I wasn't so numb, my mind probably would have snapped.

I spent the next few days away from home, walking in the woods, driving, trying to recover. I didn't want to read about it in the newspapers or see the stories on television. I just wanted to get away. Questions began to eat at me. Did he try to call me and tell me something? Why wasn't I there to help him? Why didn't anyone help him? Where was the girlfriend that was supposed to be watching him?

And the biggest question of all: What would I tell Desirée? Could I tell her anything now? Her father was gone. I'd waited too long. Why did I wait? Why? I should have overlooked everything and told him. I should have let him decide what to do about it. I should have given him at least that. Now it was too late. Desirée would never be able to know him. The guilt was as tormenting as the grief.

The stories went on for months. I found myself drawn to them like a moth toward a bonfire. Speculation about how he died, where he died, why he died, what would happen now that he was dead, and on and on. There were some horrible stories about his drug addiction and personal habits. I nearly fainted when I saw a copy of the *National Enquirer* with a picture of Elvis in his coffin. I couldn't even imagine him dead, but there he was, for all the world to see. Even in death he had no privacy.

Melody called in the midst of my mourning and began talking about her upcoming wedding. She was getting married in Ontario in December. She wanted me to design all the dresses and sing at the wedding. How was I going to get through all that?

How could I get through anything? The reminders of my lost life were everywhere. I couldn't bear to look at Desirée, so I avoided her.

I gathered the strength to call Vernon Presley. He was distraught. We both cried as we spoke.

"Honey," Mr. Presley said. "He was a gentleman. So honorable. I tried to protect him, but it was out of my control."

I told him we had to be strong, that Elvis would want us to. Then I asked if Elvis was really planning to marry Ginger. She had given long interviews about their upcoming marriage. Mr. Presley said Elvis had told him he had no intention of marrying her.

"Elvis just said Ginger reminded him of someone he used to know. That's all."

"Priscilla?"

"No, he wouldn't have wanted to be reminded of her."

I asked Mr. Presley if he would find the scapular, the small Sacred Heart of Jesus that I had given Elvis, and send it to me. Elvis had told me the binding was torn, and I was going to fix it for him. Mr. Presley promised he would look for it. He found it because it arrived in the mail the following week. He included a short note, saying simply, "I hope this is it." I held the fragile and ragged picture of Jesus to my bosom and cried.

Melody's wedding was December 10. She married an Englishman named John Taylor who was a property developer. One of the songs she requested was "The First Time Ever I Saw Your Face." Elvis told me once to listen to the words because he was singing it to me. I don't know how I made it. The audience mistook my tears as elation over my daughter's marriage. The wedding was beautiful, and it snowed all day. Afterward, the families gathered for dinner. Each member was supposed to speak. All I said was, "I know now love can move mountains. I've seen it." The hosts said they were glad that I had come so far for the wedding, and they wanted to toast me with a special song from one of their favorite people. They then played a record of Elvis singing "Memories." The choice was an appropriate one for the mother of the bride, and just a coincidence, but I again had to fight to maintain my composure. As I listened, I realized Elvis would never die, not for me, and not for anyone who loved him.

I spent the next months going through the motions of living, completely hollow. Sometimes, if I was busy, I'd go an hour or so without thinking of him. That was the longest. His memory wouldn't fade, and neither did my grief. Desirée seemed to withdraw again. I tried to talk to her, to tell her, but just thinking about it choked me up. I was afraid of losing her, too.

"When I was nineteen, I decided to send away for my birth certificate," Desirée says. "I had never seen it. Whenever I needed it to start school or get my driver's license, Mother made me use my baptismal certificate. I didn't think they'd take it, but they always did. When I'd ask her for my birth certificate she'd say she didn't have it. One time she said it was in her Bible. I looked through practically every page and couldn't find it. So now, tormented by all the unanswered questions about my father, I decided to send for it.

"I didn't think I'd get it because you have to send in all this information on the mother and father and I didn't know the names that would be on my certificate. I didn't even know what name would be listed for me. I put 'Desirée Presley' for me and 'E. A. Presley' for my father. To my surprise, it came. I was almost too scared to open it. When I did, my eyes went right to the father section. That was another shock. It said my father was 'Randolph Presley.' Who was he? And why had my mother's friend told me Elvis was my father?

"Then I noticed all this strange stuff on the certificate. It said my mother was born in Beaumont, Texas, and gave a different birthdate for her. This confused me more. I knew I couldn't ask Mother about it because she would kill me if she thought I went behind her back. But I did ask her if she was born in Beaumont. She just said 'No, why?' and laughed a little like that was ridiculous. I thought it would let her know that I'd seen the birth certificate, but she had no reaction.

"This 'Randolph Presley' began to really bother me. I asked my sisters if they had ever heard of him and no one had. Melody told me to ask Mother. I couldn't. So I just worried and wondered about it for another year. Then I decided on a new strategy. I told Mother I needed my birth certificate for a passport and was going to order it. She said she'd do it for me. Months passed and she didn't have it, so I knew that tactic was hopeless. I decided to tell her I'd sent for it and had it. She said she wanted to see it. I handed it to her. She didn't say anything, but she looked at it like it was poison. I asked her who Randolph Presley was, and she said that nothing on it was true. I asked her why. She said she'd tell me one day, but not now. Then she started telling me about when I was born and how she was unhappy and all alone, and that I had real long hair. She began to get emotional. Talking about it was torturing her. After that, I just didn't have the heart to pursue the birth certificate any further."

T HE YEARS SLIPPED AWAY. SUDDENLY it was 1979 and time to try and reconstruct my life. Jacqueline, thirteen, was studying music in Canada and was going to be confirmed at a church there. I decided to drive up in late June and asked Desirée to come with me. We had grown distant and I wanted to be with her. Before I left, I called Vernon Presley and made arrangements to see him on our way home. I wanted Desirée to meet her grandfather, even though he knew nothing about her. Visiting him and seeing Elvis's home might work to break down the barriers and enable me to tell her.

After Jacqueline's confirmation, Melody, Desirée, and I drove to Toronto. We went to a shopping mall and had a wonderful afternoon. As we were walking, my attention was focused on the faint music being piped through the mall. The music was interrupted by a news bulletin. Vernon Presley had died. That hit me hard. We were planning to see him in a few days. He was all Desirée had left, and now he too was gone. I crawled deeper into my shell. Desirée grew more distant than ever.

In 1982 I decided to move to Los Angeles to be closer to Desirée. I had to find the courage to resolve this before the damage was permanent. Jacqueline liked Los Angeles and came with me. We moved into a condo together. Desirée eventually moved in with us.

In September Desirée and I were out shopping and went to a phone booth to check our messages on the recorder. Desirée said there was a message from a friend of hers, an attorney with a number of celebrity clients. She called him and he said that he wanted her to come right over and meet some people, including a major star who knew Elvis. That panicked me. Jacqueline had said that Desirée was telling people who she thought her father was. That appeared to be the only reason why this attorney's famous client suddenly wanted to meet her.

"You can't go, Desirée," I said. "You don't know how the

people here are. Your father knew, and they destroyed him. Please don't go."

She looked at me intently and said, "Mother, who is my father?"

There was no place to hide anymore. This wasn't the way I wanted it, but I had no choice. I couldn't let her find out at some superficial L.A. party where she would be put on display like a novelty, or someone would take advantage of it and use her.

"Elvis Presley was your father."

She just looked at me and said, "I know, Mother."

"No, you don't know. You don't know the whole story. I don't want you to go there and have everyone question you. Please listen. Don't go."

She finally agreed. I began to worry about so many things. I had to tell Desirée the full story, but how could I? It was so long and complicated. My strength had left me years ago, in August 1977. Now there were new fears. How many people knew about her? Desirée said nothing more about it, but she grew cold and withdrawn again. Jacqueline did, too. They must have both decided that I was horrible. That hurt me so much. I loved them so, and now I was losing them. I returned to Dallas feeling more alienated from Desirée than ever before.

"I had confided to my closest friends that I thought Elvis was my father," Desirée explains. "This attorney was one of them.

"After Mother finally told me, it took about thirty minutes before it sunk in. It was true. Mother had admitted it. I was Elvis Presley's daughter. The impact on me was devastating. All my old feelings of, I guess you would call it bitterness, just hit me. I felt cheated. And it was still impossible to talk with Mother about it. I asked her why she didn't tell me until now, and she said it was because she thought it was better for me not to know. She said she wasn't sure it was the right decision, but she had made up her mind and just stuck with it. I still didn't get any of the facts or the story. She wasn't ready to tell me. That made it worse. My bitterness lasted for nearly a year.

"Then one day, after holding the bitterness inside for so long, it occurred to me that Mother never meant to hurt me. All these years she was really hurting and really suffering. I didn't help her because I was too afraid to broach the subject. I never pressed her or pushed her or demanded to know who my father was. She dropped hints and gave me so many opportunities to ask her, and I never took advantage of them. It was as much my fault as hers."

I N MAY 1984 I WENT TO LOS Angeles on business. I saw Desirée for the first time in nearly two years. When we saw each other all the differences melted and we embraced. Our tears mingled with laughter. Jacqueline joined in for a three-way embrace. "To understand all is to forgive all." That saying had carried me through my life and was never more appropriate than now. We had all been wrong, and we had all made mistakes that hurt each other, but our family love had survived.

There remained the question of how to tell Desirée the story. By then I realized it couldn't be a face-to-face encounter. It would take too long, and I would cry too much. I couldn't give her a short, easy version either, because the story is like a chain. If one link is broken or left unexplained, it taints the entire telling. In order to understand why I made the decisions I did, Desirée had to know it all—every detail, no matter how painful or ugly. She had to see both the horror of my life and the beauty that her father brought to it. I struggled for months with how to accomplish this. How to open the doors I had locked and reveal a secret that I suffered so long to keep.

At the same time I was wrestling with this, a solution presented itself. Desirée had been quietly approached by a writer to tell her story. She told me about it and it scared me. Who was this person trying to pry into our lives? I resented him. And it was worse. Desirée said she had no story to tell, that I would have to tell it. I emphatically told her no. She didn't give up. She told me how important it was to her for me to tell it. A mutual friend in Los Angeles, Dr. Rafael Rodriguez, helped ease my mind and advised me to consider it. Still, it took a year of anguished contemplation before I began to see the possibilities such an arrangement presented. I might be able to open up to a third party. If I could,

Desirée would be able to put herself in my shoes and live my life as she read, day by day, year by year, decision by decision. This way, she might understand.

The problem was, could I actually do it? It couldn't just be any writer. I didn't want a mercenary who just looked at it as another story. It had to be someone I trusted, someone with whom I could allow myself to open up. I doubted it could be the same writer who approached Desirée. I arranged to meet him anyway, if only to please her. There was little harm in a meeting. He would be inappropriate, and I could keep my secrets.

From the moment I met the young man, I knew he was the one. There was something about his blue eyes, a kindness, understanding, a vibrant determination to make whatever he did the best he possibly could. They were eyes that told me he would sit up with me during the long hours of forcing dark memories to the surface. He would push just hard enough to ease them out naturally instead of forcing them painfully to the surface. He'd be patient during the days or even weeks when I would be unable to go on. He'd allow me to cry when I needed to and would understand the tears.

He was the right person; I could make no more excuses. I knew in my heart I would have to go through with it. Still, it took another year before I could prepare myself for what the telling would entail.

The final stumbling block was my inability to break the trust Elvis and I shared. To talk would be a betrayal of our secret life. Elvis had never broken it. All those people around him, friends or foes, never knew. This bothered me for a long time. Then, when the awful books continued to come out about him, I began to feel that it was all right. Through my story I could let my daughter, and all those who cared about Elvis and were hurt by those terrible books, know the man I knew. He was neither a god nor a demon. He wasn't perfect, nor was he as flawed as has been written. He was just a man. A wonderful, kind, caring man who let others control him and ended up being lonely and unhappy.

I pray that I was a comfort to him and not the cause of his unhappiness.

EPILOGUE

I T WOULD HURT ME TO KNOW THAT my revelation has harmed someone. I've always tried never to infringe upon anyone's happiness. My children have all been so wonderful and loving throughout my trials. I love them all so much. I hope they understand and realize I wasn't trying to be deceptive. I had to be private. Secrecy, beyond everything else, was one of the most important things Elvis and I shared.

I know in my heart I could never have lived the life Elvis had to live. The life he so wanted to change. Our love was our greatest strength. It was a resting place, a place we could call home. As long as we kept it secret, no one could take it from us. They couldn't take our memories. I still have mine.

The first time I went to Elvis's grave was more disturbing than I ever imagined. I had been to Memphis several times after he died, but only to visit familiar places around town. In 1983 I summoned the courage to walk through the gates of Graceland as part of a tour. It was so strange, walking through an unfamiliar house with a group of strangers, yet everything about the place was familiar. There were pictures of Elvis everywhere that captured him through the different looks and hairstyles from the early years to the end. His chairs, tables, the piano, the other furnishings—it was warming and painful at the same time. Outside, his cars were on display. I recognized a few I had ridden in, including the one the last time we were together. Out in the pasture, his horse, Rising Sun, was standing proud but lonely. Despite the attempts to cheer up the place, gloom hung in the air. The garden beds were not groomed and the flowers were dead or dying. The whole compound seemed to be dying.

I waited until the crowd had left before going to his grave. Seeing it was the realization that he was gone. That acceptance was probably harder for me than any of his friends or associates because of the peculiarity of our love. He was gone many times before. Months passed. Years. During one dark stretch, ten years passed without my seeing him or hearing from him. But no matter how long the absence, he always came back. He was gone again, but it felt like another long separation. As before, he would return.

Not this time. He was dead and I had to come to grips with that.

As I knelt by his grave, a leaf fell from a nearby tree, drifted down, and landed inside my open purse beside me. It was as if he was sending a message that one day we would again be able to share the little things that had meant so much to us. I've kept that leaf to this day.

My thoughts turned to a pleasant memory. The first time we were on our hill in Memphis, in 1953, we came across a large patch of soft clover. I asked if we could stop and look for one with four leaves.

"There's no such thing," he said.

"Of course there is," I argued. "Life is full of four-leaf clovers. You just have to look hard enough."

"Well, if you find one, I'll give you a surprise."

Luck was with me. I found one within a minute. I handed it to him and just smiled. He was amazed.

"You know what this means?" he said excitedly. "It means we'll be together forever and ever." He pulled me down and kissed me in the clover.

"What about my surprise?" I asked.

"How about the best thing I have to give. My heart. It will be yours always."

Looking back at all that happened, one might find it difficult to believe that he meant it.

But he did.

BIBLIOGRAPHY

Barry, Ron. *All American Elvis* (discography). Phillipsburg, New Jersey: Spectator Service, 1976.

Camp, Wesley D., Ph.D. *Marriage and the Family in France Since the Revolution.* New York: Bookman Associates, 1961.

Dundy, Elaine. *Elvis and Gladys.* New York: Macmillan, 1985.

Goldman, Albert. *Elvis.* New York: McGraw-Hill, 1981.

Harbinson, W. A. *The Illustrated Elvis.* London: Michael Joseph, Ltd., 1975.

Hopkins, Jerry. *Elvis.* New York: Simon and Schuster, 1971.

———. *Elvis: The Final Years.* New York: Berkley Books, 1981.

Lichter, Paul. *The Boy Who Dared to Rock—The Definitive Elvis.* New York: Doubleday & Company, 1978.

———. *Elvis in Hollywood.* New York: Simon and Schuster, 1975.

Marsh, Dave. *Elvis.* New York: Warner Books, 1982.

Presley, Priscilla Beaulieu and Sandra Harmon. *Elvis and Me.* New York: G. P. Putnam's Sons, 1985.

Richmond, Mary E. and Fred S. Hall. *Child Marriages.* New York: Russell Sage Foundation, 1925.

Torgoff, Martin, ed. *The Complete Elvis.* New York: Delilah Books, 1982.

ABOUT THE AUTHORS

Lucy de Barbin lives in Texas and holds a teacher's certification in Christian Theology. She currently works as a clothing designer. A mother of six, Lucy was selected to appear in *Notable Women of Texas* in 1983.

Dary Matera was formerly an editor with Rodale Press and a reporter for *The Miami News.* He lives in Miami.